ENGAGING THE SPIRIT

ESSAYS ON THE LIFE AND THEOLOGY OF THE HOLY SPIRIT

ENGAGING THE SPIRIT

ESSAYS ON THE LIFE AND THEOLOGY OF THE HOLY SPIRIT

EDITED BY
ROBERT BOAK SLOCUM

 CHURCH

CHURCH PUBLISHING, NEW YORK

Icon on the Cover

Descending Dove: The Epiclesis in Cruciform
The Descent of the Holy Spirit on the Gifts at the Eucharist

Mixed Media on Wood

by
Johnny R. Ross

Copyright © 2001 by Robert Boak Slocum

Library of Congress Cataloging-in-Publication Data

Engaging the Spirit : essays on the life and theology of the Holy Spirit
/ edited by Robert Boak Slocum.
    p. cm.
  Includes bibliographical references.
  ISBN 0-89869-366-7 (pbk.)
  1. Holy Spirit.   I. Slocum, Robert Boak, 1952-
BT121.3 .E54 2001
231'.3--dc21

                            2001047445

Church Publishing Incorporated
445 Fifth Avenue
New York, NY 10016
5   4   3   2   1

Table of Contents

Introduction and Dedication

For too long the Holy Spirit has tended to be either disregarded or the object of fanatical exclamation in the life of the church, especially in western Christianity. However, in recent years there has been a renewal of interest in engaging the Spirit's presence and understanding the Spirit's activity. This calls for a discerning evaluation and exploration of pneumatology, the theology of the Spirit, so that we may grow in both experience and understanding of the Spirit. The essays in this collection give attention to many ways of the Spirit's life and activity—for salvation and healing, for making Christ present in our lives and in the church, for empowering our prayers and liturgies, for our inspiration and gifting, for transformation of the way we live, for the redemption of the world and the ultimate coming of God's kingdom, for the unity of our relationships with each other and God.

A variety of disciplines and perspectives are represented in this collection, but it is the one Spirit whom we seek to discern and describe. As we recognize the Spirit's activity in our traditions and doctrines, our prayers and liturgies, and in all aspects of the life we live, we may be better attuned to the leading of the Spirit into the future of faith and our life in God. I hope that purpose will be served by the writings presented here.

This collection of essays was originally published as the Summer 2001 issue of the *Anglican Theological Review*. It reflects the encouragement and support of James E. Griffiss and Jacqueline B. Winter, editor and managing editor of the *ATR*, and the careful editorial work of Susan E. Laws, assistant to the managing editor of the *ATR*. Royalties for my work as editor of this book will be given to the *ATR* Foundation in appreciation for the role of the *ATR* in this project.

I also want to thank Frank Hemlin and Frank Tedeschi, publisher and managing editor of Church Publishing Incorporated, for their support for the publication of these essays on the Holy Spirit in book form. Once again, they have helped to make a vision into a reality. It is my hope that this book will allow the insights of the contributors to be even more widely available through the coming years.

This collection is dedicated to Charles Price (Oct. 4, 1920–Oct. 13, 1999), who died while this project was underway. After I invited him to contribute to this collection of writings on the Holy Spirit, he wrote to express interest in participating and said "you've got a fascinating job ahead of you." He mentioned an essay of his on *filioque* as a possible starting point, among other ideas. With the help of Philip A. Smith, retired Bishop of New Hampshire, and Reginald H. Fuller, a colleague of Price's at Virginia Theological Seminary, his essay on *filioque* was located among his papers. Special thanks are due to Fuller, who assisted me in editing Price's manuscript for publication.

This project has been a fascinating job, and one that continues beyond the scope of this particular work. I appreciate greatly the many people—authors, editors, benefactors—who have "engaged the Spirit" generously through this project, making it a labor of love.

—*Robert Boak Slocum*

Contributors

Robert M. Cooper has served as an Episcopal parish priest, a college chaplain, a university and seminary professor, and a pastoral psychotherapist. He taught at Nashotah House and the Episcopal Theological Seminary of the Southwest. He has also been a Visiting Scholar at the Church Divinity School of the Pacific, and an Affiliate Scholar at the Boston Psychoanalytical Society and Institute. He is a Fellow of the American Association of Pastoral Counselors. He was a member of the Coalition for the Ordination of Women to the Priesthood and Episcopate. He served as a member of the National Board of Examining Chaplains and as a member and Vice-Chair of the Standing Commission on Human Affairs and Health. He was poetry editor of the *Anglican Theological Review*.

Travis T. Du Priest is Director of the DeKoven Center and Warden of the Shrine of Blessed James DeKoven in Racine, Wisconsin. An Episcopal priest, he also teaches literature and non-fiction writing classes at Carthage College in Kenosha, Wisconsin, where he was named distinguished teacher. He serves as Book Editor of *The Living Church* magazine, and is Chaplain for the Community of St. Mary (Western Province).

Tilden Edwards is an Episcopal priest, Founder and Senior Fellow of the Shalem Institute for Spiritual Formation in Bethesda, Maryland, and the author of seven books related to the spiritual life. His most recent book, *Spiritual Directors, Spiritual Companion: Guide to Tending the Soul*, was published in January 2001.

Reginald H. Fuller, an Episcopal priest, was Molly Laird Downs Professor of New Testament at Virginia Seminary, 1972–1985. He also served as Baldwin Professor of Sacred Literature at Union Theological Seminary, New York, 1966–1972; Professor of New Testament Languages and Literature, Seabury-Western Theological Seminary, 1955–1966; and Professor of Theology, St. David's College, Lampeter, Wales, 1950–1955. He was President of the Society of New Testament Study, 1983–1984. He participated in the national Lutheran-Episcopal dialogues (I and II), and the international Anglican-Lutheran dialogue. He is the author of *Foundations of New Testament Christology*, *Preaching the Lectionary* and *A Critical Introduction to the New Testament*.

Alexander Golitzin, hieromonk (priest-monk) of the Orthodox Church of America, is associate professor in the Department of Theology at Marquette University in Milwaukee, Wisconsin. He has also served as a visiting professor at St. Vladimir's Seminary in Crestwood, New York, and as a visiting lecturer at the Graduate Theological Union, Berkeley, the University of California at Berkeley, and Stanford. He was tonsured monk at the Monastery of Simonos Petras, Mt. Athos. His publications include *Et introibo ad altare dei: The Mystagogy of*

1

Dionysius Areopagita with Special Reference to its Predecessors in the Eastern Christian Tradition; St. Symeon the New Theologian on the Mystical Life: The Ethical Discourses; and *The Living Witness of the Holy Mountain: Contemporary Voices from Mount Athos.* He was a co-editor of the *Historical Dictionary of the Orthodox Church.*

Charles Hefling is a professor of systematics in the Theology Department at Boston College, and an adjunct faculty member at Andover Newton Theological School. He recently served as Priest Associate at the Church of Saint John the Evangelist in Boston, and he has been a presbyter of the Episcopal Diocese of Massachusetts since 1974. He is the author of *Why Doctrines?* and editor of two volumes in the *Collected Works of Bernard Lonergan,* and editor of *Our Selves, Our Souls and Bodies: Sexuality and the Household of God.* His current project is *The Meaning of God Incarnate: Christology for the Time Being.*

Robert Davis Hughes, III, is the Norma and Olan Mills Professor of Divinity and Professor of Systematic Theology, the School of Theology, University of the South. He has taught at Sewanee since 1977, after serving parishes in Southern Ohio and Toronto. He has been secretary-treasurer and president of the Conference of Anglican Theologians, now the Society of Anglican and Lutheran Theologians. Hughes is a Fellow of the Episcopal Church Foundation and a member of the Fellows Forum planning group. He has also served as Tennessee State Conference president and member of the National Council of the American Association of University Professors. He was also a Kent Fellow of the Danforth Foundation, and recently a Visiting Scholar at the Divinity Faculty, Cambridge. He contributes regularly to *Sewanee Theological Review* and other journals.

Thomas Hughson, a Roman Catholic priest in the Society of Jesus and Associate Professor in the Department of Theology at Marquette University, teaches Systematic Theology to graduate and undergraduate students. The work of John Courtney Murray has been a main research interest leading to *Matthias Scheeben on Faith: The Doctoral Dissertation of John Courtney Murray* (Edwin Mellen Press, 1987), *The Believer as Citizen: John Courtney Murray in a New Context* (Paulist Press, 1994), and "John Courtney Murray and Postconciliar Faith," *Theological Studies* (September, 1997), among others. An Editorial Consultant for *Theological Studies* and co-chair of the Church-State Studies Group in the American Academy of Religion, he has long been committed to the ecumenical hope that animated "Toward a Common Understanding of Ecumenism," *Ecumenical Review* (July, 1994) and "From James Madison to William Lee Miller: John Courtney Murray and Baptist First Amendment Theory," *Journal of Church and State* (Winter, 1995).

Alan Jones is Dean of Grace Episcopal Cathedral in San Francisco and an honorary canon of the Cathedral of Our Lady of Chartres. He was the Stephen F. Bayne Professor of Ascetical Theology at General Theological Seminary from 1972 to 1985. He was also the Director and Founder of the Center for Christian Spirituality at General Theological Seminary. He is the author of *The Soul's Journey: Exploring the Three Passages of Spiritual Life with Dante as a Guide; Sacrifice and Delight; Passion for Pilgrimage;* and *Living the Truth.*

Ruth A. Meyers is Associate Professor of Liturgics at Seabury-Western Theological Seminary in Evanston, Illinois and an Episcopal priest. She has served for several years on the expansive-language subcommittee of the Standing Commission on Liturgy and Music and since 1999 has been a member of the Anglican/Roman Catholic Consultation in the USA. A member of the Council of the Associated Parishes for Liturgy and Mission, she is editor of its journal, *OPEN*. She is co-editor of *Gleanings: Essays on Expansive Language with Prayers for Various Occasions*; the author of *Continuing the Reformation: Re-Visioning Baptism in the Episcopal Church*; and general editor of the *Liturgical Studies* series of the Standing Commission on Liturgy and Music (all published by Church Publishing).

Charles P. Price was an Episcopal priest and taught theology and liturgy at Virginia Theological Seminary from 1972 until his retirement in 1989. He held the William Meade Chair in Systematic Theology. Price also was on the faculty of Virginia Theological Seminary from 1956 to 1963. He served as preacher to the university and chair of the board of preachers at Harvard from 1963 to 1972, and was appointed Plummer Professor of Christian Morals in 1968. Price was a member of the Board for Theological Education, the Standing Liturgical Commission, the Standing Commission on Church Music, and the General Board of Examining Chaplains. He served on the Committee on Texts for *The Hymnal 1982*. He was a Deputy to General Convention, and served as chaplain of the House of Deputies. He was also a member of the Anglican-Roman Catholic Commission (USA). He was the author of *Introducing the Proposed Book . . . of Common Prayer; Principles of Faith; A Matter of Faith;* and co-author (with Louis Weil) of *Liturgy for Living*. He died in Alexandria, Virginia, on October 13, 1999.

Robert B. Slocum is Rector of the Church of the Holy Communion, Lake Geneva, Wisconsin, and Lecturer in Theology at Marquette University. He is co-editor of *Documents of Witness: A History of the Episcopal Church, 1782–1985*, and editor of *Prophet of Justice, Prophet of Life: Essays on William Stringfellow*. He is co-editor of the *Episcopal Dictionary of the Church*, editor of *A New Conversation: Essays on the Future of Theology and the Episcopal Church*, and author of *The Theology of William Porcher DuBose: Life, Movement and Being*. He is Review Article Editor of the *Anglican Theological Review*.

George H. Tavard is professor emeritus of theology, Methodist Theological School in Ohio. He is a Roman Catholic priest and a member of the Augustinians of the Assumption. He was *peritus* (expert) at Vatican Council II, and has been involved in the ecumenical dialogues of the Roman Catholic Church with Anglicans, Lutherans, and Methodists. He is the author of some fifty books, including *A Review of Anglican Orders: The Problem and the Solution; The Church, Community of Salvation: An Ecumenical Ecclesiology; The Thousand Faces of the Virgin Mary*; and *The Starting Point of Calvin's Theology*.

Louis Weil is the James F. Hodges Professor of Liturgics at the Church Divinity School of the Pacific, Berkeley, where he has taught since 1988. He is an

Episcopal priest. He is the co-author with the late Charles P. Price of *Liturgy for Living*, which was republished in a revised edition in 2000. He is also the author of *Sacraments and Liturgy: The Outward Signs* (1983) *and Gathered to Pray* (1986), and of numerous articles on various aspects of liturgical theology and renewal. His most recent book, *A Theology of Worship*, will be published in 2001. He was a member of the Standing Liturgical Commission from 1985 to 1991. He is a founding member of Societas Liturgica, and of the North American Academy of Liturgy, which he served as President in 1980.

J. Robert Wright has been teaching patristic and medieval church history and theology, liturgics, and ecumenical relations at The General Theological Seminary since 1968, where he is now St. Mark's Professor of Ecclesiastical History. He is an Episcopal priest. He was a Fulbright Scholar and is a Fellow of the Episcopal Church Foundation. He has been a visiting professor at St. George's College in Jerusalem, Southern Baptist Theological Seminary, Claremont School of Theology, Trinity College in Toronto, and Nashotah House. He has served parishes both in America and in England and is a past president of the North American Academy of Ecumenists. The author or editor of thirteen books including *On Being a Bishop: Papers on Episcopacy from the Moscow Consultation 1992* and *They Still Speak: Readings for the Lesser Feasts*, he was elected a life Fellow of the Royal Historical Society in London in 1981. He now serves as President of the Anglican Society, Theological Consultant to the Ecumenical Office of the Episcopal Church, and Honorary Canon Theologian to the Bishop of New York in the Cathedral of St. John the Divine. He is Historiographer of the Episcopal Church.

Rebecca Abts Wright is ordained in the United Methodist Church and has served parishes in West Virginia, Maryland and Connecticut. She is currently Associate Professor of Old Testament at the School of Theology, University of the South, Sewanee, Tennessee, where she has taught for eleven years.

Paul F. M. Zahl is Dean of the Cathedral Church of the Advent, Birmingham, Alabama. He has also served as rector of Episcopal churches in Scarborough, New York and Charleston, South Carolina, and was Curate of Grace Church in New York City. His publications include *Who Will Deliver Us?; The Protestant Face of Anglicanism;* and *A Short Systematic Theology*.

Wanda Zemler-Cizewski is an associate professor in the Department of Theology at Marquette University, Milwaukee. She has published numerous articles on theology in the twelfth and thirteenth centuries, and is currently working on a book-length study of the history of interpretations of Genesis 2:18–25, from Jerome to Nicholas of Myra.

Falling in Love:
The Work of the Holy Spirit

ALAN JONES*

What excites me about Christianity is its surprise factor. Risky, challenging, revelatory, it bubbles with new ideas and pictures, uncovering God where you least expect, and questioning many of your spiritual and social and political assumptions.[1]

This is exactly what excites me about being a Christian but sometimes it seems harder and harder to find it actually manifested in the life of the Church. The last thing we want is excitement, risk, challenge and revelation. The maddening thing about the Holy Spirit is that it is uncontrollable. That's why questions about the Holy Spirit are often questions about authority. The Spirit undermines our often limited view of authority and since most of us are control freaks—at least some of the time—we spend a great deal of energy seeing to it that nothing really changes, that nothing really happens. But the Spirit blows where it will. Perhaps that's why the Church has been somewhat weak with regard to the life of the Spirit. It cannot and will not be controlled by synods, canons and rubrics. The Church organizationally has often preferred to control rather than attract, dominate rather than invite, compel rather than win over.

Andrew Greeley has recently suggested that the Church remodel its understanding of authority in the light of a generous and open view of the way God works in the world: "God as inviting, calling, attracting, instead of God as controlling, directing, regulating. God as Omega more than Alpha; God as the one who gathers in the fragments more than the God of the Big Bang."[2] One rarely hears of the God who is breathtakingly attractive—the one who desires us and finds us desirable. In the monastic setting where I was trained as a priest, we were

---

* Alan Jones is Dean of Grace Cathedral, San Francisco, and an honorary canon of the Cathedral of Our Lady of Chartres.

[1] Brian Mountford, *Postcards on the Way to Heaven,* London: SPCK, 1997, p. 1. Brian Mountford is the Vicar of the University Church in Oxford.

[2] Andrew Greeley, "Authority as Charm" in *America,* November 20, 1999, p. 10 ff.

told that God is madly in love with us and that the life of faith is indeed risky, challenging, revelatory. The sheer beauty of it all swept us away.

Greeley believes that we have neglected the third of the great transcendentals (beauty) with our concentration on the other two (the good and true). "Often, it seems, in contemporary American Catholicism we start with the true and never get beyond it." I appreciate Greeley's point all the more because he shows how the effect of this lopsided approach to authority affects the Church at the level of the local community. Some of our parishes are dull little affairs presided over by a fearful clergy and laity. As the world seems more and more uncertain, the rigidities increase. Both the liberals and conservatives want to compel people to become virtuous. How do we encourage each other to become better Christians, better human beings? Greeley writes, "To the extent that people remain Catholic, it is because they are caught up in the beauty of sacramental Catholicism and the stories it tells, no matter how shoddy the presentation of beauty nor how inept the telling of stories. Beauty and the charm it exercises are not options." This isn't to say that synods, canon laws and rubrics don't play an important role in our common life. They do. But isn't it time to ask what we might have lost in our neglect of the sheer attractiveness of the God who was in Christ? Faith is about falling in love. Falling in love is the work of the Spirit.

In addition to this lopsided view of authority, we also need to face a serious error in the way we have come to view the role of beliefs in the life of faith. Most people still equate faith with believing certain things about God or the sacred.[3] The mistaken idea is that you have to swallow a few correct beliefs before you can embark on the spiritual journey. This, in part, is what makes religion such a dried-up miserable affair. I find it increasingly hard to tell the difference between believers and non-believers. The difference that matters is between those who are awake and those who are asleep; between those who are in love and those who are not. Karen Armstrong points out, "In all the great traditions, prophets, sages, and mystics spent very little time telling their disciples what they ought to believe." They were invited to trust that "despite all the tragic and dispiriting evidence to the con-

---

[3] See Karen Armstrong's introduction to *Every Eye Beholds You: A World Treasury of Prayer*, ed. Thomas J. Craughwell, New York: Harcourt Brace, 1998.

trary, our lives did have some ultimate meaning and value. You could not possibly arrive at faith in this sense before you have lived a religious life. Faith was thus the fruit of spirituality, not something that you had to have at the start of your quest."[4]

The Church would do well to recover this ancient wisdom of inviting people to live a certain way before it clobbers them with doctrine. How about leading a compassionate life? How about recognizing the sacredness of others? How about showing up at rituals that help us wait before mystery? How about beginning with the twin prerequisites for prayer: an acknowledgment of our own fragility, and a sense of wonder? This might also help us to be more generous to people of other faiths and to "those whose faith is known to God alone." As Brian Mountford reminds us: "The popular Christian response to this pluralism . . . has been an instinctive and defensive withdrawal behind the barricades of conservative faith. The attitude is safety first: history ended yesterday, so let's preserve what we've got at all costs, and let's not take the risk of further exploration."[5] Above all, let's not fall in love. That would be sentimental and irresponsible. So, we get bogged down with all the things we think we are supposed to believe before we can even begin the journey. Was Jesus divine? Was Mary a virgin?

When I am asked questions about the divinity of Christ and the status of Mary in the scheme of redemption, I invite people simply to look lovingly at a woman (any woman) with a baby (any baby) in her arms or at her breast, and ask themselves, "In the light of this image, how should I be in the world? How should I behave? How should I treat others and myself?"

I want to suggest three theses for our living in the Spirit in this new millennium. First, the Spirit's theater is history—messy, inconclusive, provisional. Second, we need to do for dogma what we have struggled to do with Scripture—to repudiate literalism and recover the poetic, mythic, metaphorical and playful use of the imagination so that the beauty of holiness may reappear. Third, the business of the Spirit is transformation in risk, mercy and love—shown forth in the liturgy.

---

[4]   Armstrong, p. xiv.
[5]   *Postcards on the Way to Heaven*, p. 2.

The Spirit's theater is history—messy, inconclusive, provisional.

Four events have occurred in recent years which show us just how
wonderfully messy history is. The four events are the installation of a French Roman Catholic priest as an honorary canon of an
Anglican cathedral, the Anglican/Roman Catholic Statement on Authority, the Lutheran/Roman Catholic Statement on Justification, and
a divisive ballot about the nature of marriage on the 2000 California
ballot.

Let me begin with a story about the friendship between one Anglican and one Roman Catholic priest. On June 17th, 1999, Father
François Legaux, the rector of the Cathedral of Our Lady of Chartres,
was installed as an honorary canon of Grace Cathedral in San Francisco. It was not only a significant ecumenical event but also an affirmation that what we have in common far outweighs our differences. This
celebration of the relationship between two pilgrimage cathedrals was
also a sign of mutual respect and affection between our two communions. It was a matter of falling in love.

Meanwhile, another significant event took place at around the
same time. It was the publication of *The Gift of Authority* by the An-
glican/Roman Catholic International Commission (ARCIC)—a bit of
a bombshell (a much-needed one to my mind) affirming that our two
communions could come closer together under the Primacy of Peter,
radically reinterpreted. Some evangelical Anglicans saw and see it as a
betrayal of the Reformation. Some Roman Catholics still think of
Church unity as unequivocal submission to the see of Rome. The document is useful in that it raises the question of the mess of history and
how we live in and through it. The subtext of the document (totally
unacknowledged as far I could tell) is that authority as currently practiced in our two traditions simply isn't working. Father Legaux said, in
response to his installation: to advance towards unity requires deep
prayer and is tested by

> the quality of our love for one another. The ruptures in the
> Church, over the course of its history, have been a great evil. No
> one can deny this. Because God alone is capable of drawing good
> from evil, our separations have, over the course of the centuries
> permitted the enrichment of each confession by its own history
> and its own culture. But above all, the Holy Spirit has been given
> to each of our communions as a witness to the diversity of the
> riches we share in God. This is why the future of our unity cannot

be a simple return to what was common before. We cannot reunite ourselves, in truth, unless we accept the differences of each other as an enrichment of ourselves. Unity is the fruit of prayer and must be lived out in love.

He concluded his short address with these words: "History made us who we are. Now it is up to us to make history as we hope it will be." This expresses the tension of living in time and space and affirms the work of the Spirit in and through our differences for our mutual enrichment. History, not eternity, is the theater of the Spirit and, for the most part, we don't like it. The Reformation happened as did the Counter-Reformation. The question now is, "So what?"

Thirdly, the Roman Catholics and Lutherans have just celebrated their reconciliation over the doctrine of justification. Were Lutherans better Christians than Roman Catholics for having recovered the doctrine? Hardly. Beliefs matter but do not come first. In fact, there was a nice irony in the Pope declaring a plenary indulgence for the millennium year only a few days before the Lutheran/Roman Catholic announcement on justification. One would have expected a repudiation of the practice rather than its reaffirmation and celebration.

The more important question is, what do we do now? How do we respond to the Spirit now? This, of course, drives us beyond issues of the differences between Rome and Canterbury, beyond the differences between the various denominations, even beyond issues of relations between the great religious traditions. We are driven, once again, to reflect on the very nature of God and of humanity. What is Christianity really about? The Spirit is calling us out of our tribal and national manifestations into a way of being in the world that truly expresses the universal good news of love and reconciliation.

Stanley Hauerwas, the ethicist and pacifist theologian, has a poster on his office door: "A Modest Proposal for Peace: Let the Christians of the World Agree that They Will Not Kill One Another." If accused of Christian self-centeredness he replies, "I agree that it would certainly be a good thing for Christians to stop killing anyone, but you have to start somewhere." We live in a world where people who claim to be Christians kill each other. This should cure us of moralism or of making extravagant claims about the Holy Spirit.

The fourth event has to do with California state politics (although it has national implications). In March 2000 there was on the ballot in California "A Defense of Marriage Act." Seemingly innocuous, there are, underneath this initiative, hidden and not-so-hidden agendas about the place of women, the definition of the family, the blessing of same-sex relationships, the treatment of homosexuals, the interpretation of Scripture—to name a few. The Roman Catholic bishops of the state supported the initiative.

One of the most disturbing things about the local Roman Catholic response to the Defense of Marriage Initiative is the appeal to the law of nature. Just a cursory look at history should give us pause. Arguments from so-called "nature" have been used to justify the class-system (The rich man in his castle / the poor man at his gate / God made them high and lowly / and ordered their estate); the subjugation of women; slavery and racism; and the persecution of homosexuals. How do we affirm a tradition that is alive and changing all the time?[6]

What is the Spirit teaching us? We live in the mess of history. There is no unchanging human nature. We are called into a pilgrim community through the saving images of Scripture, and we joyfully celebrate God's hospitality in a community where the unqualified and rejected are the most welcome. We are invited to fall in love. To put it another way: The theater of the Spirit is history, which means that we are in an endless conversation with the mystery of what it is to be human in the context of thrilling images of love and mercy in a community centered around a table from which no one is excluded. These images and the eucharistic table set the political and social agenda for our being in the world.

The Church then might be a place for adventurers of the Spirit rather than the refuge of the frightened in a kind of boutique Anglicanism or a rigidly certain and dying Roman Catholicism. As Father Herbert Kelly of Kelham often pointed out, "The opposite of faith is not doubt. The opposite of faith is certainty."

The world has suffered greatly from immature, violent, vindictive, fearful, tribal religion. The Holy Spirit invites us to choose gratitude over resentment, to embrace a banquet as opposed to a fortress mentality. This means giving up our judgmentalism and joining in God's lack of taste in loving everyone, even the desperately wicked. William Blake wrote in "The Divine Image":

---

[6] I think of the recent letter of some Primates of the Anglican Communion to the Presiding Bishop about our needing to get back to Scripture (which is another way of saying, "Let's ignore modern consciousness all together."). It may well be that there will be many partings of the way in the new millennium.

To Mercy, Pity, Peace, and Love
All pray in their distress. . . .
And all must love the human form,
In heathen, Turk, or Jew;
Where Mercy, Love and Pity dwell
There God is dwelling too.

These four events: the installation of Father Legaux, the ARCIC Statement on Authority, the Lutheran/Roman Catholic Statement on Justification, and the conflicting views of marriage, family and sex underlying California's Defense of Marriage Initiative are revelatory of the way the Holy Spirit works in the world and in the Church at every level. Our first point, then, is that the Holy Spirit plays in the theater of history. And one of the things we need to communicate to each other is that there was never an ideal past. There has never been "a faith once delivered to the saints," still less is there a *depositum fidei*. The early Church was confused, divided and innovative. The Church still manifests those early signs. That is the tradition!

The relationship Grace Cathedral has with Chartres is a sign of many things: the friendship between two priests of different communions; the fact that Roman Catholicism isn't as coherent a system as some people think; the way personal contacts can leapfrog over differences so that a liberal Catholic cathedral in the Anglican tradition can celebrate its relationship with one of the most distinguished cathedrals in the West and bypass the infighting within Anglicanism.[7]

In short, we are now in a situation where the divisions are not so much between the traditions as within them. I have more in common with a French Roman Catholic than many Anglican liberals, on the one hand, and the ultra-conservative group of Anglicans on the other. I find I live more in the world of the Roman Catholic weekly, *The Tablet*, than in any Anglican journal. The issue of the Holy Spirit among us? The issue has to do with the world we actually live in, not the world as we would like it to be. The issue is about history and the faithless attempt to invoke an ahistorical orthodoxy. *The Spirit's theater is history—messy, inconclusive, provisional.* The Spirit calls us to faith and trust, not to rigid tribal certainties; to a God who is inviting, calling, attracting, not to One who is controlling, directing, regulating—to a God who, Greeley insists, charms us. What a thought! A God who charms, who longs for us.

---

[7] A friend of mine recently sent me an e-mail with a list of all the Anglican sects you can find on the World Wide Web.

We need to do for dogma what we have struggled to do with Scrip-
ture—to repudiate literalism and recover the poetic, mythic, meta-
phorical and playful use of the imagination so that the beauty of holi-
ness may reappear.

When I insist on the messiness of history, I'm sometimes accused
of being a relativizer. I reply that I am a Pilgrim of the Absolute. There
are Absolute Truths. We get hints of what they are in the primordial
images of the Woman and her Baby, of the ruined Man on the Cross,
of the Community of Persons, but the last word about them can never
be spoken—at least, not by us. Our shorthand for these images is Incarnation, Redemption and Trinity. Dogma is the first word, not the
last word, about these mysteries. This brings me to my second thesis.
We need to do for dogma what we have struggled to do with Scripture—to repudiate literalism and recover the poetic, mythic,
metaphorical and playful use of the imagination. We need to learn the
game of theology in the context of liturgy. It is a game we should have
learned over a hundred years ago, but literalism/fundamentalism per-
sists. William James said it nearly a hundred years ago in *Varieties of*
Religious Experience: "We must, I think, bid a definitive good-bye to
dogmatic theology."[8] It has been a long good-bye. Without some critical distance, Jesus simply becomes a reflection of ourselves. It is no ac-
cident that the Jesus of the fundamentalists is a conservative Republi-
can. (The Liberal Jesus, too, is out there.) As A. N. Wilson comments
in *God's Funeral,* referring to the Jesus of Benjamin Jowett—"He
might very well have been to Rugby and won a scholarship to Balliol."[9]
I don't mean to encourage either our wallowing in doubt or rejoicing
in a faith eviscerated by reducing it to a warm feeling about the world.
Nigel Williams's hero in his novel *Witchcraft* complains, "My father
was a vicar. . . . One of those new vicars, who don't believe in God or
evil or any of that rubbish. Who thinks RESURRECTION is a novel
by Tolstoy."[10] This is not what I have in mind. But there are questions
we ought to be asking about the life of faith.

   Am I Still a Christian? is a book by Gordon Jeff that answers such
questions as "Do I have to accept *everything* Christians are meant to
believe? Do I have to believe everything I read in the Bible? Why do

---

[8] William James, *The Varieties of Religious Experience,* New York: Penguin, 1982,
p. 448 (Longmans, Green, and Co., 1902).
[9] A. N. Wilson, *God's Funeral,* New York: Norton, 1999, p. 338.
[10] London: Faber and Faber, 1987, 52.

Christians have so many hang-ups about sex? Why doesn't being a Christian make me more happy?" Gordon Jeff writes, "Belief, as I understand it, needs constant testing against the hard reality of experience. . . . It is becoming clear, in the light of recent scholarship, that early Christianity was far more varied than has often been imagined." We shouldn't be upset by that variety. We should rejoice. It means that there are many and varied and even contradictory voices from the past that contribute to the ongoing conversation about our faith. In other words, tradition is a living and not a dead thing. Our task is to keep questions open rather than not *asking* any at all. To ask no questions is to fall into the deadening trance of spiritual boredom. The past is always to be reinterpreted. New stories are being told about it. In the light of these new interpretations, we can retell our own story.

What image of the Spirit might be invoked for the next stage of the human pilgrimage? This brings me to the third thesis.

The business of the Spirit is transformation.

The Spirit is always drawing us into communion, calling us into love. Robert Frost writes in one of his poems of the derring-do of the Holy Spirit. The Spirit is a swashbuckling adventurer charging into earth, in birth after birth, renewing the world. The theme is that God loves us so much that the divine is willing to risk everything to be with us. The mandate for the Church for the twenty-first century? Derring-do for the love of God.

> But God's own descent
> Into flesh was meant
> As a demonstration
> That the supreme merit
> Lay *in risking spirit*
> In substantiation. . . .
> Spirit enters flesh
> And for all it's worth
> Charges into earth
> In birth after birth
> Ever fresh and fresh.
> We may take the view
> That its *derring-do*
> Thought of in the large
> Was one mighty charge

> On our human part
> Of the soul's ethereal
> Into the material.[11]

I am struck over and over again how the churches protect the tradition instead of letting it loose. I make no claims for Grace Cathedral in San Francisco. Just like everyone else, we resist the Spirit and avoid risk as much as possible. But we are, whether we like it or not, one of the great crossroads of the world. I have the privilege of being part of a community dedicated to daily prayer. This ground bass of prayer, coupled with the lively glory and tragedy of living in a modern city, bring together the two aspects of the work of the Spirit—the still small voice and its wind and fire. We are conspirators in the divine plan of transformation by our choosing God and choosing each other over and over again, forgiving each other until seventy times seven. In more prosaic terms, we are called to be involved with the world and with each other in ways we can scarcely imagine. The technical word for it is Incarnation—enfleshment in a particular time and place—and our time is now. We do not seek to escape history. I believe we are called to nothing less than the reimagination of Christianity, which will involve our reentering the tradition in such a way that we begin to trust the future because the future is God's.

Our risk lies in choosing each other over and over again in the face of failure and disappointment. This is what being in love means. The Church is a dangerous place because it calls out the best that is in us—the desire to do the right thing and to be good (not in a goody-goody way but in the deep sense of being true to who we are in God). It is dangerous because we forget that the derring-do originates with God and that it is beautiful. When we forget that our longing for the good and the true is grounded in the beautiful, the spiritual life degenerates into moralism and perfectionism. A cruel idealism overtakes us. Our resentments are mobilized and we become harsh in our judgments. Living in the Spirit is a matter of choosing not to live from our resentments and disappointments but from our new life in Christ. And we have to go on choosing right up until the end.

---

[11] Robert Frost, "Kitty Hawk," in *The Poetry of Robert Frost: The Collected Poems, Complete and Unabridged*, Edward Connery Lathem, ed. (New York: Holt, Rinehart and Winston, 1969), pp. 435–436.

There's a story of the devil confronting a rabbi on his deathbed. The rabbi had led a good and holy life. As he is dying the devil stands beside him. "Ah! So you've won!" sighs the devil. "Not yet!" says the Rabbi. This presupposes a strenuous view of life. The risk of incarnation—the derring-do of the Spirit.

The Spirit is challenging the Church with:

> our continually having to choose each other—not once but over and over again. Some of us are harder to choose than others! Some church people are professional carpers and criticizers and treat the Church as if it were a disappointing supermarket of spiritual entitlements. But we have to go on choosing each other. That's why forgiveness and generosity of spirit are givens;

> our having generously to renegotiate our partnership with one another over and over again;

> our constantly leaving "home" and building a more open and hospitable one; and

> our counting the cost.

What would a community open to the Spirit look like? One way the Spirit works on us is through repentance (saying sorry) and compunction (having the heart punctured—being cut to the quick). They provide the protocols against abuse and manipulation. The capacity to feel sorry for what we have done and the grace to admit it provide the public debate with the lucidity it needs to go forward.[12] So, one way to move ahead is to understand that community is not an end in itself but a by-product of a vision of what human beings are which stretches us beyond our limits and continually introduces us to new possibilities. The work of the Spirit is to unsettle us through love. We don't build community by building community. We build it by having our eye on something else. What is that "something else"? God in Christ. God's Great Risk as manifested in the eucharistic table.

The Spirit is also practical, pushing issues at us in the democratic experiment, in the confusion and challenge of everyday life. A democratic society requires citizens who can repent—admit their mistakes

---

[12]   Gil Bailie put it, "Contrition is the specifically Christian form of lucidity": p. 40 of *Violence Unveiled: Humanity at the Crossroads* (New York: Crossroad, 1995).

and not gloss over their shameful acts. A democratic society needs citizens who are committed to telling the truth even if they seldom get it quite right. It is our seldom "getting it right" that necessitates the ongoing conversation and our ongoing conversion. John Gardner writes: "The play of conflicting interests in a framework of shared purposes is the drama of a free society. It is a robust exercise and a noisy one, not for the faint-hearted or the tidy-minded. Diversity is not simply 'good' in that it implies breadth of tolerance and sympathy. A community of diverse elements has greater capacity to adapt and renew itself in a swiftly changing world."[13] In short, the Spirit calls us to be a compassionate and critical community with clear values. A strenuous form of spiritual maturity is demanded of us.

Finally, I want the Church—particularly on the local level—to be a voice of encouragement to all those who are attracted to God but are not conventionally religious. Brian Mountford puts it well. He has in mind

> people who stumble over bits of the creed, who don't like being herded, who are put off by organized religion or the hypocrisy of its practitioners, who feel unworthy, who think that traditional ways are not the only ways to God, who have been to the center and back again, or who are isolated from traditional Christianity by a culture shift over which they have no control. In short, most people.[14]

Let's choose each other over again and find new ways to say "Yes!" to the Spirit working in us,
Let's be generous and forgiving in our judgments.
Let's count the cost and pay joyfully in sacrifice and service.
Let's show the world who we are by the way we love one another and by our joy in the name of the one who invites us all to share in the derring-do of the Spirit.
Let's accept the messiness of history and the beauty that calls us.
Let's fall in love.

---

[13] John W. Gardner, "Building Community," Washington, D.C.: Independent Sector, 1991, p. 15.
[14] *Postcards on the Way to Heaven*, p. 70.

Spirit: Inner Witness and Guardian of the Soul

TRAVIS DU PRIEST*

A Thirst for the Vision

> The Spirit makes rivers of life flow in him for his own joy and . . .
> those who thirst for this vision (John of Dalyatha).[1]

Created in "the image of God," we have within us a template of
the divine: The same creative, coordinating Spirit which unifies
God—Trinity of Father, Son, Holy Spirit—unifies us, trinity of body,
mind and soul. The same Spirit that generates, holds together, disbands, and out of chaos expands the cosmos, likewise generates, holds
together, disbands, and out of chaos expands our inner cosmos.

In a discussion of the movement in human history from "iconic,"
or literal, analogies of the divine, to the "aniconic," or interior, spiritual analogies, Howard Wilson sums up our collective memories and
convictions in this way:

> The Divine is the great creative Spirit Within which wears the
> universe as Its body. This great cosmic, creative Spirit underlies
> all that exists and moves the world toward its completion not by
> almighty power but by kenotic self-giving.[2]

Each of us in some way knows or intuits "this great cosmic, creative Spirit" which underlies the disparate compartmentalization of
modern life. Bishop Richard Holloway of the Episcopal Church in
Scotland puts the same conviction this way: "Some great self-giving

---

* Travis Du Priest is Director of the DeKoven Center, Racine, Wisconsin.

[1] John of Dalyatha, "On The Vision Of God" (Letter 51), unpublished manuscript,
translated from the French by Sr. Helen Mary, SLG (Oxford: Fairacres, 1998), from
Robert Beulay, ed. and trans., *La Collection des Lettres de Jean De Dalyatha* in
Patrologia Orientalis, Tome 39, Fascicule 3, No. 180 (Belgique: Turnhout, 1978). See
also "John of Dalyatha" in Angelo Di Berardino, ed., *Encyclopedia of the Early
Church*, trans. Adrian Walford, Vol. 1 (Cambridge: James and Clarke, 1992), p. 445.

[2] Howard A. Wilson, "Naming the Beyond in Our Midst: Analogies for the Divine," *Modern Believing*, Vol. 39, No. 4 (October, 1998): 20.

love seems to haunt the universe."[3] Earlier in the century Swiss psychologist Carl Jung said in an interview, "Somewhere there seems to be a great kindness."[4] We know this Self-giving love, this great kindness, because this same Spirit of self-giving love "empowers us, from within, to meet . . . situations with Divine skill"[5]—at once sparking a vision of integrated harmony and rekindling Spirit's interior mission of guardianship which enables us to live flexibly in the dis-integrated, postmodern, post-Christian world.

My thesis is quite simple: Spirit coordinates, or "narrates," our inner lives, acting as inner witness and guardian. The "fruits of the Spirit" are also hidden, manifesting themselves as interior: mission, silence and solitude, still prayer, community, and guardianship.

First, though, let us review the ironic neglect of Spirit in our Western Christian tradition. We do so with thankfulness for this irony, because as the sometime Dean of Emmanuel College, Oxford, Don Cupitt, writes, "Irony is spiritually liberating. It delivers one from the tyranny of power, and from idolatry."[6]

Forgetting Soul, Neglecting Spirit

"Why are you so full of heaviness, O my soul? and why are you so disquieted within me?" (Psalms 42 and 43).

Our souls, the divine within the body, are disquieted within us. We sense this not so much from the muddle of our minds—this seems to be the natural human condition—but rather from the ache of distance from the Great Kindness of the universe and from our own sense of self-worth. One reason for this ache is that the soul itself is sorely neglected, crouching in the dark corner of her inner temple, as psychologist Marion Woodman describes her: a little girl—weak and insecure, wondering if she has anything to offer the more dynamic duo of body-mind.[7] Soul has been passed over, as it were, in favor of

---

3   Richard Holloway, *Dancing on the Edge* (London: Harper Collins, 1997), p. 44.

4   Brewster Beach, "The Theology of Jung's Psychology," Third Lecture in a Series of Three, presented at "A Journey Into Wholeness Conference" (Greenville, S.C.), Audio Tape No. 3.

5   Wilson, p. 21.

6   Don Cupitt, "My Postmodern Witch," *Modern Believing*, Vol 39, No. 4 (October, 1998): 10. See also *After God: The Future of Religion* (London: Weidenfeld and Nicolson, 1997).

7   Marion Woodman, "The Soul in Exile and How to Bring it Home," lecture given at "Civilization in Transition: Jung's Challenge to Culture in Crisis" (Chicago: C. G.

mind and body. The mind is fed with ideas and exercised with challenges, the body, with food and physical activity, but the soul is no longer fed with symbols and metaphors necessary for imaginative liveliness and fortitude.

Moreover, the very context of soul's nurture is in flux: We live in a time of "faith-quakes . . . chaotic and transitional."[8] In this era of chaos and transition, ironically there has been, as there was in a similar transitional period of culture in the seventeenth century, a great revival of interest in spirituality among all peoples. Old systems and languages are either being cast off or experimented with. As Howard Wilson has said, "The Divine has not died, but our language about it has proved inadequate to our contemporary needs."[9]

A third reason for soul's disquietude is that the guardian of our souls is frequently forgotten in prayer and attentiveness: God the Spirit is sorely neglected.

The anchorperson of a religious talk show recently commented to a caller: "Even those who have no earthly family are part of a larger family: We have God our Father, Jesus our Brother, Mary our Mother and the Saints." Where, one wonders, is Holy Spirit? Catherine Mowry LaCugna wonders the same thing in her book, *God For Us: The Trinity and Christian Life*, in which she says that if the concept of the Trinity were to drop out of Christianity altogether, it would hardly be missed or noticed by most contemporary Christians, so focused are Christians on the singular person of the Trinity, Jesus—perhaps remembering God the Father, but consistently neglecting the co-equal and co-eternal God the Holy Spirit.[10]

In Christian gatherings, if Spirit is mentioned, it is usually something of an afterthought—a bow to the Trinity on Trinity Sunday, or in a supercharged—almost apologetic—way on the Day of Pentecost. As the late liturgical scholar H. Boone Porter has pointed out,

---

Jung Center), audiotape. See also *Addiction To Perfection* (Toronto: Inner City Books, 1982 and Boston: Shambhala Lion Audio Tapes).

[8] L. Robert Keck, "Defining Our Moment in History," *Snapshots of the Wind*, (September–October, 1998), p. 1.

[9] Wilson, p. 18.

[10] Catherine Mowry LaCugna, *God for Us: The Trinity and Christian Life*. See also her "Re-Conceiving the Trinity as the Mystery of Salvation," *Scottish Journal of Theology*, Vol. 38, No. 1 (1986): 1–23, and Kilian McDonnell and C. M. LaCugna, "Returning From 'The Far Country': Theses for a Contemporary Trinitarian Theology," *Scottish Journal of Theology*, Vol. 41, No. 2 (1989): 191–215.

The only familiar and easily recited prayer directed to the Holy Ghost (*Veni, Creator Spiritus*) is no longer printed out anywhere in the Prayer Book. . . . It may be regretted that in the last revision (of The Book of Common Prayer) we did not seize the opportunity to restore strong emphasis on the Third Person of the Holy Trinity. . . . Of course both books (1928 and 1979 BCPs) missed the boat in not clearly connecting Holy Communion with the Holy Spirit.[11]

On most Sundays, and in most people's experience, the Spirit is the forgotten person of the Godhead. In the words of one theologian, Spirit seems nothing more than an "edifying appendage to the doctrine of God."[12] Anglican theologian John Macquarrie says the Spirit is "shadowy"; another great Anglican theologian, Norman Pittenger, calls the Spirit "anonymous." Thus, Spirit, like an abandoned child, has been forced to the outer realms of consciousness in the mainline churches and to the inner depths of forgetfulness for many Christians. Forced, as it were, into a submerged corner of consciousness—awaiting our affection, our invocation, awaiting the voice that tells Spirit we love her not as appendage but as God the Spirit herself.

As a result of this neglect and sequestering, the closeness of Spirit-experience—that is, the radically personal, sometimes mystical, sometimes mystifying directness we term "spirituality"—has likewise been sequestered and, consequently, distanced from theology. With the rise of interest in spirituality prompted through such books as *Reclaiming Spirituality*[13] in our own time, the topic again seems frightening to many in the Church: "Once the exclusive property of Western monasteries and Eastern mystics, the term 'spirituality' has now become one of the disturbing metaphors that lingers . . . to remind us of more ancient cosmologies and anthropologies."[14]

---

[11] H. Boone Porter, "What Can 1928 Teach Us?" *The Anglican*, Vol. 28, No. 2 (April, 1999), p. 14.

[12] Heribert Muhlen, "The Person of the Holy Spirit" in Kilian McDonnell, *The Holy Spirit and Power* (Garden City, N.Y.: Doubleday, 1975), p. 12; Elizabeth A. Johnson, *She Who Is: The Mystery of God in Feminist Theological Discourse* (New York: Crossroad, 1977), p. 130.

[13] Dairmuid O'Murchu, *Reclaiming Spirituality* (New York: Crossroad, 1998).

[14] Lawrence Brown, Bernard C. Farr, and R. Joseph Hoffman, eds., *Modern Spiritualities* (Amherst, N.Y.: Prometheus, 1997), p. 9. See also Raimundo Panikkar, who urges us to unite cosmology and anthropology in his phrase "Cosmotheandric Intuition," in L. Anthony Savari Raj, "Overcoming Fragmentation: Discovering the Context of Raimon Panikkar's Cross-Cultural Contribution," *Modern Believing*, Vol. 39, No. 1 (January, 1998): 4; and "Some Basic Assumptions of Spirituality at Work

The Hiddenness of the Spirit

> "We have to realize . . . that any kind of external word, preaching and teaching, is secondary to the inner reality, the inner self, the inner experience" (Bede Griffiths).[15]

One Sunday evening years ago, my wife and I heard a sermon at Westminster Abbey, and I shall always remember the opening: "In the name of God: Spirit, Son, and Father." The young priest certainly got our attention when he reversed the usual Trinitarian formula, and he went on to make his point: It is the work of the Spirit which is primary—leading us to Christ who leads us to the Father. As Brian Gaybba has put it, "The history of doctrine shows that the Spirit, while the first and most intimate way God is experienced, was yet the last to be named explicitly divine."[16] Spirit, throughout the history of Christianity, has been a bit like the Book of Revelation—included but to a large degree overlooked.

The hiddenness of the Spirit, therefore, is nothing new. Hiddenness, in fact, is Spirit's milieu, contrary to what we popularly think when we speak of the manifestations of the Holy Spirit. As a priest preaching in the Cathedral of Santiago de Compostella, Spain, put it on a Trinity Sunday several years ago: "Today we take a glimpse at the inner life of God." It is the Spirit that coordinates, if you will, the inner life of God, providing the means whereby Father is revealed in Son and Son is revealed in Spirit and Spirit is revealed in Father. Spirit "unites" God, as indeed it is Spirit's essential nature to coordinate our being—body, mind, and soul.

In *She Who Is*, Elizabeth A. Johnson writes:

> What is most baffling about forgetfulness of the Spirit is that what is being neglected is nothing less than the mystery of God's personal engagement with the world and its history of love and disaster. . . . Forgetting the Spirit is . . . ignoring the mystery of God

---

(http://www.spiritatwork.org/basic.html); and Richard Cimino and Don Lattin, *Shopping for Faith: American Religion for the New Millennium* (San Francisco: Jossey-Bass, 1998).

[15]   Bede Griffiths, "The Silent Guide," *Parabola*, Vol. 11, No. 1 (February, 1986): 45.

[16]   Brian Gaybba, *The Spirit of Love* (London: Geoffry Chapman, 1987) in Elizabeth A. Johnson, *She Who Is*, p. 128.

closer to us than we are to ourselves, drawing near and passing by
in quickening liberating compassion.[17]

This "closer than closeness" derives from the very nature of God, as
Gerard Longhlin says in "Writing the Trinity": "The Spirit 'narrates'
the Son . . . one can say that the Spirit 'narrates' both Father and Son,
and thus that the Father and Son 'proceed' as much from the Spirit
as that the Spirit 'proceeds' from one or both of them. There is a radical coinhering of the three stories or 'persons.'"[18] Likewise, body
proceeds from mind, and mind proceeds from soul, and soul proceeds
from body and mind—all in a "radical coinhering" of the human
interior.

Spirit coordinates, or "narrates," our inner lives, and the "shadowy" and "anonymous" qualities of the Spirit in traditional theology
are, then, actually positive in the realm of spirituality and personal
experience. One might even say that it is the "shadowy anonymity" of
Spirit which allows her to do her important work, that is, function as
Inner Witness seeking to bring into consciousness her role of
guardianship—of protecting and nurturing the soul, that is, the self-
united-with-God, which is so often bruised or unattended.

In fact, the deeper into the well of the human psyche one peers,
the more likely one is to glimpse Spirit's dynamic energy and power:
She works most intently in the cave of the interior. Her "language" is
symbol and metaphor, and she communicates through dreams and
daydreams, visions and musings. Spirit is alive and well in our unconscious mind and dream life, sending up clues, in the "language" of
image and metaphor, about the status of our souls. She also oversees
interior dialogue, allowing us to "hear within" both our negative and
often-inflated self images and opinions of others.

The Spirit of Interior Mission

"He dwells within man in his innermost heart as the Spirit, the
ultimate witness of all things" (Victor Danner).[19]

---

[17]   Elizabeth A. Johnson, *She Who Is: The Mystery of God in a Feminist Theological
Perspective* (New York: Crossroad, 1992), p. 131.
[18]   Gerard Longhlin, "Writing the Trinity," *Theology*, Vol. 97, No. 776 (March–
April, 1994): 82.
[19]   Victor Danner, "Shahadah," *Parabola*, Vol. XI, No. 1 (February, 1986): 48. See
also Travis Du Priest, "Turning Inward, Facing Outward," *Reflections* (Advent, 1987):
2–4, reprinted in *Voices: The C. G. Jung Center of Milwaukee* (February/March,
1988): 1–2.

Dom Bede Griffiths, a Roman Catholic Benedictine, founded and lived in an ashram in Southern India where he taught the crucial importance of Eastern and Western religions to each other. He speaks in an interview of "the silent witness . . . which is the witness behind the active self. I always understand it in the Christian sense of the spirit, the pneuma of St. Paul." This, Dom Griffiths says, is "the point of our openness to the Divine . . . the point of witness and self-realization."[20] The silent guide is the Holy Spirit working as interior missionary seeking to bring the self to the self, to that point of "the Divine self manifesting in that human self," to the point, as a Quaker writer has phrased it, "where God and I mingle," that is, to the soul.

So, the radical or root work of the Spirit is ongoing interior mission—"the witness behind the active self"—not the more easily identifiable outward manifestations of the Spirit; and not even the energy of the "creative" person. To make possible external manifestations is not Spirit's primary work: External manifestations garner thanksgivings, but often the gratitude is for what Spirit does for me, or for us, and not for Spirit as Spirit. Indeed, what Spirit actually does for me is to ensure that there is an authentic "me." In other words, Spirit brings consciousness itself into being.

Even in our unconscious state, in our lack of alertness, however, Spirit's work is quietly being done without recognition of any kind. There are many inner voices making claims on us each minute of each day, and when we turn inward through mental prayer or meditation we often overhear our own "interior talk show," and often we are startled by what we overhear—conversations of a conflicted inner community. But to overhear our own interior conversation is affirmative, for this "interior talk show" is sponsored and narrated, as it were, by Spirit.

Anyone who doubts that he or she is a community of voices need only turn inward and sit silently in meditative awareness for a few minutes. One quickly experiences something akin to an inner zoo with thoughts like monkeys swinging wildly from tree to tree. Behind all of these competing thoughts and voices, though, is a still small voice of generosity seeking either to bend our awareness once again toward a "centered unity," or to equip us with ironic fortitude to live among the dissembled scraps of the postmodern, post-Christian world. Again, as

---

[20]   Griffiths, *Parabola*, 45. See also *The Golden String*, in which Bede Griffiths records the inner experiences that begin his spiritual quest.

the master of such experiences, John of Dalyatha, writes, "Happy is he who fixes his eyes continually on You, oh my Paradise which appears in me."[21] Whether for a few moments only or as ongoing presence in the lives of certain mystics, the Kingdom of God is to be found "within us," as our Lord said—Spirit's domain of guardianship.

There is, then, at the core of our being, a missionary—proclaiming, primarily in symbol and metaphor, the recovery of self, the recovery of what former Benedictine Abbot Benedict Reid refers to as "spiritual worth," lack of judgment, acceptance of self and openness to others.[22] In light of the mean-spirited forms of fundamentalisms in all religions, which assault and grieve the soul, the awareness and honoring of this missionary Spirit is needed today, perhaps as much if not more than ever. Also needed are the very pathways this inner witness invites us to travel, the pathways of silence, solitude, and still prayer toward a new mission field of community.

The Spirit of Interior Silence and Solitude

"Happy is he whose thoughts are reduced to silence" (John of Dalaytha).[23]

This Spirit of silence places on the lips of Christ, "Say nothing / "Don't tell" (Mark 5:43, 7:36). The Spirit of silence, manifesting a Spirit of solitude, urges Christ's withdrawal from the crowds (Matthew 14:13), away from the activity and debates of the people, to quiet and deserted places to be in communion with self and God.

This same Spirit of silence and solitude wants to arrest inwardly the evaluative obsessions and negative evaluations of ourselves and others, and our own glib and fatuous thoughts (manifested in talk) about God and religion. It is one of Spirit's more obvious manifestations to arrest an ill-conceived action or comment from within, that is, to assist us, inwardly, in finding the place of silence and to touch that interior spot which poet William Blake calls "the healing moment."[24] So it is the protective work of Spirit, in a hidden sense, to bridle our tongue, thereby guarding our soul. Christ was so consciously aware of

---

[21]   John of Dalyatha, Letter 51.
[22]   Benedict Reid, OSB, "Meditation," in *Regula: The Newsletter of the Friends of St. Benedict*, Vol. 1, No. 2 (Fall, 1998): 1. See also *A Spirit Loose In The World* (Summerland, Calif.: Harbor House [West], 1993).
[23]   John of Dalyatha, Letter 51.
[24]   Marion Woodman, *Addiction To Perfection*.

the workings of the inward Spirit, so consistently living out of "the healing moment," that he remained in silence and solitude equally during the cleansing of the temple and as he hung on the cross.

Just as silence is often the most appropriate response to a beautiful painting or poem or film, so too, silence is often the appropriate response to the image of Christ on the cross drawing the whole world to himself, or to Christ in glory robed as our great high priest, rather than any words of analysis or preachment. Of course, interior silence is much more difficult to attain than a mere absence of noise from the external world, and though related, far more difficult than bridling one's tongue. Yet it is stillness and a relative quietude releasing us from chit-chat which allows us to scan the multifarious activity of our mind and see what is coming into consciousness for review and reflection.

It is the interior Spirit of silence and solitude that will eventually take us beyond the physical realm into the realm of "transcendent mystery within."[25] Our bodies are, indeed, the temples of the Holy Spirit, and we discover the kindness and the heart of compassion from which all creation emanates.

In the conscious seeking out of silence and solitude, especially in acts of meditation and still prayer, we ourselves become "the silent witness" to the compassion of the universe—acceptance of ourselves and of others—and, indeed, of the easy-going, ever-shifting flow of life. This witness is far more salutary than a public, verbal witness that seeks to convert others.

Silence and solitude are commissioned and dispatched to our consciousness as partners, two by two, for interior mission: silence and solitude are curative, that is, meditative and medicinal—for the deep silence of the heart experienced in solitude is the medication of the Spirit, unifying through rest, body, mind, and soul. This meditative and medicinal curative of silence and solitude is Spirit's evangelistic work as inner missionary.

The Spirit of Interior Still Prayer

"Now this transformation by the renewal of our mind is entirely the work of the Spirit" (Sister Edmée, SLG).[26]

---

[25] Griffiths, p. 46.
[26] Sister Edmée, SLG, "Prayer: The Work of the Spirit" (Oxford: Fairacres SLG Press, 1985/1996), p. 5.

Stealing away in time and space, bending toward inward and outward silence, listening to our own inward chatter until it dissipates or as it lifts up topics and images needful of attention—these are experiences of "real presence." They are brought about through the emptiness of silent solitude, Spirit's interior manifestations. To be in this place—the heart of prayer—is both to "experience" the Holy Spirit and to be under Spirit's guardianship.

In the heart of prayer, the Spirit becomes, as it were, the active agent of all our praying. This activity, this prayer, is ongoing whether we are aware of it or not. When we are conscious of "being at prayer," we are actually "practicing," that is rehearsing, our own availability or openness to the Spirit's prayer.

Always, even when we are conscious of being at prayer, it is the Spirit who prays, not us. As St. Paul says in Romans 8:25, "If we don't know how or what to pray . . . the Spirit does our praying in and for us, making prayer out of our wordless sighs, or aching groans."

Indeed, as Julian of Norwich put it in her *Showings*:

> God teaches us to pray, and to have firm trust that we shall have what we pray for, because everything which is done would be done, even though we had never prayed for it. But God's love is so great that he regards us as partners in his good work; and so he moves us to pray for what it pleases him to do. . . . Therefore we pray much that he may do what is pleasing to him.[27]

What we consciously think of as prayer—what I call our "practice"—is inarticulate precisely because silence is the language of God. God spoke but one word for all eternity, and that word, spoken in silence, is Christ, to paraphrase St. John of the Cross, conceived by the power of Holy Spirit.

In one sense our yielding to prayer signals our heart's desire to be connected to God, no matter the particular type of prayer—verbal or non-verbal, individual or corporate. Yet in reality it is more likely that what we have yielded to—or picked up out of the spirited wind—is God's prayer of creation throughout the universe or Christ's ongoing intercession on our behalf, or the prayers of the saints who cloud around us as witnesses to the Spirit's presence and the world of ongoing prayer. It is this cosmic prayer of God that directs us inward.

---

[27] Julian of Norwich, *Showings*, Short Text, trans. by Edmund Colledge and James Walsh (New York: Paulist Press, 1978), Chapter 19, p. 158.

It is the Spirit who prays, even when "we" are at prayer. There is only one prayer, and that prayer is the Spirit's. The Cistercian monk and writer Thomas Merton wrote, "The danger is that our very prayers get between God and us. The great thing in prayer is not to pray, but to go directly to God."[28] This giving up of prayer is the work of the Spirit. The pathway of going to God is the way of the Spirit. That God we reach is Spirit.

These prayers, uttered in silence, are offered as silence itself, and become invitations into the great silence, the quietness at the center of cosmic and personal consciousness. The moments of epiphany in our lives that allow us a glimpse into the cosmic-personal consciousness are the essence of bonding, union, and friendship. Hence, we can say that even on the interior—unseen and hidden from outward manifestation—Holy Spirit is creating community.

The Spirit of Interior Community

"Every conversion is a discovery of the absolute in some measure, within a particular, limited human context" (Bede Griffiths).[29]

The Spirit pulls to the future. Yet we are uncertain about the future and how to deal with change. The Spirit pulls together. Yet we are uncertain about unity and how to deal with solidarity. As Anglicans understand her, Spirit coordinates in a spirit of catholicism, that is, pulls forward and pulls together in an all-encompassing sense. Alan Jones once offered at a conference Oscar Wilde's definition of the Catholic Church: Here comes everybody. Spirit's work is always to lead, coordinate, and unite the disparate.

The Spirit is pulling together people of all races, cultures, and religious backgrounds into a family of spirited folk through the world. The challenge to the churches, Anglicans included, is that more and more young people have little to do with religion or even spirituality which does not check out with personal experience. As nettlesome as this challenge is, it is one that we dare not avoid, as different people of different religions increasingly acknowledge, especially among the young.

To some extent, the fruits of interior community are manifested externally in actual, visible communities, as cell groups and spiritual

---

28 Thomas Merton on Prayer, quoted in Sr. Brigit-Carol, SD, "A Lenten Meditation," Cypress Mill, Tex.: The DeKoven Hermitage, February 28, 1998): 1.
29 Griffiths, *Parabola*, p. 47.

friends meet to share silence and discussion; but for the most part these visible manifestations remain "hidden" from institutional structures and churches which think and organize themselves in terms of definitions, limits, and distinguishing characteristics, hence perpetuating the great public divisions among Christian churches—not to mention perpetuating the great divide between the different religions of the world. To quote Benedict Reid: "The Spirit is teaching us that there is but one community made up of all people. How do we talk to, and love, each other in this one-world family?"[30] Here is an area where the outward manifestations of Spirit are as needed as they are missing. Several "manifestations" are, however, on the horizon.

A document produced in England called "A New Theological Vision" suggests that "The neglect of other faith traditions is willful. In a culture where religious choice has become a significant issue, the lack of interest in other religions is an abdication of responsibility."[31] Bishop William Swing of the Diocese of California has recently set forth his vision of "United Religions," affirming that "There will be no wholeness for the created order until there is peace among religions," creating an "Olympic village of the sacred."[32]

The Holy Spirit draws into oneness all humanity. The Holy Spirit is the essence of catholic faith, uniting the living and the dead, the hot and the lukewarm, the believer and the unbeliever, the reflective and the silly, the weak and the strong, the rich and the poor, the sanctimonious and the blasphemer. The Holy Spirit believes, the Holy Spirit holds faith, the Holy Spirit ministers, as there is one belief, one faith, one ministry—hidden yet powerful—throughout all religions of the world (see 1 Corinthians 2:1–11).

Just as the Spirit of silence and solitude generates a coordinated sense of wholeness in body, mind and soul, so the Spirit of interior community bonds our inner communities of disparate voices and concerns, as She bonds people of Spirit throughout the world. Nowhere is this truth of one silence and one humanity so profoundly obvious as when we are silent in community—meals during a silent retreat, silent periods of reflection after Scripture readings during the liturgy, or

---

[30] Benedict Reid, p. 1.
[31] "A New Theological Vision: A Call to Join the Forum for Religion and Theology," *Modern Believing*, Vol. 39, No. 4 (October, 1998): 32–40.
[32] William E. Swing, *The Coming United Religions* (Ada, Mich.: CoNexus, 1999), reviewed by J. Barrington Bates (San Francisco, CA), manuscript.

communal silent sittings at meditation centers or houses of prayer, during which the silence "says," if you will, "We're all in this together."

The Spirit of Interior Community converts individual hearts and is converting nations, not only in but also through silence and hiddenness. As the magnificent Good Friday collect in The Book of Common Prayer puts it, "by the effectual working of your providence, carry out in tranquility the plan of salvation." This "effectual working" of God's providence can often best be glimpsed through a spirit of unlearning and of letting go of structures and strictures that are outdated and ineffective. Spirit says, along with French mystic Charles Péguy, "Go and learn to unlearn."

Spirit as Interior Guardian

> "Happy is he who at all times carries in his heart the remembrance of You, for it is his soul which is intoxicated with your sweetness" (John of Dalyatha).[33]

A large part of our unlearning is the letting go of ineffectual language systems and the attainment of new metaphors, as we gather in a spirit of global community and solidarity. In an essay on the rootlessness of our modern culture, Christopher Savage writes:

> The churches, if they are to witness effectively in a pluralistic multi-faith post-modern society, have to find metaphors for God that convey to the current age its message—its gospel. That will mean telling the stories, but part of the process of becoming will also mean recreating the possibility of shared values and consensus living alongside the many and varied features of our post-modern society.[34]

It is the search for these metaphors that is the challenge to the contemporary Church, indeed to all contemporary people of faith throughout the world. The Spirit is, of course, already providing these metaphors—for those who have eyes to see, ears to listen, inner sanctuaries in which to reflect. Bishop Swing's "Olympic village of the sa-

---

[33] John of Dalyatha, Letter 51.
[34] Christopher Savage, "Postmodernism, Theology and Rootlessness," *Modern Believing*, Vol. 39, No. 4 (October, 1998): 39. See also Clifford Longman, "Kicking the Abbey Habit," *The Church Times*, via Gregory Singleton, e-mail, IPC News Corporation (April 1, 1999): 1.

cred" is one such metaphor, built on the "outrageous confidence" that divine unity centers the universe.

The Spirit envelops our whole being—body, mind and soul. Hence, the language of the Spirit is that of image and metaphor, the aesthetic "language" that speaks to the heart and gut as well as the mind—at times even befuddling the rational mind. No one understands or articulates this holistic language better than psychologist Marian Woodman, who says, "Metaphor heals because it speaks to the whole person . . . without the metaphor the mind may be fed, but the imagination and heart go empty . . . and the Soul starves."[35] Bishop Richard Holloway calls metaphor "the poetry of God," and goes on to say, "Much of it has lost its surprise and has been used wrongly by insecure believers as code or password to test the authenticity of others."[36] He postulates that one reason people with inquiring minds feel there is no place for them in churches is "the apparent fixity of our symbolical systems."[37]

To embrace Spirit and to have Spirit embrace us as churches and communities of faith, we must turn to the collective imagery and metaphors of poetry, fable, mythology, legend, folklore, story, art, music, architecture, sculpture—the world of graphic and verbal metaphor. This is a world largely outside of rational analysis and comprehension: a world of symbol that transports us from one realm to another. In our poetry, literature and art, in our songs and dances, Spirit nourishes us and our individual souls as well as our collective, cultural souls. She nourishes us anywhere she can rise to consciousness through image and metaphor, even in archaic and ancient tales and symbolic myths.

With poetry, symbol, and metaphoric art, we enter a world of apprehension. We enter a world where we are ourselves apprehended, a world in which we can only apprehend in awe and silence what has embraced us—gifts of the Spirit. Literary critic George Steiner puts it like this: "Any coherent understanding of what language is and how

---

[35] Marion Woodman, "The Soul In Exile."

[36] Holloway, *Dancing*, p. 44.

[37] Holloway, *Dancing*, p. 159. See also W. T. Brattson, "The Insufficiency of Scripture,"in *Theology*, Vol. 101, No. 803 (September–October, 1998): 351: "The insufficiency of Scripture necessitates that Christians employ an auxiliary method of determining their doctrinal and ethical norms, such as tradition, the guidance of the contemporary Church, direct inspiration by the Spirit."

language performs . . . [is] underwritten by the assumption of God's presence."[38]

In both our personal lives and in society at large, Spirit sends up and out the language of Spirit—metaphor, image, and symbol, but always hidden from analysis and rational explication, even from verbal articulation. This is "God's wisdom, secret and hidden . . . for the Spirit searches everything, even the depths of God" (1 Corinthians 2:7, 10).

The primary manifestation of Spirit as guardian of soul is in igniting interior metaphors which generate what William Blake calls "the healing moment," that is, waking up to what we are about to do. When we are about to have a knee-jerk reaction to a comment or situation, when we are about to utter false witness or are about to repeat an unhealthy compulsive pattern, Spirit is there in the split-second gap, as it were, offering the alternative gift of silence or interior retreat to a place of solitude. Spirit's ongoing interior work over and over safeguards and restores the soul.

Such emerging metaphors as "one community," "Olympic village of the sacred," "family of families" are already healing and nurturing the souls of many spirit-filled people around the world. If attended to inwardly, these same metaphors may eventually manifest themselves in an exterior reality. And most certainly, where there is outward manifestation of Spirit's interior mission, there is redoubled nourishment inwardly at that meeting place of the human and the divine: soul.

The Spirit's interior mission, then, is to set our minds toward that which is eternal within ourselves, within our world, within the cosmos, to "declare the mysteries of ancient times" (Psalm 78:2). The Spirit is interior preacher, witness, missionary, and guardian. And the Spirit is forever communicating through silence, solitude, still prayer, imagery, and metaphor—all languages of love. The Spirit is guiding us each day back to love of self, love of others, and love of the eternal, the transcendent divine. Thereby, for a moment at least, the Spirit is restoring soul to herself, allowing soul to live free and unencumbered like her inner witness and guardian: Spirit.

---

[38] George Steiner, *Real Presences* (London: Faber and Faber, 1989), p. 3. See also Karl-Josef Kuschel, "Presence of God? Towards the Possibility of a Theological Aesthetic," in "An Analysis of George Steiner," trans. by Andrew Hass, *Literature and Theology*, Vol. 10, No. 1 (March, 1996): 1–19.

Speaking Personally of You, Holy Spirit

TILDEN EDWARDS*

Words about you, Spirit Divine, reverberate around my caged mind, seeking fragile order. I can only stutter about your vast-intimate Nowness, about which my mind knows nothing but rumors—rumors seeping out from my spiritual heart's more directly attuned antennae, and from others' spiritual hearts reflected in Scripture and tradition. Yet my mind's stutter is a calling, a gift from you, my mind's way of getting in on your Mystery a little. My prayer is that in the probing of your Presence, you indeed will feed my mind with the word-food that enriches my appreciation, and perhaps others' appreciation, of your ever-inspiring reality.

I write in the humility of knowing that you finally will turn my words about you to writing on water, fading into your vast sea. Yet my mind wants to probe your uncreated energy anyway. I want to ponder these great waves that rise up and move me only you know where. I want to gaze upon your fire that burns in and around me. I want to ask whether I can sustain trust in your uncontrollable freedom. When that trust is empowered, I am moved to participate in your vision for fresh life and beauty at every level of living. I am able to embody your love and receive your many life-giving, community-bonding gifts, however incompletely. I have come to know so well that I can receive none of these favors without your inspiration and timing.

I want so much from you. I think it is you who place these yearnings in me. You are in the wanting of what I most deeply want, even when this deep wanting is hidden within my lesser desires. And how else could it be, since my very being is a temple for you? Indeed, I am a clay form you shape into life and invite into a dance. It is a dance whose steps you do not command but simply show me, leaving me to take them only as I am willing, and in the form befitting my unique way of moving. You dignify me with such freedom, and together we

* Tilden Edwards is an Episcopal priest and Founder and Senior Fellow of the Shalem Institute for Spiritual Formation in Bethesda, Maryland.

improvise a dance that has never been done before, yet mysteriously blends with the steps of all your other dancers.

Your steps lead me to the arms of Jesus. The chaff of my life burns up in his fiercely loving gaze. You bring his Mind into mine as he shows me his life and way, and his old and new spiritual families. You open my eyes and heart in child-like wonder as I absorb the burning wisdom—love flowing through his words and deeds. You show me his way of death as an empowering and all-embracing act of love, holding every paradox, every contradiction, every living being in its redeeming embrace. You show me his living Spirit as your own.

Through Jesus' whole life and death and life beyond, you draw me ever deeper into the One from whom he comes. Yet that One Personal Source of all includes you, and the ever-expressive One shaped into Jesus Savior, all three moving together as completely One, one eternal Circle of Love, energizing all that is. Who can understand this infinite mystery? And yet I sense a dim reflection of it in the very depths of my soul. Awed by my unique participation in your divine creating, reconciling, loving Being, I feel a special belonging to your Love Circle, and a connectedness with everything your energy forms in creation. I sense my incipient wholeness, everyone's incipient wholeness, in your ever-inviting Wholeness, and I rejoice in this great good news for us all.

That goodness is qualified by the ways I see how fallen my mind and will can be from your Truth. Indeed, there are many fallen spirits within and around me that inspire turmoil, fear, self-absorption, and division. I ask you to give me a discerning heart so that I can recognize and embrace your real Spirit of Truth. I ask you to continue to draw me deeper into your Circle of Love, where there is nothing but your Truth. I know I can never grasp its endless dimensions, but I trust you will empower what I need to realize for your glorification in each dimension of my life, and I trust you will forgive me for those times that I do not respond to your invitations.

You give me the special community of your Church with all its treasures, born and shaped in your Fire. You give it as an arena for ever more full awakening to the great united Circle of Love deep in the heart of all things. And you give it as a means of encouragement to live out of that awakening with others, with all of your gifts and fruit reverberating between us, within and beyond the Church. You show me the Church as a sign for everyone in the world of his or her own varied spiritual callings and ultimate mutual belonging, all united by an orientation to your creative and reconciling love.

Often you seem so hidden in the Church that confusion, delusion, and willfulness take over its active life. Fearful, self-securing ways sow bitter dissension rather than respect for rich diversity, and self-justifying projects rather than ones discerned from listening to you, and holding on to stale bread rather than opening in trust to the ever-fresh Bread of Life you offer. The heart of the community's holiness then is eclipsed and it is left with hollow words about your Circle of Love that are not truly believed and followed. Yet I trust that you can never be finally eclipsed. It is our empty ways that in time will be shown up for the sad substitutes they are for your life-giving ways. I think you will in time let such communities die to their falseness through your inspiration, or else you will simply allow them to die completely so that a truer community can eventually come into being. Sometimes, though, you seem to let a particular church die not because of any falseness, but because it has lived out its purpose, and you are calling its members to other communities now. Such a community can go in peace, to love and serve your Love-Circle in new ways.

You seem to be inspiring a more fluid Church community life today, heavenly Spirit. You don't give me the security of clear boxes with strong walls, floors, and ceilings, with the same people committed there for a long time. Instead, you seem to be creating a more membrane-like Church, one with more permeable boundaries, permeable to people, ideas, practices, coming and going, and more willing for a full array of your gifts and fruit to show themselves, for the sake of your kin-dom. You are asking for a lot of openness and turning to you for discernment as you shape your Church in new ways whose consequences I don't know, but can only trust. In this flux your wide-open name rests on my lips, and those of many others, as a constant we can share and turn to for guidance, a name that invokes your living Presence to take us through times of unknowing to fresh life ever-forming.

Because you are so wide-open, Living Spirit, your name has become the divine name of choice for millions of people today, both in and out of the Church, who sense your hidden movements drawing them beyond their little selves. You allow them to see you as a great Mystery deep within and around them, too great to be contained by any doctrine narrower than the sky. You let them see you as universal Spirit winding through all religions and cultures and creation itself. In you they find a connection with everyone, everything. Any other divine name they often find too confining, too divisive. They yearn for whatever divine name can bring the world together in a common trust and sense of unity. If they read about it, they would rejoice in the inclusive, life-renewing covenant with Noah that was made with all earthly beings. They would rejoice even more in a sense of divine covenant with creation itself, formed from the beginning in your creative womb. They would see all more particular covenants, such as the ones with the patriarchs, Moses, and Jesus, as gifts of yours within this shared, inclusive covenant.

I share these people's yearning for a holy name, a sense of loving, holy power that can show me our unity beyond our endless personal and sectarian differences. I, too, feel the world's fragmentations. You are giving me your name with special strength today, because I need your direct, pervasively uniting guidance in this volatile global community. Even as you are so infinitely intimate, you are so infinitely boundaryless in my imagination that you escape many of my narrowing human projections. You elude anything I can finally wrap my mind around, anything I can domesticate. You cannot be captured in any mind-net, which I am sure is why you have been written about so little compared to the other names of your holy Circle of Love.

And yet you are given to my faith as an integral part of that larger Circle. I need your love made visible in Jesus and drawing me to the heart of your Circle, as I have said. But I need you to show Jesus as big as yourself. That means showing me not only Jesus of Nazareth, but also the great I AM in him, in whom I and every living being can find fullness of life. Jesus that big belongs to more than the Church, just as you do. The Church itself belongs and witnesses to this vast-intimacy of your Circle of Love, and it bursts its own frail containers again and again as you awaken it to your transforming Presence.

I could go on and on with the ways you have im-pressed me, Holy Spirit, both through the tradition of your Presence and through my own experience. But these feel like enough impressions to refresh my mind with an awareness of your Livingness so beyond my mind's grasp, yet closer than each forming thought. Now you seem to be calling me to an open silence, where my words can rest and my heart can be simply present in you, through everything that appears. In that place we all share before interpretive words rise, you let every appearance be accommodated, just as it is; you show everything in community, just as it is. There I listen to your murmurings too deep for words. There I find life connected in a way that no thought can de-construct, because it is the way you allow life to be appreciated before my mind begins to grasp for any construction. Before my silence now, my mind-in-heart would offer you this fervent plea:

Stirring Creator Spirit,
   spring open our hearts with the divine scent of your breath,
     move us to shared life guided by your fire,
       carry us to the Light One shining in Jesus,
         ground us in the Dark-Radiant One whose life you share,
     that we may live freely in the ever-fresh unity and vision of your
       Circle of Love.

The Holy Spirit:
Source of Unity in the Liturgy

LOUIS WEIL*

For Anglicans, discussion of the role of the Holy Spirit in the liturgy has tended to focus on two specific issues in sacramental theology: first, there is the long debate among a wide range of Anglican theologians and liturgists concerning the action of the Holy Spirit in Christian Initiation. More specifically, this debate has focused on the Spirit's role in confirmation.[1]

At least with regard to the authorized liturgical texts, this debate has been concluded for the American Church in the rites of baptism and confirmation in the 1979 Book of Common Prayer: the rite clearly indicates (BCP, p. 298) that "Holy Baptism is full initiation by water and the Holy Spirit into Christ's Body the Church." This assertion is affirmed also in the prayer (BCP, p. 308), which follows the water rite:

> Heavenly Father, we thank you that by water and the Holy Spirit
> you have bestowed upon *these* your *servants* the forgiveness of sin
> and have raised *them* to the new life of grace.

The text then continues with the prayer for the gifts of the Spirit that had appeared in earlier versions of the Prayer Book (in a somewhat different form) in the rite of confirmation:

> Sustain *them*, O Lord, in your Holy Spirit. Give *them* an inquiring
> and discerning heart, the courage to will and to persevere, a spirit
> to know and to love you, and the gift of joy and wonder in all your
> works.

---

* Louis Weil is the James F. Hodges Professor of Liturgics at the Church Divinity School of the Pacific, Berkeley, California.

[1] The literature on this subject is vast. The most convenient survey of the issue may be found in: Daniel B. Stevick, *Baptismal Moments, Baptismal Meanings* (New York: Church Hymnal Corporation, 1987). A more recent update on developments in the Episcopal Church may be found in: Ruth A. Meyers, *Continuing the Reformation* (New York: Church Publishing Incorporated, 1997), esp. pp. 104–112. See also the discussion in: Charles P. Price and Louis Weil, *Liturgy for Living*, revised edition (Harrisburg, Pa.: Morehouse Publishing, 2000), pp. 65–89.

Archbishop Cranmer's inclusion of this prayer at confirmation obviously contributed to the confusion within Anglicanism over the role of the Holy Spirit in baptism. It contributed to the idea that confirmation was an essential aspect of the initiatory process, and the claim that confirmation was the primary sacramental action associated with the gift of the Holy Spirit. This latest revision in the American BCP resolves that problem by clearly identifying the Spirit's activity with the "full initiation" which baptism effects.[2]

The second area where one may find a reasonable amount of material among Anglican authors, although much less than that concerning Initiation, is with regard to the role of the Holy Spirit in the eucharist. More particularly, this relates to the inclusion of an *epiclesis* or Invocation of the Holy Spirit in the text of the eucharistic prayer. For the Eastern Orthodox, this crucial element in the various forms of the eucharistic prayer is absolutely fundamental to the integrity of the prayer. In the West, on the other hand, the primary prayer of the Western Church prior to the Reformation—that is, the Roman Canon—was notably weak in its proclamation of the role of the Spirit in the eucharist.[3]

This difference is an important reminder of the much more central place that the Holy Spirit has held in the theology and spirituality of the Eastern traditions than has been true in the West. It is appropriate to begin our discussion on the role of the Holy Spirit in the liturgy with some comments on the difference between the Eastern and Western traditions. This will lead, in turn, to a suggestion as to the underlying theological issue concerning the Spirit in the liturgy.

A story is reported from the first session of the Second Vatican Council in 1963. The work of the Roman Catholic bishops on the text of the *Constitution on the Liturgy* was moving toward completion. It was decided that the text should be shown to the ecumenical observers at the council and that their reactions to it would be solicited. Comments were positive, on the whole, except for one matter. The observers noted that, apart from formulaic references to the Holy Trinity, the document did not ascribe any significant role to the Holy Spirit in the Church's liturgical worship.

---

[2] The classical study of this question is that of G. W. H. Lampe, *The Seal of the Spirit: A Study in the Doctrine of Baptism and Confirmation in the New Testament and the Fathers,* second edition (London: SPCK, 1967).

[3] A useful summary of the evolution of the *epiclesis* in the eucharist may be found in: W.R. Crockett, *Eucharist: Symbol of Transformation* (New York: Pueblo Publishing Company, 1989), pp. 54–63, and passim.

When we read the text of the *Constitution* as it was finally promulgated on December 4, 1963, we can see that some attempt was made to respond to this criticism through the insertion at a number of points in the text of such phrases as "in the Holy Spirit" or "through the Holy Spirit." Although these insertions were intended to address this lack of attention to the Spirit's role in the liturgy, they seem little more than tokenism. The document does not give serious attention to the place of the Holy Spirit in Christian worship. In this, the document embodies the generally inadequate theology of the Spirit that has characterized the Western theological and liturgical tradition.

For the Eastern Orthodox, this lack indicates a serious theological imbalance in the Western tradition. In Western Christianity, on the other hand, there has been a strong Christocentric focus both in its theology and in its liturgical prayer. This is seen, for example, in the debate between East and West on the inclusion of the *filioque* clause in the Nicene Creed: "who proceeds from the Father *and the Son*," which the Eastern Church has never accepted as a legitimate addition. The *filioque* was first introduced in Spain without conciliar authority.[4] For the West, the words were an affirmation of the full divinity of the Son in its confrontation with the Arian heresy. From Spain, the inclusion of the word in the Creed spread throughout the rest of the Western Church.

My purpose in raising the issue of the *filioque* is not to contribute to the debate as to whether or not it should be omitted from the authorized text found in such Western liturgical documents as The Book of Common Prayer. Rather, I think the inclusion of the *filioque* in the West is indicative of the Christological prism through which we in the West interpret all divine action. Both our theological tradition, and Western spirituality as well, tend to be shaped by this Christocentric orientation. The characteristic Anglican focus on the Incarnation is our own particular expression of that orientation.

As a consequence, our theology of the Holy Spirit has not received a comparable emphasis. There has thus resulted a failure to lay claim to the balance and complementarity between the work of the Incarnate Son and the Holy Spirit that has been consistently maintained by the Orthodox East. In writings of the Eastern Fathers, one finds an image that embodies this complementarity: the Son and the Spirit are spoken of as the right and left hands of God. This image im-

---

[4]   At the Third Council of Toledo in 539.

plies not only the complementarity of their work, but also the distinc-
tiveness of each.

This metaphor of the two hands is characteristically Eastern. The
mission of the Incarnate Lord in history is, as it were, complemented
by the free and unconditioned activity of the Holy Spirit. The Son's
work is revealed in the historical and institutional structures of human
society, and in a particular way, in the institutional life of the Church
understood as his Body. The work of the Spirit serves as the needed
counterpoint to the work of the Son by bringing new life and breath to
institutions that would otherwise rigidify. In this sense, the Holy Spirit brings God's judgment upon the tendency to absolutize any human
institution, even the most sacred. If that work of the Spirit is not affirmed and welcomed, religious institutions can become idols, self-
serving rather than serving the goals for which they exist.

What does all this suggest about the role of the Holy Spirit with
regard to the liturgical life of the Church? More specifically, how does
the work of the Spirit manifest itself in liturgical prayer? The forms of
eucharistic prayer found in the various versions of the American
Prayer Book, for example, have included an Invocation of the Holy
Spirit, an *epiclesis*, which is not found in the authorized eucharistic
prayers of some other provinces of the Anglican Communion. Why
was this a matter of such urgency for Samuel Seabury, the first bishop
of the American Church? The English Prayer Book of 1662 had been
used in the American colonies prior to the revolution of 1776, and in
most ways the first American Prayer Book of 1789 took that book as its
model. And yet the eucharistic prayer in the 1789 BCP included an
Invocation of the Spirit.

It is not necessary to repeat in this article the well-documented
history of Samuel Seabury and the reasons for which he went to the
bishops in Scotland for episcopal ordination.[5] But it was that link with
the Scottish Episcopal Church which led to a commitment on
Seabury's part to bring to the American Church a eucharistic prayer
which more fully expressed the Trinitarian character of the prayer, and
thus to bring back into the Anglican tradition the Eastern Church's
emphasis on the role of the Holy Spirit. Because of the providential
contact between Seabury and the Scottish Episcopal Church, the
Prayer Book of the American Church has always included a eucharis-

---

[5]   Cf. W. W. Manross, *A History of the American Episcopal Church* (New York and
Milwaukee: Morehouse Publishing Company, 1935), pp. 154–201.

tic prayer structured in the tradition of the Eastern Antiochene Church in which the divine action of the Son and of the Spirit are seen to be complementary:

> And we most humbly beseech thee, O merciful Father, to hear us; and, of thy almighty goodness, vouchsafe to bless and sanctify, *with thy Word and Holy Spirit*, these thy gifts and creatures of bread and wine. . . .[6]

We see in this recovery an underlying sense of the integral relation between the Memorial of the Son in the Institution at the Last Supper and the present activity of the Holy Spirit in the eucharistic assembly. The consecration of the bread and wine is thus seen as more than merely a repetition of the *Verba*, the Words of Christ, which had become the focus for all the Reformers and thus, ironically, a perpetuation of the mediaeval isolation of the Words of Institution as the moment of consecration. This recovery of the theological integrity of the prayer points us beyond some minimalist focus on a formula of consecration to the reclaiming of the prayer as a proclamation of the Church's Trinitarian faith.[7]

The eucharistic *epiclesis* in its classical form is a potent indicator of the deeper question concerning the relation of the Holy Spirit to the liturgy: the various forms of the Invocation have a twofold sense. They see the work of the Spirit as the divine agent through Whom the bread and wine are transformed to become the sacramental Body and Blood of Christ. But this Invocation is twofold in that it also proclaims our petition for the Spirit's action upon the gathered people of God: that all of us who receive the holy gifts will be united as the Body of Christ. In other words, the *epiclesis* reminds us that communion is not a private act between an individual Christian and God; rather, it is always a corporate act whose purpose is to build up the unity of the Body of Christ.

---

[6] BCP, p. 335 (italics added). Cf. the version in the eucharistic prayer by Archbishop Cranmer found in the 1549 BCP. There the Invocation appears prior to the Words of Institution. This phrase was incorporated in *Bishop Seabury's Communion-Office* (New York: T. Whittaker, 1874; reprinted in facsimile), p. 13, and was drawn from the eucharistic prayer of the Scottish Episcopal Church. In these versions, the Invocation appears after the Words of Institution according to the model of the Antiochene tradition.

[7] Cf. Louis Weil, "Proclamation of Faith in the Eucharist," in *Time and Community*, ed. J. Neil Alexander (Washington, D.C.: Pastoral Press, 1990), pp. 279–90.

The fundamental action of the Holy Spirit is seen in this prayer for unity: the work of the Holy Spirit in us is to nourish the unity of all Christians that is created through baptism. As St. Paul writes, "By one Spirit we are all baptized into one Body" (1 Cor. 12:13). So the action of the Spirit is not narrowly individualistic but rather is ordered toward the unity of the whole Body. When a person is baptized, it is not the creation of a private bond between the individual and God, but rather the incorporation of that person into the corporate life of the community of the faithful.

We see in this the role of the Spirit in the whole liturgical life of the Church: the call to all of us to worship is itself the activity of the Spirit of God. And through us this call extends to the entire human race. The vision of that call is human solidarity and unity as God's people. On the whole, the Church has failed to claim this imperative of the Holy Spirit toward unity. Yet this is what we pray in our eucharistic assemblies:

> Sanctify (these gifts) by your Holy Spirit to be for your people the Body and Blood of your Son, the holy food and drink of new and unending life in him. Sanctify us also that we may faithfully receive this holy Sacrament, and serve you in *unity*, constancy, and peace. . . . (BCP, p. 363, italics added).

This is not merely a formula that a priest recites because it is in the Prayer Book: it is in the Prayer Book because its meaning and significance are essential to the liturgical action. The action of the Spirit in our liturgical prayer is to compel us toward the unity that God wills.

Much theology has been written over the centuries that has attempted to set forth the Church's understanding of the Real Presence of Christ in the eucharist. But if what has been presented in this essay is convincing, then the Church must be equally concerned about the Real Presence of the Holy Spirit in the Eucharist, which is what the *epiclesis* clearly implies. By extension, every liturgical act of God's people when they gather for prayer is done in the power and presence of the Spirit. The Church is the Spirit-filled Body—that is what Pentecost is all about. Likewise, each Christian from baptism is a temple of the Holy Spirit. In other words, not only is Christ present when "two or three are gathered together in his name," but the Holy Spirit is also present and active in the community of faith, the people of God. One must acknowledge that the pentecostal movement has shown itself far more alert to this reality than the Church as a whole. This is not a minor theological issue: it is central in our experience of God's presence in our lives. And the work of the Spirit who abides in us is always to draw us from our adversarial postures into a unity that embraces the rich diversity of the Spirit's gifts.

In the highly polarized situation in the life of the Church today, there would seem to be no greater imperative for all of us to hear. The unity which the Holy Spirit creates through baptism and which is proclaimed when we gather for eucharist is fundamental to the life of the Church. The Church is *"one,* holy, catholic and apostolic." Our polarization over issues and our complacency about disunity and threats of schism are a fundamental betrayal of the unity that we are called to share through the Spirit's action and that we proclaim as our faith each time we recite the Nicene Creed. Indifference to the imperative of that aspect of our proclamation of faith erodes the integrity of the liturgical act itself.

By Water and the Holy Spirit: Baptism and Confirmation in Anglicanism

RUTH A. MEYERS*

The work of the Holy Spirit is expressed in widely varying ways in contemporary Anglican worship. In congregations influenced by the charismatic renewal of the late twentieth century, vivid expressions of the power of the Spirit abound—praise music with worshipers raising their hands and swaying to the music, healing and other extemporaneous intercessory prayer with laying on of hands, testimony by worshipers, speaking in tongues. At the other end of the spectrum, no special attention is given to the power of the Spirit in worship. For example, mention of the Spirit in the invocation in the eucharistic prayer is formulaic and appears unremarkable: Eucharistic Prayer A simply states, relative to the bread and wine, "Sanctify them by your Holy Spirit to be for your people the Body and Blood of your Son. . . ." (BCP 1979, p. 363).

Yet all Christian worship is—or ought to be—Spirit-filled. It is the Spirit who inspires our praise of God and brings us into the divine life, that is, into the mystery of God revealed in Christ. The entire act of worship is empowered by the Holy Spirit, and through the Spirit, we are drawn into participation in God's triune life.[1]

In Anglican worship, the texts of the liturgy ensure that there is reference to the Spirit. But mention of the Spirit in the rites of baptism and confirmation did not stop Anglicans from a prolonged debate, beginning in the late nineteenth century, about how and even whether the Spirit is at work in those rites. While this may seem to be an arcane theological controversy, it has implications not only for our understanding and practice of baptism and confirmation, including

---

*   Ruth A. Meyers is Associate Professor of Liturgics at Seabury-Western Theological Seminary, Evanston, Illinois. She is indebted to her colleague David Cunningham, who read and critiqued an early draft of this manuscript.
[1]   Catherine LaCugna, *God for Us: The Trinity and Christian Life* (San Francisco: HarperSanFrancisco, 1991), pp. 362–363; Geoffrey Wainwright, *Doxology: The Praise of God in Worship, Doctrine, and Life* (New York: Oxford University Press, 1980), pp. 103–109.

the role of the bishop in those rites, but also for decisions about who may be admitted to communion and how we approach questions of empowerment for ministry.

The Seal of the Spirit

The 1979 Book of Common Prayer makes a bold claim about baptism: "Holy Baptism is full initiation by water and the Holy Spirit into Christ's Body the Church" (p. 299). The assertion that baptism is *full* initiation and includes the work of the Spirit was a direct response to the protracted Anglican controversy about the role of the Holy Spirit in baptism and confirmation. While the debate was engaged far more vigorously in England than on the American side of the Atlantic, the Drafting Committee on Christian Initiation was well aware of the scholarly arguments and considered them carefully as they developed a new initiatory rite for the Episcopal Church.

The "Mason-Dix line"[2] made a sharp distinction between baptism of water, which provided cleansing from sin, and baptism of the Spirit, bestowed through the imposition of hands. In its most extreme form, this view insisted that the Spirit was operative not in baptism but in confirmation, the seal of the Spirit that completed Christian initiation. Gregory Dix's distinction between baptism of water and baptism of the Spirit was rebutted by Geoffrey Lampe, who argued in *The Seal of the Spirit*[3] that the indwelling gift of the Spirit is one aspect of the Christian's participation in the resurrection life of Christ that is begun in baptism.

Though few were willing to go as far as Dix in denying any action of the Spirit in water-baptism, his two-stage understanding of initiation is evident in several publications widely used in the Episcopal Church during the 1950s and 1960s.[4] Lampe's position, on the other hand, received far less attention. When in 1964 Massey Shepherd pro-

---

[2] So named because its principal proponents included Arthur James Mason, author of *The Relation of Confirmation to Baptism* (London: Longman, Green and Co., 1891), and Gregory Dix, *The Theology of Confirmation in Relation to Baptism* (Westminster, Md.: Dacre Press, 1946).

[3] London: Longmans, Green and Co., 1951.

[4] See Massey Shepherd, *The Oxford American Prayer Book Commentary* (New York: Oxford University Press, 1950), p. 271 and *The Worship of the Church* (Greenwich, Conn.: Seabury Press, 1952), pp. 166–186; and Associated Parishes, *Christian Initiation: Part I–Holy Baptism* (1953) and *Christian Initiation: Part II–Confirmation* (1954).

posed a single initiatory rite, for infants or adults, with the bishop presiding, he described this as reintegrating baptism, confirmation and admission to communion, although he did not discuss the work of the Spirit in the rite.[5] Leonel Mitchell, who had recently completed his doctoral dissertation on baptismal anointing, made a similar proposal.[6]

These and other proposals for a unified rite of initiation informed the work of the Drafting Committee on Christian Initiation from the beginning of Prayer Book revision in 1967, in part because Mitchell was a member of the committee throughout the process. In light of the heated debate in the early 1970s regarding the meaning and practice of confirmation, it is remarkable that the prayer and actions that follow the water baptism in the 1979 baptismal rite are so similar to the rite presented to the General Convention in 1970.[7] Of particular significance is the inclusion of the prayer for the gifts of the Spirit, a paraphrase of the prayer for the sevenfold gift of the Spirit found in every Anglican *confirmation* rite since 1549, and the imposition of a hand, historically the essential ritual action of Anglican confirmation rites. The presence of these elements reflects the intent to include in baptism the central sacramental aspects of confirmation as it had been practiced in Anglicanism.

The prayer and the handlaying, optional chrismation and consignation, with the formula "N., you are sealed by the Holy Spirit in Baptism and marked as Christ's own for ever," can be interpreted in various ways. Leonel Mitchell asserts that there is a deliberate ambiguity in the text, allowing the "seal" to be identified either with the consignation or as the inward part of the water action (the position of Lampe). Mitchell prefers the former interpretation, that is, that the seal is "closely identified with, but not identical to, the water bap-

<hr />

[5] Massey Shepherd, *Liturgy and Education* (New York: Seabury, 1965), pp. 103–107; the substance of this book was originally presented in the Bradner lectures delivered at the General Theological Seminary in February 1964. For further discussion of Shepherd's views, see Ruth Meyers, "Scholarship Shaping Liturgical Reform: Massey Shepherd's Influence on Rites of Christian Initiation," in J. Neil Alexander, ed., *With Ever Joyful Hearts: Essays on Liturgy and Music Honoring Marion J. Hatchett* (New York: Church Publishing, 1999), pp. 116–138.

[6] Leonel Mitchell, "The 'Shape' of the Baptismal Liturgy," *Anglican Theological Review* 47 (1965): 410–419.

[7] *Prayer Book Studies 18: On Baptism and Confirmation* (New York: Church Pension Fund, 1970), pp. 39–40; cf. BCP 1979, p. 308.

tism."[8] For the Roman Catholic liturgical scholar Gerard Austin, the 1979 baptismal rite is laudable because it reunites the rites of initiation, that is, baptism and confirmation, although Austin expresses concern that the inclusion of the phrase "in Baptism" in the formula at the handlaying could imply that this is not a distinct sacramental action.[9]

Identifying distinct sacramental actions within the baptismal rite preserves the medieval distinction of baptism and confirmation, now "reunited" in a single rite. But locating the seal of the Spirit in a specific ritual moment, whether that moment is the signing after the bath ("confirmation") or the bath itself (as Lampe argued), may limit our perception of the work of the Spirit throughout the initiatory process. If we understand the Holy Spirit as one who prompts our praise of the triune God and draws us into the divine life, then we must begin with an expectation that the Spirit is at work in every part of the baptismal rite and in those who come to be baptized.

Toward a New Consensus?

A new Anglican consensus in this matter became evident at the 1991 International Anglican Liturgical Consultation, which asserted unequivocally that baptism is complete sacramental initiation, including the gift of the Holy Spirit, but did not identify the seal of the Spirit with any particular portion of the rite.[10] Yet a survey of contemporary Anglican rites of baptism and confirmation, including those revised since the 1991 consultation, suggests that this consensus among the liturgical scholars and leaders at the consultation has yet to be fully received throughout the Anglican Communion.

In many ways, the work of the consultation is an affirmation of the 1979 baptismal rite. But questions can be raised about the order of the prayer and action that follow the water baptism. The rite in *The Book of Alternative Services* of the Anglican Church of Canada, which in

---

[8] Leonel Mitchell, *Worship: Initiation and the Churches* (Washington, D.C.: Pastoral Press, 1991), p. 144. The formula accompanying the postbaptismal action changed several times during the revision process; Mitchell (pp. 143–144) traces the development of this text and its interpretation.

[9] Gerard Austin, *Anointing with the Spirit: The Rite of Confirmation: The Use of Oil and Chrism* (New York: Pueblo, 1985), p. 76.

[10] "Walk in Newness of Life: The Findings of the International Anglican Liturgical Consultation, Toronto 1991," in David Holeton, ed., *Growing in Newness of Life: Christian Initiation in Anglicanism Today* (Toronto: Anglican Book Centre, 1993), pp. 227–253; see especially pp. 229–230, 243–245, 252–253.

many respects follows the 1979 BCP rite, places the signing and optional chrismation before the prayer for the gifts of the Spirit, with no option for an alternative order.[11] The 1979 order, with prayer followed by action, can be interpreted as a distinct sacramental act (a form of confirmation) and was intended as such, although the rubric permitting the action to precede the prayer militates against a definitive interpretation along these lines. The Canadian order (and the alternative U.S. order) may make a stronger statement about the unity of the baptismal rite, which in turn may underscore the work of the Spirit throughout the rite rather than focusing it at one moment in the rite.

Other contemporary Anglican revisions have not followed the lead of the U.S. and Canadian churches in including the prayer for the gifts of the Spirit in baptism. Rather, in most, including those rites revised after the 1991 consultation, this prayer has remained in confirmation.[12] While this provides continuity with previous Anglican confirmation rites, including the medieval Sarum rite, earlier sources—the fourth-century writings of Ambrose of Milan and the eighth-century Gelasian sacramentary—include the prayer in the baptismal rite. The contemporary Anglican rites that leave the prayer in confirmation emphasize the bestowal of the Spirit in that rite.

It is not, however, only a matter of when the Spirit is invoked, but how the action of the Spirit is understood in baptism and in confirmation. During most of the twentieth century, proponents of a two-stage approach to initiation often described the distinctive grace of confirmation as "the ordination of the laity," empowering laity for their ministry in the world.[13] The 1989 South African rite implies such a view: "[In Baptism] we are raised with [Christ] to new life in the Spirit. In Confirmation we come to be filled . . . with the power of the Spirit for

---

[11] *The Book of Alternative Services* (Toronto: Anglican Book Centre, 1985), p. 160.

[12] See Church of the Province of New Zealand, *A New Zealand Prayer Book* (London: Collins Liturgical Publications, 1989), p. 392; Church of the Province of Southern Africa, *An Anglican Prayer Book* (London: Collins Liturgical Publications, 1989), p. 376; Anglican Church of Australia, *A Prayer Book for Australia* (Broughton Books, 1995), p. 61; Church of England, "Baptism and Confirmation at the Order for Celebration of Holy Communion" (2000), http://www.cofe.anglican.org/commonworship. In the Church of the Province of Kenya, the prayer for the gifts of the Spirit is found neither in "Baptism" nor in "Draft Confirmation and Commissioning" in *Modern Services* (Nairobi: Uzima Press, 1991).

[13] See, for example, Edward Lambe Parsons and Bayard Hale Jones, *The American Prayer Book: Its Origins and Principles* (New York: Charles Scribner's Sons, 1937), p. 224; Convocations of Canterbury and York, *Confirmation Today* (London: Press and Publications Board of the Church Assembly, 1944), pp. 11–13, 31–32.

worship, witness and service."[14] Yet the Spirit who draws us into the life of the triune God at baptism also transforms us and enables our lives to be conformed to the image of God as revealed in Christ. This transformative action is not withheld for bestowal at some time after baptism, but is integral to the baptismal gift of the Spirit, as the 1991 Anglican Liturgical Consultation acknowledged: "Baptism affirms the royal dignity of every Christian and their call and empowering for active ministry within the mission of the church."[15]

The Australian and English rites, both revised since 1991, give some attention to commissioning for ministry as part of baptism. The prayers in the Australian rite include a petition that those baptized may "continue in the fellowship and service of [Christ's] Church [and] . . . proclaim, by word and example, the good news of God in Christ."[16] But the Australian book also appoints texts for use at confirmation that state that those who are baptized *and confirmed* are empowered by the Holy Spirit for ministry and service.[17] It is not altogether clear from the rite whether this empowerment is effective in those baptized but not yet confirmed. In contrast, in the English baptismal rite the water-bath is followed by the "Commission," which articulates the baptismal commitment to ministry. For baptizands unable to answer for themselves, the minister reminds the congregation that these children will need the assistance of the Christian community "to follow Jesus Christ in the life of faith" and "serve their neighbor after the example of Christ." Candidates able to answer for themselves are asked to respond to questions of commitment similar to the questions in the baptismal covenant in the U.S. and Canadian rites.[18]

Understanding baptism as complete sacramental initiation, including the gift of the Spirit who empowers Christians for ministry, means that baptism must also be the basis for admission to communion, the principal sacramental means of nurturing members of Christ's body. This is a radical change for Anglicans, whose Prayer Books since 1549 included a "confirmation rubric" requiring confirmation before admission to communion. The churches in New Zealand, the United States and Canada led the way in introducing this

---

14 *An Anglican Prayer Book*, p. 369.

15 "Walk in Newness of Life," in *Growing in Newness of Life*, p. 236.

16 *A Prayer Book for Australia*, p. 57.

17 Ibid., pp. 52, 61, 69.

18 Church of England, "Holy Baptism" (2000), http://www.cofe.anglican.org/commonworship.

change, which was recommended to the entire Anglican Communion by a liturgical consultation in 1985 and reaffirmed by the 1991 consultation. Since the 1980s, communion of all the baptized has been discussed in many but not all Anglican provinces, and while practice has changed in some places, in other provinces there has been no change in the historic Anglican initiatory pattern of baptism, confirmation and admission to communion.[19]

The recent rites of the Church of England, which has retained the historic pattern, allow adults to be baptized and confirmed by the bishop at the same service and so admitted to communion. When adults are baptized in the parish and later confirmed by the bishop, they may be admitted to communion at their baptism or after confirmation.[20] The Australian prayer book states that the baptism of adults should include their confirmation and first communion, "making one unified rite of Christian initiation."[21] The attempt to provide a single initiatory rite, at least in the case of adults, is laudable. But requiring confirmation, whether at baptism or at a later time, undermines an understanding of baptism as full initiation, including the gift of the Spirit. A similar problem is evident in the 1979 BCP, which includes an expectation that those baptized as adults, unless baptized with laying on of hands by a bishop, will make a public affirmation of faith and receive the laying on of hands by a bishop (p. 412). In contrast, the Canadian rite has no requirement for baptized persons to receive laying on of hands by a bishop, and it describes confirmation, reception and reaffirmation as "various modes of response to baptism," not as initiatory rites.[22]

In the case of those baptized as adults, since their baptism includes the gift of the Spirit and so fully incorporates them into the life of the triune God, confirmation can only add imposition of hands by a bishop. The commentary on the Church of England rites specifies that the requirement of episcopal confirmation is a principal expression of the bishop's oversight of the entire initiatory process. Yet Anglicans must consider how important it is to require Christians to re-

---

[19] For the statement and recommendations of the 1985 consultation, see Ruth A. Meyers, ed., *Children at the Table: The Communion of All the Baptized in Anglicanism Today* (New York: Church Hymnal Corp., 1995), pp. 127–144. See also "Walk in Newness of Life," in *Growing in Newness of Life*, pp. 229, 232.

[20] Church of England, "Initiation Services—Commentary by the Liturgical Commission" (1998), http://www.cofe.anglican.org/commonworship.

[21] *A Prayer Book for Australia*, p. 70.

[22] *The Book of Alternative Services*, p. 149.

ceive laying on of hands by a bishop. Eastern Orthodox baptismal rites have historically included chrismation by a presbyter, and no ritual action by a bishop, at baptism or in some subsequent rite, has been expected or required. Increasingly in Roman Catholicism, confirmation—laying on of hands with prayer for the sevenfold gift of the Spirit, followed by chrismation—is administered by presbyters when adults are baptized at the Easter Vigil. In the Lutheran churches with which Anglicans are now in full communion, confirmation—laying on of hands—has historically been administered by presbyters. The 1991 Anglican Liturgical Consultation encouraged a broader view of the bishop's ministry: as chief pastor, the bishop expresses the unity of the Church by presiding at baptism and the eucharist and by delegating or presiding at other rites of commitment, such as confirmation.[23]

For those baptized when unable to answer for themselves (e.g., infants and young children), confirmation not only may add laying on of hands by a bishop but also provides opportunity for individuals to make the profession of faith previously done on their behalf. Yet because their baptism fully initiated them into the body of Christ, confirmation must be seen as a rite of renewal of faith, an event within Christian life. The principal sacramental means of renewing that faith is participation in the eucharist. An opportunity for ritual profession of faith along with prayer for strengthening with the Spirit may also be desirable, although requiring such a rite diminishes the claim of full sacramental initiation in baptism.

While the life of faith may involve gradual awakening, being drawn by the Spirit ever more fully into participation in God's triune life, Christian life is often punctuated by times of sin followed by repentance and renewal, and it may also have moments of sudden awareness and dramatic transformation by the Spirit. Most contemporary Anglican revisions recognize this by providing rites of reaffirmation in addition to a rite of confirmation. A number of these revisions allow a presbyter to administer some rites of renewal, particularly the renewal of baptismal vows at the Easter Vigil. But they require a bishop to administer rites of reaffirmation that are parallel to confirmation, a restriction that is even less justifiable than requiring that confirmation be administered by a bishop.

---

[23] "Walk in Newness of Life," in *Growing in Newness of Life*, pp. 249–251; see also p. 229.

An understanding of baptism as full Christian initiation is undermined by requirements that baptized persons subsequently be confirmed by a bishop and by the requirement of confirmation prior to admission to communion. Rites that place commissioning for ministry as an effect of confirmation rather than baptism also diminish the significance of the baptismal gift of the Spirit. In addition, the language and structure of some contemporary Anglican rites may imply that the Spirit is bestowed at a specific moment at baptism rather than being active in every part of the rite, while others may give more attention to the action of the Spirit in confirmation than in baptism. In light of both contemporary pneumatology and the Anglican debate about the bestowal of the Spirit at baptism and at confirmation, it is important to develop rites of initiation and reaffirmation of faith which articulate an understanding that the Spirit is fully bestowed at baptism and leads the baptized ever more fully into participation in the mystery of the triune God.

"The Spirite searcheth the botome of Goddes secretes"

Robert M. Cooper*

If we are "thinking reeds" as Pascal has claimed, then are our memories yet more feeble than our thinking? I do not think I can remember a time when my mind and soul were not filled with images and fantasies that I would later come to call imagination, an imagination, in turn, overrunning with metaphors. And, for years and years now I have been intensely aware that I think primarily in images. Often it has been for me that as I spoke or wrote I was *seeing* what I was speaking or writing. I might even say that in a way it was dream-like. When you and I report our dreams to another or when we write them down afterwards for ourselves, we try to *tell* what we dreamed. But if the dream-seeing never moves on to a public and (usually) narrative account, it remains a cul-de-sac or a private mysticism. What follows is an essay about the spirit, about the spirit of God. I do not clearly know how to discern the difference between "the spirit of God" and the "Holy Spirit" (of God) any more, I believe, than Paul the Apostle did in the phrase from one of his Corinthian letters which provides this essay's title: using Paul's language, I claim that the Spirit of God is what I will call "the fore-feeler" and that feeling after that Spirit and along with that Spirit we trace the spoors where the Christ has gone on before us. Hence, we can say that what follows is an essay in *experientia quaerens intellectum*, experience seeking understanding. This will be accomplished largely by means of bodily based images and metaphors. It is hoped that these images and metaphors—as if they were to appear in a *strong* poem—will widen and deepen our own experience, amplifying and renewing it, illuminating and even glorifying it. Hasn't Irenaeus averred that the glory of God is a human being alive? Who *is* this then, who encounters us, who glorifies us *and* the world about us?

---

* Robert M. Cooper has served as a parish priest, a college and university chaplain and teacher, a university and seminary professor, and a pastoral psychotherapist.

Like joy, which we can never plan on, or for, the Spirit always takes us by surprise. We think of Wordsworth's line, "Surprised by joy—impatient as the Wind." We cannot plan on or for joy, surprise, or the Spirit because they all arrive as gifts. Everything interesting in life happens at the edges of things.[1] Everything that surprises us [sur-pris-es, lays hold of us or takes us over] happens at the extremities of our lives—and our bodies whose largest organ is our skin, the medium of touch, evidence this truth. Aristotle said this long ago, opening his *Metaphysics* by claiming that "All men by nature desire to know and the evidence for this is the delight (*agapēsis*) that they take in their senses." The basis for such a claim, however, is laid in his treatise "On the Soul," and elsewhere. Wonderfully, in writing on the soul the animal/human *body* foregrounds all else, although he has claimed that "Sight is the chief sense (*malatista aisthēsis*, 429a) in humans: touch (*haphē*) is a kind of mean (*mesotēs*) between all tangible qualities. . . . [D]eprived of this one sense alone animals must die" (435a,b).

The sense of being at the edge, borders, or boundaries is captured in the lines from a poem by Yehuda Amichai, "My Children Grew":

> I remember giving them a stern warning:
> "Never, never stick your hand out of the window of a moving bus."
> Once we were on a bus and my little girl piped up, "Daddy, that guy stuck his hand into the outside!"
>
> That's the way to live: to stick your hand into the infinite outside of the world, turn the outside inside out,
> the world into a room and God into a little soul inside the infinite body.[2]

The hand here is a means, a medium. "Mean" is our keynote in all that follows. For it is in the mean where the edges of things and expe-

---

[1] See Robert M. Cooper, "Joy, Ecstasy, and Loss of Control," *St. Luke Journal of Theology* 28:2 (March, 1985), reprinted with author's changes in *The Clergy Journal* 75:2 (Nov./Dec. 1998).

[2] "My Children Grew," *The New Yorker* [Sept. 27, 1999], trans. from the Hebrew by Chana Bloch and Chana Kronfeld, p. 58. Concerning *hands*, see David Michael Levin, *The Body's Recollection of Being: Phenomenological Psychology and the Destruction of Nihilism* (London: Routledge & Kegan Paul, 1985). Three more recent books are important here. See George Lakoff and Mark Johnson, *Philosophy in the Flesh: The Embodied Mind and its Challenge to Western Thought* (New York: Basic Books, 1999); Antonio Damasio, *The Feeling of What Happens: Body and Emotion in the Making of Consciousness* (New York: Harcourt Brace, 1999); and Elaine Scarry, *On Beauty and Being Just* (Princeton: Princeton University Press, 1999).

riences come together, where they touch each other. Sigmund Freud
understood this so well (as have since him, Karl Abraham, Norman O.
Brown, and Leonard Shengold, among others). We see this in his
pointing out the central importance of the alimentary canal, especially in people. All of our mucous membranes are at the edges of—on the
surfaces of—our bodies where inside and outside meet and "turn the
world inside out."

If we grant that God is the one who makes, and is making, us—as
we are indeed granting—then let us come to expect to meet the spirit
of God at the edges, the borders, the limits, and the boundaries of our
bodied lives. It is *in extremis*—at the extremities—that *we can expect
to be surprised*. At the edges and in the in-betweens the spirit search-
es and we find that spirit where and when we are *in extremis*. "It's only
at the edges of life, when I have put myself at risk, that faith vindicates
itself."[3]

The angels—I am thinking primarily of the Gospel narratives—
are boundary-beings also. Always at least two worlds come together at
every angelic experience, and in their appearing our fear and our wonder kiss each other. Such angelic epiphanies occasion both fear and
wonder because they are also *kratophanies* (manifestations of power);
they always emphasize a joining of the temporal and the eternal for
they mark the location of an *effractura*, a gate where *kairos* breaks
into, opens upon *chronos* ("that guy stuck his hand into the outside!").

Amichai's phrase, quoted again, is joined by a small host of
metaphors that are ordinary terms used to describe aspects of our
physical world. These are our principal metaphors: feeling after, laying hold of; edges, borders, boundaries; touch, bodies; inside, outside;
end, finite, infinite; surfaces, apertures, closures; membranes, pene-

---

[3] Dr. Ann Hedge-Carruthers, private communication. That we especially attend
to, and *emphasize*, borders and boundaries is evidenced powerfully in our use of
halos, the nimbus and the aura in the arts. Jews and Christians are familiar with the
shekinah (a word not actually in the Hebrew Bible, but whose root [importantly, I be-
lieve] means to dwell). Hans Urs von Balthasar, a number of years ago, wrote, in three
volumes, *Herrlichkeit: Eine Theologische Ästhetik. Herrlichkeit* can be translated as
splendor, magnificence, glory, grandeur, etc. *Ästhetik* and our "aesthetic" translate the
Greek *aisthanomai*—I feel, sense, perceive (see Hebrews 5:14).
    A sense of the pertinence of *Herrlichkeit* is strong in Phil. 3:21: Paul contrasts
"vile bodies" with the glory of the body of Jesus Christ—literally, "in the body of his
glory" (*tōi sōmati tēs dokēs autou*).
    It will interest some to notice here, from (Mahayana) Buddhism, the "enjoy-
ment—body" (*Sambhogakāya*) of the Buddha.

tration, testing; and finally, wounding and healing in the tension that life is.

Surprise and angels also come together. The spirit cannot be seized or pinned down any more than can the individual electron in the synapses *connecting* neurons be. When you and I are interested in something, when we find ourselves interested, we are already in a be-tweenness, between where, for example, I am already leaning into somewhere, someone, else, which is the object of my interest. In that instant I have already begun *to be* something else, someone other than I was when the interest grasped me, took hold of me—perhaps, took me over—indeed, *sur-prised* me.

Truly, "the Spirite searcheth the *botome* of Goddes secretes" (my emphasis, 1 Corinthians 2:9–10, The Geneva Bible), and every-thing that follows in this essay is bent upon tracking the traces (see Derrida) of that searching spirit in order to "feel after God" (Acts 17:27, [*psēlaphēseion*]) that I may lay hold of (*katalambanō*). This lat-ter Greek verb also means *"to surprise"* or "to discover" [Philippians 3:12] the one who has *laid hold of* me—Christ, as Paul puts it.

We do well to look for the spirit in the interstices of our lives, in the "betweens," of life, at the edges, the borders, of our lives.[4] I con-cede that the Spirit comes whence it will, coming from whence we know not, and going where we do not know. I mention now two other things concerning the Spirit of God: first, I emphasize that I am speak-ing almost exclusively of our experience of the Spirit of God, looking primarily to biblical, especially New Testament, literature. Secondly, I will show what I claimed in the opening sentences: our experience of God is most vivid at the edges and in the interstices of our lives dis-cerned at the exterior and the interior *aporias* of our existential think-ing, in our thinking as *Dasein*, in our *Verworfenheit*. I use *"aporia"* to indicate that which is inherently, rationally insoluble and/or that about which rational conclusions *cannot* be obtained. Alfred North White-head, in a different context, put this poetically: "What we perceive as present is the vivid fringe of memory tinged with anticipation."[5] We can put this in another idiom, that of Josiah Royce. It was his claim

---

[4]   I have developed these ideas at length elsewhere. See especially my George Craig Stewart Memorial Lectures on preaching at Seabury-Western Theological Seminary, "Preaching Between a Rock and a Hard Place," unpublished manuscript, 1978.

[5]   *The Concept of Nature* (Cambridge: Cambridge University Press, 1930), p. 73.

that we live in "a community of interpretation." At our best, I believe, we live simultaneously in a community of memory *and* one of hope.[6] And because our *bodies* remember and because they (rest in) hope, hence our whole lives are *tensed* as "very members incorporate" in the community of the *Spannungsmensch* (Bultmann's term for the crucified Jesus [in his commentary on the Fourth Gospel] stretched between heaven and earth).[7]

Three other references at this point will further indicate how I am framing this discourse. First, Nemesius of Emesa (late fourth century) has spoken of us humans as *amphibians* living *between* heaven and earth in the same instant, and in the same *present,* if you will. Second, Heraclitus (530–470 B.C.) called our attention to the basic tensionality of our existence by playing upon the two Greek words (*biós*) and (*bíos*)—bow, "a strung bow," on one hand and "life" on the other. Third, there is Freud. I have in mind not so much his positing of a life *Instinkt* and a death *Instinkt* as his powerfully insightful articulation (an important term for us) of the individual's movement (trajectory) from the utter helplessness and dependence (upon others) of infancy and early childhood and beyond, and thence on into whatever are the between years of *relative* helplessness—to ourselves—and finally on into decline, senescence, and death. The trajectory is from total lack of control to relative control to total loss of control in death. A crucial portion of Jesus' own trajectory is that of his being thrown out (his *Verworfenheit*) into the desert. So to be thrown is to become largely out of control.[8]

---

[6] See his 1899–1900 lectures, *The World and the Individual* (New York: Dover Publications, 1959). A different but related turn on this notion of "a community of interpretation" can be seen in H. G. Gadamer's *Truth and Method.*

[7] See how Augustine treats "tension" in *Confessions, XI,* xxviii, in its *temporal* aspects. On how "tension" appears importantly in our English word "attention," see James H. Austin, M.D. (a neurologist). He writes, "*Attention* (his emphasis) reaches. It is awareness stretched *toward* (his emphasis) something. It has executive, motoric implications. We attend to things." *Zen and the Brain: Toward an Understanding of Meditation and Consciousness* (Cambridge: The MIT Press, 1998), p. 69. Note here the physical, gestural and *visual* aspects. Compare my doctoral essay, *Silent as Light: a Christian-Zen Inquiry*, especially Chapter I, "A Phenomenology of Attention," pp. 9–39 (Nashville: Vanderbilt University, May, 1972).

[8] Robert M. Cooper, "The Fantasy of Control," *St. Luke's Journal of Theology* XXXIII/4 [September 1990]. This is a much-expanded version of my remarks at the annual Krost Symposium at Texas Lutheran College, in a "response" to the keynote address by Dr. Bruno Bettelheim.

"And the spirit threw Jesus out into the wilderness and for forty days he was with the wild beasts and the angels served him." The wilderness is at the *limen* of what we are pleased to call civilization, i.e., what is citified: *Civis* (in our *hubris, civis* easily becomes *cosmos*); Jesus is thrown *out* and *into* the desert (*erēmos*) to become a forty-day hermit. *Civis*, of course, is Latin. Its rough Greek equivalent is the word *polis* (Aristotle, *Politics*: "Man is a political animal, *politikon dzōn*)," a view, although only partially correct, which lends weight to the saying from classical Greek antiquity: Only a beast or a god can live outside the *polis*. We believe that Socrates's only known time out of Athens, aside from his military excursuses, was when he ventured *outside* the walls of the city—the city which gave him birth and which subsequently required that he take his own life—for an ambling talk with Phaedrus concerning pleasure.[9]

But why, one may well ask, these Greek excursions? First, they provide instances for the human experience of difference. In fact, it is only humans who *experience* anything. Everything else, animate or inanimate is "there" in the world of occurrence or in the world of happening (*tynkanō*, "to happen") in the world of chance or luck (*tychē*). We humans can be said to have experiences only when happenings or occurrences are made into experience by interpretation or by our giving meaning to them (why else would Hermes [cf. "hermeneutics"] be a god; indeed, a god of the in-betweens?).[10]

Happening and occurrence given meaning become event. Hence we come to speak of what we experience. Jacques Derrida has written, "I prefer to speak of *experience* (his emphasis), this word that means at the same time traversal, voyage, or ordeal." "Experience" embodies the Latin *per* which with "*ex*" yields the sense of what may derive from

---

[9] Underlining the power of this "outside" is the Greek fear of, shrinking from, the *apeiron* (the unbounded). See, among the Pre-Socratics, especially Anaximander, and my treatment of this material in "Preaching Between a Rock and a Hard Place."

[10] Hermes is a liminal figure (as "the Trickster" generally is. See Lewis Hyde, *Trickster Makes this World: Mischief, Myth and Art* [New York: Farrar, Straus and Giroux, 1998]).

Other such border figures are Plato's *eros* (See *Symposium*), and his *Pharmakos* (*Republic*), Shakespeare's fool in *King Lear*, and Kierkegaard's *en vims lille Person*. See Jacques Derrida's important treatment of *Pharmakos* in his *Dissemination,* trans. Barbara Johnson (Chicago: University of Chicago Press, 1981), pp. 95 ff. See my "Preaching Between a Rock and a Hard Place," and especially my "Plato on Authority, Irony, and True Riches" in Vol. 14, *Bibliotheca Kierkegaardiana, Kierkegaard's Classical Inspiration*, eds. Neils Thulstrup and Marie Mikulová Thulstrup (Copenhagen: C. A. Reitzels Forlag, 1985), pp. 25–62.

what one has gone *through* (See Derrida's "ordeal").[11] There are also embedded here the Greek words *peras* (border or boundary) and *per-adzein* (to tempt, test, probe, etc.). I hold that the Spirit always search-es with us at these edges of our lives.

We live out our days as westerners between the two worlds of "pagan" antiquity with its myriad myths and gods, on the one hand, and on the other hand we live in the world of what H. Richard Niebuhr characterized as one of "radical monotheism." Our simulta-neously living in these strongly and starkly differing worlds is one more powerful instance of our living in a between, living liminally, in-terstitially where we attempt *aporias* and try to stay alive at the same time. In this pagan/biblical in-between we all are afflicted to some de-gree by what Rafael López-Pedraza called "cultural anxiety" in his im-portant 1990 book *Cultural Anxiety*. In the midst of this further ten-sionality, in this special anxiety, we find ourselves *impinged* upon in such a way that we experience a being narrowed by the coming to-gether of two worlds: It is the experience of being leapt upon (note the strong [quasi-]violent language) and being set upon by, for example, "the sickness that destroyeth at the noon-day" (the noon-day demon). It is an experience known to those who have suffered "pseudo-angi-na"—the feeling of constriction and suffocation. We breathe literally anew when the "demon" departs and spirit/breath come into us afresh.[12]

To this point the language and the metaphor of our discourse have been mostly those of laterality or of the planar (this "planar" is an important term, more of which later). Obviously, if we continue, as we really *humanly* must, to think directionally we will come now to think *vertically*, to think of "up and down," and hence cover the six cardinal directions. The vertical dimension has, of course, already been no-ticed in terms of the crucified Jesus and Bultmann's term *Spannungs-mensch*, or we may want to speak of Christ always as the/our *Zwischensmensch*: our in-between, our *mediating*, one. (It is impor-tant to notice that in Buddhist sculpture and iconography Gautama

---

[11]   See his piece "A 'Madness' Must Watch Over Everything," *Points . . . Interviews, 1974–1994*, various translators (Stanford: Stanford University Press, 1995), p. 362. Again, I refer the reader to my extended discussion of "experience" in "Preaching Between a Rock and a Hard Place," chap. 4, pp. 85–114.

[12]   See *Cultural Anxiety* (Einsiedeln, Switzerland: Daimon Verlag, 1990), pp. 29–54; cf. Jacques Derrida, *Archive Fever: A Freudian Impression*, trans. Eric Prenowitz (Chicago: University of Chicago, 1996), p. 97.

the Enlightened one enters *parinirvana* reclining peacefully on his right side: There is no agony here, no tension.)

We observed at the outset Aristotle's emphasis upon touch as the mean; we may think of touch as a mediator. In customary Christian terms, we think of Christ not only as the mediator between God and ourselves, but also as mediator between our so-called civilization(s) and the wastelands and deserts of our world as well as between our interior selves and our exterior lives: "To whom all hearts be open. . . no secrets hid." One has but to think here of Gerard Manley Hopkins's poem:

> O the mind, mind has mountains; cliffs of fall
> Frightful, sheer, no-man-fathomed. . . .[13]

We have already noted our turn from the lateral or the planar to the vertical dimension so that we can readily see, simply put, that we are speaking about heights and depths, or to put it in other terms, of *altitudo* and *profundum (de profundis)*. In Latin, of course, *altitudo* can mean either height or depth and in itself is occasion for an etymological meditation, something observed differently by both Sigmund Freud and Carl G. Jung. This image of verticality leads us by another route to the phrase from Paul which has given this article its title, "The Spirite searcheth the botome of Goddes secretes." This translation is from the Geneva Bible of 1560.[14] What indeed is *au fond de dieu*—at the bottom of God—not "just" God, but "the botome of Goddes *secretes*"? [my emphasis]. Here is a monumental *aporia,* and however we might presume to approach it, we must ponder (deeply) Paul's claim that the spirit is to be found there also—and is at work there. The Greek text gives us *bathē tou theou* and the Latin *etiam profunda Dei* and either of these will allow "botome" as an adequate and proper rendering of the Greek *bathe* and the Latin *profunda*.

---

[13]   *Gerard Manley Hopkins: A Selection from his Poems and Prose,* by W. H. Gardner (Middlesex: Penguin Books, 1953) p. 61. For the central theme of this essay, see his "God's Grandeur" which begins:

> The world is charged with the grandeur of God.
> It will flame out like shining from shook foil (p. 27).

[14]   I am relying here on Harold Bloom, *Shakespeare: The Invention of the Human* (New York: Riverhead Books, 1998), p. 147, in his animadversions on Bottom in "A Midsummer Night's Dream." I have direct access only to the 1602 version which reads, "The Spirit searcheth . . . the deepe things of God" (1 Cor. 2:11–12).

But who can think at the "botome of Goddes secretes"? If we *could* think to, up to, or toward the bottom as toward a limit, (as we might feel in the dark for the edge of a table where we think we have set down a water glass in the night), we can get a distant glimpse of this. We grope about for a boundary that we believe we know to be there. It makes good sense to find Paul speaking of our "feel[-ing] after God." *Both the aporetic and the physical are as one when the limits of our language meet the boundaries of our dwelling in the only physical world we are able to inhabit.* We notice the linear progress in the way the language (of the Geneva Bible) proceeds—how many *aporias* there are! We would approach finally (*finis*) the nethermost boundary. We (and the Spirit) seek the bottom not for the sake of the bottom itself, but rather because it is the bottom *of God*, but that is not yet the *end* for us; it is the bottom of the *secrets: of* God, *within* God, and *about* God.

The profound distancing reverence in this sort of language is so wonderfully Hebrew! YHWH allows Moses to see only his "hinder parts" as Moses hides himself face-first in the cleft of a rock. We see this screening—as it were about the holy of holies—again in Paul's letters to the Corinthian Christians: "We have seen the light of the glory of God in the face of Christ" (2 Corinthians 4:6). How many removes from God! How much distance to be traveled or mediated in order to *get to* God, so to speak? How many *aporias*? For us, Paul avers, to "get to" God (and for us in English to "get to" means "to obtain") we look behind the *face* of Jesus who is the Christ, in which we see the *glory* of God, and by the light of that glory—"beyond" the glory which Moses was allowed to see the backside of—is, we trust, *the God* whose glory it is. Metaphors and images are as close as we ever get to God, to the secrets of God. That is why metaphors and images are so precious to us. And it is in, by, and through them that the Spirit meets us—already searching, already "ahead of" us. This searching Spirit is the same Spirit who threw Jesus out into the wilderness after his (holy-setting-apart) baptism to dwell with both wild beasts and angels between them (Mark 1:13).

This is the kind of wilderness place in which Jesus has been before (the journey to Egypt with his parents). This is the physical terrain of rocks and a mountain, a place of desolation, and it is also a place of the dereliction of the soul. There is in this wilderness, indeed, "a high mountain" and there are also pits and there are declivities; there are wells there, and there are always depths yet unfathomed. *O altitu-*

do! And *we* face this sort of condition whenever "words fail us," when our language cannot fit what we experience when we are without resource.[15] In his poem at the death of William Butler Yeats (September 1, 1939), the poet W. H. Auden spoke of "the deserts of the heart," going on to say that this is where we may learn to "let the healing fountain start." Desert is a place in which we have been before; we will be there again; we are in it now.

Auden utters his own poetic expression of what is a commonplace psychologically and spiritually, namely what we find in his phrase, "the deserts of the heart." A major watershed in the life of the soul occurred when we in the West interiorized the notion of wasteland, desert or wilderness. One of the first and most profound articulators of this was Augustine of Hippo, who in his *confessio* ("testimony") wrote this sentence of but four words: *mihi quaestio factus sum* ("I became a debating point to myself," *Conf. XII.x*). What we know from the sorry history of our recent past is that it is beyond the edges and borders of so-called civilization that we want to put our prisons (recall not too long ago the existence of penal colonies); outside the city walls is where Jesus is crucified. It was not within Deutschland that the Third Reich put what came to be called in its own time *anus mundi*, but beyond its own borders—in southern Poland, in the town of Auschwitz. And just as human waste, perspiration, etc., comes to the surface where we can get rid of it through a variety of cleansing (see the earlier mention of mucous membranes), so we take trash to the edges of the city and rid ourselves of it.[16] Some things do not change and some things never change. Golgotha is outside the walls of the city of peace, *salem*.

The forty-year wandering of the Hebrews in the desert, in the wilderness, can never be far from mind when the Bible is read by Jews and Christians, or indeed by the followers of Islam. The desert time is linked to slavery—to Egypt and to Exodus—to freedom, to wandering. (In fact, to be free is probably by partial definition to wander.) Linguistically, wandering, deceiving and being deceived are closely linked. One simply cannot miss this in Jesus' forty days of thrown-out-

---

[15]　See my recent essay, "Who is Like God? On Not Mistaking the Pointing Finger for the Moon," in *A New Conversation: Essays on the Future of Theology and the Episcopal Church*, ed. Robert Boak Slocum (New York: Church Publishing, 1999), pp. 94–108.

[16]　See Christian Enzenberger, *Smut: An Anatomy of Dirt*, trans. Sandra Morris. (New York: Seabury Press, 1972).

ness in the wilderness. The planets, it was once believed, *wandered* about the heavens. The Greek verb is *planaō,* which means not only to wander but to deceive (or be deceived). Both of these meanings come close together in Jesus in the desert and with the Hebrews in exile. The god Hermes who gives his name to "hermeneutics" was not only a thief, but also a mover, a shifter, of border and boundary markers—a warning to all interpreters!

A continuing motif of the warnings of the Old Testament prophets to the Hebrew people over the centuries was that they should take heed lest they stray away from, forsake or desert God— usually for idols, for what is *not-*God. "Desert" as a place or a locale is not only a certain climate and terrain, it is an *experience* of waste, of absence of customary definition (we use this kind of language some- times psychologically when we speak of decompensation—when whatever it had been that held us together no longer does so and we fall apart or dissipate); being without support, the experience of aban- donment. This was an intimate aspect of Augustine's own experience: *Ideo . . . dissipabar a me ipso* (a rough translation would be: "then . . . was I scattered from myself," *Conf. VIII.x.24*). There is nothing par- ticularly surprising or strange about this, given the fact that the Eng- lish verb "desert" is given to us from the Latin *desevere,* to undo or to sever one's connection, that is to be cut off (from).

Jesus in the wilderness into which he has been thrown (out) by the Spirit is cut off from the usual compensations of home, friends, synagogue, culture, etc. This kind of cut-offness is dereliction—a pro- found foretaste of the cross. Having been cut loose (*severed*) from what had hitherto compensated him, he finds again and anew that the only lasting mysterious compensation is God, is the spirit-of-wander- ing-in-the-wasteland God. Most strangely and wonderfully *the desert is always "the continuing city" of the Spirit.* This is the land also of the beasts and the angels in between which Jesus dwelt for "forty days."

The desert is a place of wandering (a mode of physical existence). We must try to find adequate language for the *experience* of waste- land. (The best English language effort to do so in the past century is T. S. Eliot's 1922 poem, *The Waste Land*). If we cannot find the lan- guage we have not found the *clear thought,* for aporias are met when we arrive at thought's extremity: some matters are simply, and *finally* unable to be settled by human intellect and thought. In fact, the word "aporia" as we have it is a (letter-for-letter) transliteration of the Greek *aporia,* and the Greek verb *aporeō* means "to be at a loss, to be without resources," hence, helpless, hapless, forlorn.[17] John Calvin's claim is both powerful and profound: *experior magis quam intelligam* ("I experience more [rather] than I understand").[18]

The desert, then, is a place of abandonment from all certainties and securities of quotidian life, its joys and exigencies, and its conventional thought. What had daily compensated Jesus' life, we may presume is gone.

In the desert terrain—whether hilly or mountainous is not the point—the world flattens out, dissipates. The Latin word is *dissipo*, a familiar word to Augustine, as we have seen, when he speaks of himself as being scattered, which is precisely the word's meaning. In the Greek language, of course, *diabolos* is a scatterer. All customary borders or boundaries are gone.

This is where Dante finds himself, imaginatively/poetically, at the edge of a "dark wood where the right way is wholly lost and gone" (Dorothy Sayers's phrase; Dante's Italian is *smarrita*).[19] It is the work of the devil to scatter, to throw things apart, to cast things down and bewilder. There is no more effective way to do that than to lead those of us who live by the usual common*places* and compensations of life to a place where we are relatively or wholly de-compensated. A superficial inquiry into the experience and the language of wilderness filled with pits will reward even the most casual reader. We find in the Psalms the power of this notion as experienced by the Hebrew people. Also, in his own desert time Jesus could have identified with Joseph, who was thrown into a pit, and also with the prophet Jeremiah, who was later thrown into a pit in which water was standing. Such an association can quickly lead the Jew to recall that it is the water under the earth which has been put there in the creative act of God's spirit moving over the face of *tohu wa bohu*, but which also will suggest most powerfully the waters of dissolution, the waters that flood and strangle and choke—an image we see again and again among the Psalmists. We have already seen that it is in the wastelands where we wish to put our trash; it is where we wish to store our human trash—our prisoners. (I

---

[17]   See Jacques Derrida, *Aporias*, trans. Thomas Dutoit (Stanford: Stanford University Press, 1993). Martin Heidegger could have lived only in our time, and the same *mutatis mutandis* can be said of Jacques Derrida.

[18]   See Cooper, "Who Is Like God?"

[19]   The verb is *smarrira*: to lose (one's senses), to mislay, to miss (the way), to bewilder. All of these translations are apt in Dante's poem (*la diritta via era smarrita*, *Inferno* 1.3).

was called, as a child, "white trash.") It is the place where we want to take our nuclear wastes. Within the boundaries of our compensations, within our cities, we want to find and *confine* in our "tenderloin" areas, red-light districts and so-called "adult entertainment," what we deem "trash." Trash and waste have their places (see Enzenberger, *Smut*) but at the same time they are places where we may well imagine and indeed believe that the Spirit is searching the bottom of God's secrets.

Perhaps the best single place to get a clear view of this trashy business is in the Psalms—and I use the translation in the 1979 Prayer Book of Psalm 116:2, "The grip of the grave took hold of me." There are, of course, a multitude of other citations that could be made. Not only is the grave a pit (cf. Gehenna as a burning pit) in the earth, but we have also this wonderful and frightening metaphor: the grave lays hold of us, has a grip upon us. It snares us, and having snared us, it becomes a beast seizing its prey; it draws us under the earth again, from whence we came. Thus the place of creation becomes the place of desolation and eventual destruction. "Out of the depths have I cried to you, O God."[20]

Notice especially the vivid physical aspect of the language: the "grip of the grave took hold of me." We can read this as an echo of the language of "feeling, after God," of God laying hands on us in and through Jesus. The Spirit which searches the bottom of God's secrets is the fore-feeler of the grip of God *and* "the grip of the grave." We began this essay by making the claim that everything that is interesting to us happens at the surfaces (of our lives). We may add to that claim now this one: nothing in the world happens apart from *force*. We have seen this just now again in placing in juxtaposition various phrases from biblical literature. "Force" is a very common word in English, but it is well to remember that the word in Greek is *bia*, which means both force and violence, and its meaning is near the word for life, *bíos* (and *biós*), as we have seen (cf. Matthew 11:12, "and the violent carry it away" [*kai biastai harpadzousin auton*]). Further, note especially the *bia* in *biastai*. In every important and surprising event in our lives there is always an in-breaking. There is an *effractura* or in German an *Einbrechen*. In the latter word we have the clear sense of someone who breaks in, as someone who breaks in to rob, etc., the dwelling

---

[20] We do not leave this verb *harpadzō*—to seize and overpower—without noting its relation to *harpē*, a bird of prey, and thence to the terror-striking Harpies, the three daughters of Thaumas and Electra, or of Poseidon and Gaea.

place of another. So we are well advised to keep in mind here the aspect, the element, of what we might call—although this is a curious way to talk—*a benign violence*.[21] Perhaps we might think of this as a *benign trauma* which ever after alters our lives. We are all, like Jacob, walking wounded. The activity of the Spirit is searching, is probing: The healer wounds, to use an expression from Greek antiquity: *ho trōsas kai iasetai* (the wounder also heals).[22]

"Probe"[23] contains a sense of testing, of penetration, of in-breaking, and from "the other side," so to speak; we can think of it as an acceptance or a yielding of ourselves up to that which comes into us from God and God's forerunning, fore-feeling, searching Spirit.

I began this essay autobiographically and I bring it to a close autobiographically. I was asked years ago to give a brief address at a meeting of the Conference of Anglican Theologians. I entitled it, "I Believe in Bodies, Wonder and Grace." Only in mercifully brief moments have I lapsed into insanity by failing to find the world charmed, enchanted—nay! rather *graced*. Perhaps it's an overly romantic way of seeing/reading—although I am far from being alone in this: the gods, goddesses, heroes and heroines of the *Iliad* and the *Odyssey* light up the world of mortals, and "flame out like shining from shook foil," to use the phrase of Gerard Manley Hopkins. The great Shakespeare puts it in *Hamlet*, "There's such divinity doth hedge a king" (IV.v.123) and goes on to claim the same for all who "see the sky or feel the sun." It was Athanasius of Alexandria who taught us that God became human being in order that we mortals might become God. Yes, "the world is charged with the grandeur of God" (Hopkins).

Finally, we have the strongest sense that God is engaging us always, but we have too the heightened sense that it is at the edges of our lives where we find interest; that it is at the borders and bound-

---

[21] Psychoanalytic aspects of trauma, *effractura,* etc., are extremely interesting here, but space limitations do not permit further discussion. See, however, the important book by Jean Laplanche, *Life and Death in Psychoanalysis,* trans. Jeffrey Mehlman (Balitmore: Johns Hopkins University Press, 1976).

[22] See Carl Kerenyi, *Asklepios: Archetypal Image of the Physician's Existence,* trans. Ralph Manheim. Bollingen Series 65/3. (New York: Pantheon Books, 1959), p. 112, n. 7. Kerenyi remarks that "Telephos, wounded by Achilles, receives from the oracle" the sentence quoted. The oracle told that the cure would come to Telephos by means of rust from the sword of the very Achilles who had wounded him. See also the very interesting and learned work by the physician, Guido Majno, *The Healing Hand: Man and Wound in the Ancient World* (Cambridge: Harvard University Press, 1975).

[23] On "probe" (and "impinge"), see my "Preaching Between a Rock and a Hard Place."

aries, so we think, that we find the possibility of surprise and that these experiences are always coupled with the language of being grasped or taken hold of or laid hold of. None of this is surprising since if Christianity is a religion of *incarnation*, *it is in the body that we experience these things,* and as far as we know now, apart from the body there is nothing certain.

So be it! But faith and trust give it to us that the one who encounters us at the edges of our lives is the Spirit of the Holy One—the always-coming-upon-us-God—who continually illumines us, both dwelling *upon* us and dwelling *among* us.

Holy Spirit in Holy Church:
From Experience to Doctrine

J. Robert Wright*

The history of the Holy Spirit in the early Church can best be understood as a development from experience to doctrine: from experience in prayer, worship and charismatic gifts as seen especially in Origen, Hippolytus, Tertullian, and Montanus, to a development of doctrine as written in St. Basil of Caesarea and formulated in the third paragraph of the Nicene Creed. I shall begin where the scriptural accounts end. The general outlines of pneumatological development evaluated in this essay are already well known, and hence the facts that are summarized here are not all individually annotated.[1]

The Early Church After the Time of the New Testament

The vagueness of the scriptural evidence concerning the Holy Spirit in the early Church, especially regarding the Spirit's identity and distinction from the Son, was noted as early as St. Gregory Nazianzen in the later fourth century, who remarked that Scripture itself does not "very clearly or very often call the Spirit God in so many words, as it does call God first the Father and later on the Son." Indeed, before the Second Ecumenical Council added the third paragraph to the Niceno-Constantinopolitan Creed in 381, most creeds both eastern and western ended simply with the words "and in the Holy Spirit." In fact, it is not entirely certain that the entire expanded form of the third paragraph as we have it actually came from Constantinople in 381. How the Church's faith moved from such a statement found in the Nicene version of 325 to the 381 formula "Lord and giver of life, proceeding from the Father, who with the Father and the Son

---

* J. Robert Wright is St. Mark's Professor of Ecclesiastical History at The General Theological Seminary and Historiographer of the Episcopal Church.

[1] They are principally excerpted or paraphrased from John Burnaby, *The Belief of Christendom* (London: SPCK, 1959), and Jaroslav Pelikan, *The Emergence of the Catholic Tradition* [*The Christian Tradition*, Vol. 1], (Chicago and London: The University of Chicago Press, 1971). See also Michael O'Carroll, *Veni Creator Spiritus: A Theological Encyclopedia of the Holy Spirit* (Collegeville: The Liturgical Press, 1990).

is together worshiped and glorified, who spoke through the prophets"
is a major consideration in this essay.

Origen, ca. 185–254, emphasizes in his *Treatise on Prayer* that the
characteristic sphere of the Spirit's operation is the Church, especially
in prayer, as contrasted with the whole of creation, which is the operative sphere of the Logos. Origen states that all things derive their existence from the Father, their rational nature from the Logos, and their
holiness from the Holy Spirit, which is given in water-baptism. Em-
phasizing the Spirit's role in prayer, Origen stipulates: "Neither can
our understanding pray, unless previously the Spirit prays" (*Treatise
on Prayer* 2.4).

In *The Apostolic Tradition* of Hippolytus, a treatise whose unity
and authorship have been under much question of late but which for
the purpose of this essay will be regarded as a substantial body of evidence pointing to the early third century, there is an explicit connection of the Holy Spirit with baptism or Christian initiation, as is also
the case in Justin Martyr, Athenagoras, and the Didache. However,
Hippolytus connects the Spirit also with ordination and the eucharist.
The biblical association of Spirit and breath (the Hebrew word *ruach*
is translated both ways) is recalled by Hippolytus, as the bishop
breathes into the faces of the recently exorcized catechumens, as well
as in the threefold baptismal immersion, in the signing of oneself by
the cross with one's moist breath, in the Spirit's breathing the adver-
sary away, and, possibly, in the eucharistic epiclesis. When a bishop is
being ordained, and the other bishops have laid their hands upon him,
Hippolytus says, "All indeed shall keep silent, praying in their hearts
for the descent of the Spirit," and one of the ordaining bishops prays,
"Pour forth now that power which is thine, of thy royal Spirit, which
thou gavest to thy beloved servant Jesus Christ, which he bestowed
upon his holy apostles." Here is suggested the empowering which the
Holy Spirit effects, but we must note that this power of the Spirit is
something in particular given to persons in ordination. Hippolytus
refers to the "Spirit of high priesthood" as giving authority to remit
sins. Yet in another context Hippolytus indicates that all believers have
the Spirit. Finally, Hippolytus ends his prayers with a doxology, which
includes mention of "the Holy Spirit in the holy church."

Tertullian (ca. 200) seems to have had a rather prematurely clear
Trinitarian formula of three persons and one substance, in which the
Spirit equally with the Father and the Son is called "God and Lord"
and in which the Spirit proceeds from the Father through the Son.

For the present purpose, however, our major interest in Tertullian is in his relationship to the late second-century apocalyptic movement known as Montanism, which Tertullian eventually joined ca. 206–207. Traced back to Montanus, who lived in the region of Phrygia in central Asia Minor in the mid-second century, the adherents of this movement lived in expectation of the speedy outpouring of the Holy Spirit upon the Church as well as the imminent return of Christ. They believed they were already experiencing the first beginnings of all this in their own prophets and prophetesses and especially in Montanus. The Montanist movement, however, did not claim to be entirely new. Rather, it looked to the Scriptures of the New Testament and found there the sort of Church that it claimed to be continuing.

At Pentecost the Holy Spirit was said in Acts 2:1–13 to have descended in fullness upon the Church. This descent was marked by the gift of tongues, and St. Peter is recorded in Acts (2:16 ff.) as seeing in this the new dispensation that had been prophesied by Joel (2:28–32). We are indebted to the works of the seminal thinker Roland Allen for his emphasis upon the Gospel of St. Luke as presenting the history of the earliest Christian missionary enterprise as guided directly by the Holy Spirit, and for his emphasis upon the Book of Acts as portraying the apostles as conscious of receiving direct communications from the Spirit. In the theology of St. Paul, however, the exalted Christ is associated so closely with the Spirit that often the two seem almost identical. Life in Christ is, alternately, life in the Spirit, and both are contrasted by Paul with "life in the flesh." The Spirit, for Paul, intercedes for us with the Father and divides his gifts severally as he will; it is the Holy Spirit's presence that makes a Christian's body the temple of God. There are, moreover, many fruits and gifts of the Spirit, all of which indicate a rather immanent, presentist activity and experience of the Spirit in the early years of Christianity, and it was to this activity and this experience, so vividly described in the New Testament, that the Montanists looked back.

As the historian of early doctrine, Jaroslav Pelikan, has shown, and to whose works for these points I am much indebted, the rather extraordinary gifts of the Spirit seen in the New Testament Church had all but died out both in frequency and in intensity by this time, the apocalyptic and eschatological vision had become less vivid, and the Church's institutional structure more rigid. The origins of Montanism, then, as Pelikan points out, seem to lie in disaffection with these developments, which its followers regarded as a settling and adjustment of the Church to the world's terms. Earlier Justin Martyr had based his case against Judaism partly on the claim that "among us until now there are prophetic charismata," although they had died out among the Jews, and St. Irenaeus had spoken of and described the many persons in the Church of his day who had such gifts, speaking in tongues by the Spirit. There seems indeed to have been some degree of truth in the Montanist claim that all this was passing away in the great Church, but, alas, with the Montanists this protest seemed to go too far.

The great Tertullian was attracted to the African offshoot of this new movement, not so much for its theological novelty but for its asceticism and moral zeal, which were very great indeed. Montanism asserted that the gifts of the Spirit had fallen away from the greater Church on account of its moral laxity. Widows and widowers were now being permitted to remarry, fasting was not strictly enforced, penitential discipline was lax, leadership and organization were corrupt, and flight from martyrdom and even persecution was permitted. Against all this, Montanism called the Church to tighten the reigns and repent, for the kingdom of God was now finally at hand. By contrast, the sort of Church that Montanus offered was one of ecstatic prophecy, immediate eschatology, ascetic moral rigorism, and, at the same time, institutional chaos. It led, moreover, to the impression that the Church, the Body of Christ, was nothing more than a loose aggregation of Spirit-filled individuals.

In the absence of this sort of internal prophecy, the official Church—the great Church, the Church catholic—could hardly reply that the Montanists' prophecies were simply false. The challenge was therefore met by catholic writers on the ground that the Church was no longer living in the so-called "last days" of the age to come that had been set forth in Scripture. The Church was beginning to reconcile itself to the delay in the Lord's second coming, and as the time of the second coming was projected further into the future, so also the time of prophecy was being pushed back into the past, even to the Apocalypse of John (the Book of Revelation). In spite of various synodal condemnations of Montanism in the third century, the sect itself did not finally die out until the fifth century.

Jaroslav Pelikan, from whose work much of the immediately foregoing has been summarized, has perceptively contrasted the development of the Church's organization and ministry by the time of Montanus with that of a half century earlier:

The simple fact was that in the context of the course that church doctrine was taking by that time, Montanism was obsolete and could not succeed or survive. Its principal significance for the development of church doctrine was to serve as an index to the gradual solidification of the church's message and work, and to its inevitable need for fixed forms of dogma and creed. Montanism was obsolete because the church had begun to find its most trustworthy guarantees of the presence and functioning of the Holy Spirit in the . . . apostolic authority taught by Irenaeus [against Gnosticism] rather than in the ecstasy and prophecy that the Paraclete granted to the adherents of Montanism. . . . And by the adoption of [such a] norm for the church's life and teaching . . . the church looked increasingly not to the future, illumined by the Lord's return, nor to the present, illumined by the Spirit's extraordinary gifts, but to the past, illumined by the composition of the apostolic canon, the creation of the apostolic creed, and the establishment of the apostolic episcopate. To meet the test of apostolic orthodoxy, a movement or idea had to measure up to these norms. In this way the apostles became a sort of spiritual aristocracy, and the first century a golden age of the Spirit's activity. The difference between the Spirit's activity in the days of the apostolic church and in the history of the church now became a difference not only of degree but fundamentally of kind, and the promises of the New Testament on the coming of the Holy Spirit were referred primarily to the Pentecost event and only through that event, via the apostles, to the subsequent ages of the church. The promise that the Spirit would lead into all truth, which figured prominently in Montanist doctrine, now meant principally, if not exclusively, that the Spirit would lead the apostles into all truth as they composed the creed and the books of the New Testament, and the church into all truth when it was built on their foundation.[2]

Lex Orandi Lex Credendi

Relatively little can be said about the Holy Spirit in the history of the Church's doctrine for some one hundred and fifty years after the Montanist outburst. Professor Maurice Wiles of Oxford has perceptively described the major evidence for the Holy Spirit after Montanism in the century or so prior to the Cappadocian fathers of the late fourth century in this way: "It was the continuing fact of baptismal

---

[2]   Pelikan, pp.107–108. Bracketed words mine.

practice which did most to keep alive the idea of the Holy Spirit as a third alongside the Father and the Son."[3] Thus it was baptismal practice, already reflected in the Trinitarian addition to the Great Commission of Matthew 28:19, to which appeal could be made in the fourth century as evidence of the divine and distinct nature of the Spirit. St. Athanasius argued in his letters to Serapion that since the name of the Holy Spirit is solemnly conjoined with those of the Father and the Son in the most fundamental experience of baptism, the Spirit cannot be fundamentally disparate in nature from the other two. St. Basil of Caesarea, similarly, in setting out his beliefs about the Spirit, cites the practice of baptism as the first and basic evidence of his convictions. Hence it was the devotion of prayer, of sacramental practice, here reflected in baptism in the name of Father, Son, and Spirit, that fed the Church's doctrinal stream and encouraged it to reflect upon Scripture in developing its doctrine in this direction. The principle under development here was stated in writing over the years 435–442 by the lay theologian St. Prosper of Aquitaine, and it has come down to us by its Latin tag *lex orandi lex credendi,* literally "the rule of praying is the same as the rule of believing," and idiomatically, "what we pray is what we believe."

This principle of *lex orandi lex credendi* is often cited and employed by Anglicans in explaining how they derive their own doctrine from the words they pray in The Book of Common Prayer. Its precise original formulation in the actual words of Prosper of Aquitaine is even more suggestive and appealing to the typical Anglican mentality: *legem credendi lex statuat supplicandi,* literally "the rule of praying *establishes* the rule of believing," i.e., it is prayer that establishes doctrine, not doctrine that establishes prayer. Both, of course, must be subject to the sufficiency of Holy Scripture, according to Article 6 of the Articles of Religion.

Apart from this evidence of the practice of prayer that fed the development of doctrine in the early centuries and kept alive the idea of the Holy Spirit as a third person of a trinity, there is little else that can be discerned about the Holy Spirit in the history of the Church's doctrine for some one hundred and fifty years from the early third century to the second half of the fourth century.

---

[3]   Maurice Wiles, *The Making of Christian Doctrine* (Cambridge: The University Press, 1967), pp. 80–81, from which the following is both paraphrased and corrected.

Shift from Experience to Doctrine in Basil and the Third Paragraph of the Creed

By this time, however, the Church's concern is less about the active *experience* of the Spirit and more about what should be *taught and believed* about the Spirit. The *doctrine* of the Spirit, called "pneumatology," now became a matter of acute controversy, and the first major doctrinal treatise on the subject was the work of St. Basil of Caesarea in the later fourth century, *On the Holy Spirit* (ca. 375). For this reason it is sometimes said that the first two ecumenical councils (Nicea and Constantinople) were really about Trinitarian controversy, whereas the last two (Ephesus and Chalcedon) were about Christology. The Arian denial of the Godhead of the Son (at the time of Nicea) had carried with it the corollary that the Spirit too might be inferior to the Son, as the Son was to the Father. But even when Arianism had been rejected, there was still some reluctance to call the Spirit God. It fell to St. Athanasius, followed in the later fourth century by all three Cappadocian Fathers, to urge the same arguments with respect to the divinity of the Spirit that had already been predicated of the Son. It was St. Basil's claim, vindicated in 381 at the Council of Constantinople, that both the language of Scripture and the faith of the Church required the same honor or glory or worship to be paid to the Spirit that was already being ascribed to the Father and the Son, i.e., that this *ruach* or *pneuma* or *spiritus* was truly a person or hypostasis of the Godhead. Thus it was entirely proper, Basil asserted,[4] to adore God in liturgical prayer not only by the traditional formula "Glory be to the Father *through* the Son *in* the Holy Spirit," but also by the form "Glory be to the Father *with* (Greek *meta*) the Son *together with* (Greek *sun*) the Holy Spirit," to which his opponents objected as an undesirable innovation.

And so the third paragraph of the Niceno-Constantinopolitan Creed was developed, at least probably, at the Second Ecumenical Council held at Constantinople in 381 to assert distinctively the divinity of the Spirit: "Lord and giver of life, proceeding from the Father, who with the Father and the Son is together worshiped and glorified, who spoke through the prophets." As for the individual words, St. Paul had used the word "Lord" of the Spirit in 2 Cor. 3:17 in order to affirm

---

[4] *On the Holy Spirit*, 3 and 16. A convenient modern English translation is by David Anderson, *On the Holy Spirit/St. Basil the Great* (Crestwood, N.Y.: St. Vladimir's Seminary Press, 1980).

that the Spirit's divinity is exactly the same as that of the Father and of the Son, a point also noted by St. Basil of Caesarea. Paul had also spoken of the Spirit as "the Spirit of Life" (Rom. 8:2), and the description "life-giver" had been used of the Spirit in verbal form in John 6:63, 1 Cor. 15:45, 2 Cor. 3:6, and 1 Peter 3:18. The phrase "proceeding from the Father" was borrowed from Jesus' own words in John 15:26 ("The Spirit of truth, who proceeds from the Father," will bear witness to the Son; although the New Testament Greek word for *from* at this point is *para* rather than *ek*). The phrase "who spoke through the prophets" came from 2 Peter 1:21. All this language was largely scriptural, we may note, and was calculated to give as little offense as possible to the opposition and middle views. The key clause at Constantinople, however, was a bold statement of equality reflecting the terminology of both Athanasius and Basil: "who with the Father and the Son together is worshiped and glorified": *sun patri kai huio sunproskunoumenon kai sundoxazomenon*. The unity and equality of all three persons is underscored by the threefold repetition of the preposition "with," echoing Basil's own terminology. Here, we may observe, is the affirmation of the divinity of the Holy Spirit in terms of worship or glory (*doxa*), rather than as the same substance (*homoousios*), which would have been logically possible (and, indeed, would later be the way that would be chosen by Article 5 of the Articles of Religion). All this at Constantinople was then affirmed by canon 1 of that council in condemning the Macedonians or Pneumatomachoi ("Spirit-fighters") who had denied the Spirit's divinity. (At this point it is reported that thirty-six Macedonian bishops packed their bags and departed!)

We should note the observation of Bishop Kenneth Woollcombe, formerly Bishop of Oxford and before that Professor of Theology at The General Theological Seminary, in his keynote address in support of the ordination of women before the General Synod of the Church of England, that the evolution of the credal doctrine of the Holy Spirit's divinity was basically accomplished and completed in the half-century from 325 to 381, with most of the theological development that made this possible coming in the last two decades before 381. The Church does not necessarily have to debate a major doctrinal development for centuries before acting upon it!

With this portion of the third paragraph of the Niceno-Constantinopolitan Creed, then, which was affirmed at the Fourth Ecumenical Council of Chalcedon in 451, the Church's classical doctrine of the Holy Spirit is complete: "Lord and giver of life, proceeding from the

Father, who with the Father and the Son is together worshiped and glorified, who spoke through the prophets."

Filioque

Doctrinal development continued in the West, and continued to be expressed in the Nicene Creed. The major western addition to this doctrine was the *filioque*, the words "and the Son" added to the phrase describing the Spirit's procession. This notion of a double procession of the Spirit gained currency in the West through the teaching of St. Augustine,[5] who sought the most effective way to assert both the equality of the three persons and the nature of the relationship between them and therefore to affirm that the Spirit is the Spirit of the Son as well as of the Father. It would seem that this affirmation can hardly be denied, although we must note that no statement of the double procession occurs in the actual text of John 15:26, which is the source of the "procession" phrase itself ("the Spirit of truth, who proceeds from the Father," will bear witness to the Son). The Spirit is called the Spirit of the Father in Matthew 10:20 but the Spirit of the Son of God in Gal. 4:6.

The first major use of this addition to the Creed appeared at the Third Council of Toledo in 589 (not, of course, one of the seven ecumenical councils), when it was ordered to be sung at Mass to emphasize the divinity of the Son as a testimony of the conversion from Arianism to catholic orthodoxy of King Reccared and the Visigoths. To affirm that the Spirit proceeds from the Father *and* the Son thus emphasized the Son's full divinity. The single procession, on the other hand, was elevated to especially high dogmatic level in the Eastern Church under the Patriarch Photius in the late ninth century. The Eastern Orthodox have objected to the addition of the *filioque* because it was not approved by an ecumenical council and because they believe it introduces two principles or sources into the unity of the Godhead.[6]

---

[5] *On the Trinity*, 26. A convenient modern English translation is by Stephen McKenna, *St. Augustine. The Trinity* [Fathers of the Church, Vol. 45] (Baltimore: Catholic University of America Press, 1963).

[6] Perhaps the best solution to the *filioque* problem has been the one that was actually agreed on for a time between East and West in the mid-fifteenth century at the (ecumenical) Council of Florence. There, the Latins held that the Holy Spirit proceeds *from* the Son (and *from* the Father), using the Latin preposition *ex*, whereas the Greeks held that the Holy Spirit proceeds *through* the Son (but *from* the Father),

The *filioque* was intentionally retained in the Nicene Creed when the first Book of Common Prayer was published (1549), and it had also been included within the third invocation of the English Litany produced by Cranmer in 1544: "O God the Holy Ghost, proceeding from the Father and the Son." [In the 1979 American BCP the adjectival phrase about the double procession is changed to "Sanctifier of the Faithful."] That the *filioque* should be retained because it expressed the teaching of Scripture and the early Church was, also, the all-but-unanimous teaching of Anglican divines in the later sixteenth and seventeenth centuries. The *filioque* is now common in the West, and it has been included in the contemporary English version of the Creed in the Episcopal Church's Book of Common Prayer.

However, in response to the objections of Eastern Orthodox and others as well as to resolutions of the Lambeth Conferences of 1978 and 1988, and in keeping with a worldwide Anglican tendency, the Episcopal Church's General Convention of 1994 voted its intention to remove the *filioque* from the third paragraph of the Nicene Creed at the next revision of The Book of Common Prayer, and directed that it be omitted even now whenever the English Language Liturgical Consultation's text (ELLC) is used, "such use always to be under the direction of the diocesan bishop or ecclesiastical authority, and with an appropriate educational component." *Enriching Our Worship* (New York: Church Publishing, 1998), the fourth edition of the Episcopal Church's *Supplemental Liturgical Materials*, prints the Nicene Creed with the words "[and the Son]" in brackets (p. 54) and adds an explanatory note (pp. 74–77). Since 1994 the *Alternative Services Book* of the Church of England has printed the same creed without *filioque* in an appendix.

---

using the Greek preposition *dia* for *through*. By the conciliar decree *Laetentur caeli* of 1439, both sides at Florence agreed that in this case *ex* ("from") in Latin was to be understood as the equivalent of *dia* (through) in Greek; i.e., that there is only one causal source of Godhead, but expressed differently by different linguistic formulas in different cultural contexts. (Interestingly, the very same principle from Florence was cited approvingly by the official Anglican-Roman Catholic Consultation in the USA in its agreed statement on theological methodology and doctrinal pluralism of 1972). In spite of great promise, however, Florence unfortunately failed for other reasons, mainly political, and today neither side officially accepts that solution to the *filioque*. The Roman Catholic Church today insists that all "Uniats" of the Eastern Rites must believe the doctrine of the *filioque*, and acknowledge that they belong to a church which teaches it, even though they are not required to insert it into the creed (*The New Catholic Encyclopedia*, vol. 5, p. 914).

Article 5 of the Thirty-Nine Articles of Religion is but a reaffirmation of the classical doctrinal development of the *filioque* that has been traced above: "The Holy Ghost, proceeding from the Father and the Son, is of one substance, majesty, and glory, with the Father and the Son, very and eternal God." What this article does do, however, which the original text of the creed did not, is to predicate divinity of the Holy Spirit in the same way that the Nicene Creed predicates it of the Son, by using the term "one substance" (*homoousios*). Article 1 of the Articles of Religion does also use the phrase "three Persons, of one substance."

Epiclesis in the Eucharist

Another important aspect in the development of doctrine about the Holy Spirit concerns the Spirit's action in the eucharistic consecration, which is called the *epiclesis* (from *epi* + *kaleo* = to call down upon; hence, the calling down of the Holy Spirit upon the elements). Both St. Cyril of Jerusalem and Theodore of Mopsuestia in the later fourth century emphasized this action in their writings. There is also a non-consecratory *epiclesis* in the eucharistic prayer of Hippolytus, ca. 210, but it may be a later addition. The earliest clear assertion of eucharistic consecration only by *epiclesis* and not by words of institution, however, does not come until St. John of Damascus in the eighth century.[7] From then on, this view of eucharistic consecration has been generally accepted in the East but not in the West.

In the Episcopal Church's 1979 Book of Common Prayer, the epiclesis comes *after* the Words of Institution in all eucharistic prayers except Prayer C (p. 371), and thus is often regarded as being "consecratory" *together with* the Words of Institution. In Prayer C, however, it comes *before* the Words of Institution and so is often regarded as "non-consecratory." (It also comes before the Words of Institution in the Roman Catholic Church's Eucharistic Prayer 4). One should also note that the Prayer Book's form for additional consecration (p. 408) implies that consecration occurs by the Words of Institution with epiclesis coming *before* them.

---

[7] *On the Orthodox Faith*, IV.13. A convenient and relatively modern English translation is by S. D. F. Salmond, *John of Damascus: Exposition of the Orthodox Faith* [Nicene and Post-Nicene Fathers, second series, Vol. 9] (New York: Charles Scribner's Sons, 1899).

The Spirit-Filled Church

It should also be noted, finally, that the doctrines of the *Spirit* and the *Church* come down to us appearing in the same third paragraph of the creed, and this does suggest, credally, that it is in the Spirit-filled Church that we believe. Credally, the Church is subordinate to the Spirit. Probably reflecting the thought of Origen and Hippolytus as well as Irenaeus, the Creed bids us to profess our belief in the Church as an outgrowth of, and directly related to, the Spirit. We are, as it were, bidden to think of the Church of the apostles receiving the Holy Spirit on the first day of the week, on Pentecost, after the Resurrection in John 20:19–23. There is a connection, interdependence, and mutuality between the doctrines of the Spirit and of the Church that is clearly indicated. Therefore the Church is, or should be, the place where the doctrine of the Holy Spirit is experienced, lived and perceived.

Starting Over: The Holy Spirit as Subject and Locus of Spiritual Theology

ROBERT D. HUGHES, III*

The burgeoning interest in "spirituality" is too obvious to be missed. Alongside tendencies towards a New Age[1] there is a genuine revival of classical Christian spirituality. This more focused movement can be seen in new seminary courses, training programs at diocesan and local levels, and new scholarship embodied in the formation of the Society for the Study of Christian Spirituality and a number of scholarly journals devoted to the subject. Seemingly endless debates about what "spirituality" means as practice and as an academic discipline have arisen.[2] Nevertheless, both studies and pastoral practice have flourished in four areas: (1) resources for introducing people to the disciplines and traditions of the spiritual life;[3] (2) courses, programs, and literature on the theory and practice of spiritual direction/spiritual formation;[4] (3) recovery of the history and literature of

---

* Robert D. Hughes, III is the Norma and Olan Mills Professor of Divinity and Professor of Systematic Theology at the School of Theology of the University of the South.

[1] See Owen C. Thomas, "Problems in Contemporary Christian Spirituality," *Anglican Theological Review* 82:2 (2000): 267–281.

[2] The literature is vast. Most important here at present are, I believe, Sandra M. Schneiders's many contributions, recently "A Hermeneutical Approach to the Study of Christian Spirituality," *Christian Spirituality Bulletin* 2:2 (Spring, 1994): 9–14; Walter H. Pricipe, "Spirituality, Christian," *New Dictionary of Catholic Spirituality*, ed. Michael J. Downey (Collegeville: Liturgical Press, 1993, hereafter *NDCS*), pp. 931–938; Bradley C. Hanson, "Spirituality as Spiritual Theology," in *Modern Christian Spirituality: Methodological and Historical Essays*, ed. Bradley C. Hanson [American Academy of Religion Studies in Religion 62] (Atlanta: Scholars Press, 1990), pp. 45–51; and Philip Sheldrake, *Spirituality and History: Questions of Interpretation and Method*, rev. ed. (London: SPCK, 1995), esp. pp. 40–64. See also the works by Sheldrake and McIntosh cited below, fn. 7.

[3] The immense popularity of Richard J. Foster's *Celebration of Discipline: The Path to Spiritual Growth,* now in its third edition (San Francisco: HarperSanFrancisco, 1998) may be taken as representative of the genre.

[4] William A. Barry and William J. Connolly, *The Practice of Spiritual Direction* (New York: Seabury Press, 1982), remains the contemporary classic. Anglicans will be familiar with the important works of Alan Jones, Margaret Guenther, Tilden Edwards, Gerald May, Kenneth Leech, Martin Thornton, Peter Ball, Morton Kelsey, etc.

classical Christian spirituality;[5] and (4) a hermeneutical or phenomenological approach, highly interdisciplinary, relating Christian spirituality to philosophy of religion, psychology, and non-Christian religious traditions.[6]

Missing from this blossoming resurgence, until recently, has been spiritual theology, that is, disciplined Christian theological reflection on the source, nature, and shape of the Christian life in the Holy Spirit. Important recent works have explored the territory and offered powerful suggestions for moving forward;[7] but as far as I know there has been no attempt in this new situation to provide a systematic spiritual theology of the sort that was ubiquitous in Catholic (including some Anglo-Catholic) circles for the two centuries preceding Vatican II.[8] There are a number of reasons for this, including a deep sense that there has been too vast a shift in world-horizon for the older manuals to have much relevance, even while many of us recognize real wisdom in what they contain.[9] It seems terribly difficult to get started today on such a project, because the old foundations of the discipline do not provide a place to begin, and the current discussions on "spirituality" do not further the conversation.

There are many tasks relevant to making a new beginning for the discipline. In this essay, I want to suggest a systematic and construc-

---

[5] The many-volumed Classics of Western Spirituality series from Paulist Press is the major phenomenon here. It has been a world-altering event for those of us who teach this material.

[6] This is the approach advocated by Schneiders.

[7] See especially Mark A. McIntosh, *Mystical Theology: The Integrity of Spirituality and Theology* (Oxford and Malden, Mass.: Blackwell Publishers, 1998); and Philip Sheldrake, *Spirituality and Theology: Christian Living and the Doctrine of God* (London: Darton, Longman, and Todd, 1998). Kenneth Leech, *Experiencing God: Theology as Spirituality* (San Francisco: Harper and Row, 1985) is a classic attempt to show the spiritual grounds of theology. The closest effort to what I have in mind is Yves Congar, *I Believe in the Holy Spirit*, trans. David Smith (New York: Crossroad Herder, 1997), especially Vol. 2, "He is Lord and Giver of Life."

[8] The one exception would appear to be Jordan Aumann, O.P., *Spiritual Theology* (Allen, Tex. and Chicago: Christian Classics [Thomas More Publishing], 1980, 1987). As Philip Sheldrake notes, however, this is very much a spiritual theology on the old model (*Spirituality and History*, pp. 54–55), and Aumann himself notes that much of the work is taken directly from his previous collaboration with Antonio Royo, O.P., *The Theology of Christian Perfection* (Dubuque: Priory Press, 1962).

[9] See Diogenes Allen, *Spiritual Theology: The Theology of Yesterday for Spiritual Help Today* (Boston: Cowley Publications, 1997), which attempts to mine the past but does not offer a new synthesis. Margaret R. Miles, *Practicing Christianity: Critical Perspectives for an Embodied Spirituality* (New York: Crossroad, 1988), provides a more critical framework.

tive contribution: one of the difficulties we have in getting started or restarted is that the Western theological tradition has saddled us with a wrong systemic location for the discipline, and current discussions have not really resolved that difficulty. I propose to do three things here to contribute to a new start: (1) to provide a quick review of the reasons for the collapse of the tradition of spiritual theologies; (2) to note briefly the current discussions about approaches to the study of Christian spirituality and the place of theology in that study; and (3) to articulate three propositions for moving forward: (a) the proper subject of a theology of the Christian life is the Holy Spirit and her[10] mission; (b) more immediately, the object of study of spiritual theology is primarily the movement of the Holy Spirit in the *Missio Spiritus*, and only secondarily the impact on the human community or individual life; and (c) the proper locus for spiritual theology, therefore, as a theology of the Christian life in the Holy Spirit, is pneumatology. More precisely, I propose that spiritual theology proper is structurally to pneumatology as soteriology is to Christology. These propositions, taken together, at least provide us with a place to restart the discipline.

The Rise and Decline of the Classic Model

The rise and precipitous decline of spiritual theology as a discipline has been well documented in recent years, most especially by Philip Sheldrake and Eugene Megyer, from whose accounts the following summary is largely drawn.[11]

It is generally agreed that in early patristic times there was no separation of theology and spirituality, a characteristic that remains

---

[10]   Which personal pronoun to use for the Spirit is a vexing but unavoidable question. Scripture does not decide it, Spirit being feminine in Hebrew, neuter in Greek, and masculine in Latin. Despite awareness of the attendant difficulties (see Cynthia Bourgeault, "Why Feminizing the Trinity Won't Work: A Metaphysical Perspective," *Sewanee Theological Review* 44:1 [2000]: 27–35), and despite my own preference for seeing each person of the Trinity as bi-gendered (Father/Mother, Logos/Sophia), I shall follow in this essay M. John Farrelly, "Holy Spirit," *NDCS*, 492–503, in using the feminine pronouns for the Spirit. The major contribution here is now Elizabeth A. Johnson, *She Who Is: The Mystery of God in Feminist Theological Discourse* (New York: Crossroad, 1992).

[11]   Eugene Megyer, "Spiritual Theology Today," *The Way* 21:1 (1981): 55–67, and Sheldrake, *Spirituality and History*, pp. 40–61. For the sake of brevity I shall not footnote all my dependencies on these two sources in this section.

true of Eastern Orthodoxy to this day.[12] "True theologians were those who saw and experienced the content of their theology."[13] Except for occasional treatises on prayer, such as Origen's, most of what we know about what we would now call spirituality is in dogmatic and controversial treatises, letters, sermons and scriptural commentaries. Indeed, much (like Basil of Caesarea's *De Spiritu Sancto*) grows directly out of the dogmatic controversies of the time. Most of the theologians were also bishops with active pastoral responsibilities, and monks, so that dogmatic, spiritual, pastoral and monastic theology all grow apace and together. Sheldrake also reminds us that virtually all were men, and from the elite, educated classes of Hellenistic/Roman society.[14]

In the early medieval West, it was the monastic theme that came to predominate, right through Bernard of Clairvaux; some treatises did begin to focus specifically on the mystical life, but still in the overall context of monastic theology. While this genre continued to bear fruit in the High Middle Ages, the Scholasticism of the thirteenth century brought a major shift. For the first time, dogmatic, moral and theological concerns were separated. Although his great *Summa* struggles to maintain a real unity of disciplines, Thomas put most of what he had to say about the Christian life in the Second Part of the *Summa theologiae*, the return of all things to God, beginning a trend which would subordinate spiritual theology to moral. Despite Thomas's desire to maintain the notion of loving knowledge of the Trinitarian God as the unity of speculation and affection, the die was cast.

Also at this time, the "Mystical Theology" of Pseudo-Dionysius, a fifth-century Syrian monk, which divided the spiritual life into three successive stages of ascent (purgative, illuminative, unitive), re-emerged into popularity in the West, but was largely taken out of its original context, and was often conflated with another set of three successive stages, that of the Beginner, the Proficient and the Perfect. There was also a systematization of teaching on meditation and prayer. These three tendencies—Scholastic organization and differentiation, Dionysian stages, and systematized teaching on prayer—had already come together in the immensely influential teachings of the Canons

---

[12] At least in the classic work of Vladimir Lossky, *The Mystical Theology of the Eastern Church* (London: J. Clarke, 1957).

[13] Sheldrake, *Spirituality and History*, p. 57.

[14] Ibid., p. 48.

of St. Victor in Paris, notably Richard and Hugh, in the late twelfth century. A new subjective and affective piety emerged with its own literary genres, as did the very early roots of subsequent individualism. Systematic treatises on the spiritual life began to emerge, including Richard of St. Victor's *Benjamin major* and *Benjamin minor*; *The Cloud of Unknowing*; and Bonaventure's *Journey of the Mind/Soul into God* and *The Triple Way*. Christian women from Hildegard of Bingen to Julian of Norwich contributed to the growing genre of personal theological reflection on one's own mystical experiences. Popular works such as Marguerite Porete's *The Mirror of Simple Souls* and the *Theologica germanica,* a fourteenth-century work by a Germanic monastic knight, later admired and translated by Martin Luther, show the impact of these developments on more popular piety. The shifts in the movement known as the *Devotio Moderna* in the fourteenth and fifteenth centuries deepened these trends.

In the period of the Catholic Reformation, the Carmelites (Teresa and John of the Cross) and the Jesuits and their followers, including Francis de Sales, solidified the final subjective turn of the discipline to close observation of the movement of individual souls, especially in the "higher" stages of spiritual development, completing the separation from academic theology. As the early modern period with its Enlightenment consciousness progressed, the notion of mysticism as a separate range of phenomena, and of mystics as an elite religious class, arose in seventeenth-century France.[15] As the triumph of pure reason proceeded, what was now the province of an elite also became identified as paranormal, completing the separation from "rational theology." Subsequent to the Romantic movement and its concept of artistic genius (with its own links to something much like the mystical and paranormal, as in the fascination of the Shelley, Byron, Keats crowd with the "Gothic," with vampires and werewolves, to say nothing of drug-induced states of altered consciousness), there finally emerged in William James, perhaps with some help from Kierkegaard, the ulti-

---

[15] The remarkable account of this turn is Michel de Certeau, *The Mystic Fable,* trans. Michael B. Smith (Chicago: University of Chicago Press, 1992). This work is rapidly becoming the touchstone of all truly postmodern approaches to mysticism and spirituality.

[16] A stunning postmodern reflection on and critique of this development, with a major focus on James, is Nicholas Lash, *Easter in Ordinary: Reflections on Human Experience and the Knowledge of God* (Charlottesville: University Press of Virginia,

mate expression of elitist spiritual subjectivity in the concept of the heroic religious genius.[16]

The first systematic spiritual theologies were the *Direttorio ascetico* (1752) and *Direttorio mistico* (1754) by Giovanni Scaramelli, a Jesuit. There followed a series of classic manuals, which fall into two major camps. One maintains the distinction between the ascetical and truly mystical, and believes the latter is reserved for a small elite. Typical of this school is Adolphe Tanquerey.[17] A second stream taught the unity of the spiritual life and the belief that all Christians are called to the highest degrees; R. Garrigou-Lagrange is typical of this stream.[18] Joseph de Guibert would subsequently argue for the unity of the ascetical and the mystical under the single rubric of "spiritual theology."[19] All of this was synthesized in what has remained a classic textbook, *The Theology of Christian Perfection*,[20] just as Vatican II was rendering the whole enterprise as so conceived highly problematic. Earlier, an Anglican classic, F. P. Harton's *The Elements of the Spiritual Life: A Study in Ascetical Theology,* had emerged, drawing wisdom from these sources but, as usual, in a less systematic fashion.[21]

Two starting points characterized these manuals. The first is a theology of Christian perfection which assumes moral theology covers the ground of Christian action required by commandments and precepts of obligation, and hence what is required for salvation; spiritual theology is then for those who go on to the counsels of perfection, hence works of supererogation (Tanquerey, de Guibert, Royo-Aumann). The second is simply a theological reflection on the three Dionysian stages as a kind of law-like ascent of the spiritual ladder (Garrigou-Lagrange). Neither of these starting points is any longer tenable. The former has

---

1988). The impact of this movement on contemporary evangelical theologies of the twice-born experience needs much more critical examination.

[17] *The Spiritual Life: A Treatise on Ascetical and Mystical Theology*, trans. Herman Branderis (Tournai: Desclée & Co., 1932).

[18] Of his many works, the ultimate classic is *The Three Ages of the Interior Life: Prelude of Eternal Life*, trans. M. Timothea Doyle (St. Louis and London: B. Herder Book Co., 1947, 1948). Anglicans should note that much of the point of Kenneth Kirk's famous Bampton lectures of 1928, *The Vision of God: The Christian Doctrine of the Summum Bonum* (London, New York: Longmans, Green, 1932) is on this very issue, and that he takes the same side as would be advocated by Garrigou-Lagrange.

[19] *The Theology of the Spiritual Life*, trans. Paul Barrett (New York: Sheed and Ward, 1953).

[20] Royo and Aumann, *The Theology of Christian Perfection*.

[21] F. P. Harton, *The Elements of the Spiritual Life: A Study in Ascetical Theology* (London: SPCK, 1950).

never been acceptable to Protestants, and is entirely undone by the theology and anthropology of Vatican II. The second is more hopeful, but Karl Rahner had already given a devastating critique of a rigid elevation of stage theory to the level of theological principle.[22] Sheldrake summarizes the problems with the old manuals thusly:

> Firstly, while not crudely dualistic, this approach often conceived of the supernatural life as distinguishable from, or grafted on to the natural. As a consequence it was possible to identify specifically spiritual areas for exclusive treatment. Secondly, while differing on the classifications and distinctions in the spiritual life, spiritual theologians saw the journey towards perfection in terms of degrees and consecutive or separate stages. Thus, the ultimately mysterious nature of human existence was reduced to detailed analysis according to predetermined general laws. Finally, there was a tendency to be individualistic, to ignore the social dimensions of Christian spiritual life and to reduce the ecclesial aspects of spirituality to participation in the sacraments.[23]

If the wisdom summarized in the classic manuals is to be preserved in a new attempt at spiritual theology, these difficulties must be overcome.

Theology in Current Discussions of "Spirituality"

Many authors have traced a general trend in contemporary literature to move from separate ascetical and mystical theologies, to a unified "spiritual theology" as advocated by de Guibert, to new, multidisciplinary approaches which go by the name "spirituality" and have a broadly ecumenical and experiential base. This latter approach has been most firmly proposed by Sandra Schneiders in a variety of essays, in her efforts to carve out a unique room for the study of spirituality in the contemporary academy.[24] Schneiders has suggested that there are three complementary approaches to Christian spirituality, each of

---

[22] "Reflections on the Problem of the Gradual Ascent to Christian Perfection," *Theological Investigations III: Theology of the Spiritual Life* (Baltimore: Helicon Press, and London: Darton, Longman & Todd, 1967), pp. 3–23.

[23] *Spirituality and History*, p. 54.

[24] Schneiders herself provides summary and bibliography in "Spirituality as an Academic Discipline: Reflections from Experience," *Christian Spirituality Bulletin* 1:2 (Fall 1993), p. 15. Her more mature thought is given in "A Hermeneutical Approach to the Study of Christian Spirituality."

which has an appropriate contextual locus: the strictly theological approach is best used in a denominational seminary setting focusing on formation in a particular tradition; the historical/critical approach[25] Schneiders sees as most appropriate for the nondenominational divinity school or university religious studies department; her own hermeneutical approach she sees as most appropriate to an interdenominational, interreligious graduate theological institution such as the one in which she teaches. Even this position of Schneiders, which made far more room for theological critique as an element in her own broadly conceived hermeneutical method,[26] has been subject to criticism from the beginning.[27] Walter Principe put it well: "Could it not be asked whether this ultimacy of hermeneutical criteria in fact leads spirituality thus conceived and practiced finally to approach the method of secular religious studies?" And "Any Christian spirituality involves theological positions in these areas [all the mysteries of the faith] either explicitly or implicitly."[28]

Philip Sheldrake has provided a theory of theology and spirituality as inherently and essentially related in a dialogical partnership in which each has a role of normatively evaluating the other, each being a discrete discipline, without being distinct or autonomous.[29] The fundamental reason for this is that the Christian spiritual life, precisely as life in the Spirit of committed Christians, does not have a pre-thematic or pre-theological basis[30] because as Christian experience "Christian spirituality exists in a framework that is Trinitarian, pneumatological, and ecclesial."[31]

As long as spirituality and theology remain in this kind of mutual-

---

[25] Advocated by Bernard McGinn in "The Letter and the Spirit: Spirituality as an Academic Discipline," *Christian Spirituality Bulletin* 1:2 (Fall 1993): 1–10. McGinn has embodied this approach in a variety of books, most notably in his monumental series still in process from Crossroad, *The Presence of God: A History of Western Christian Mysticism* (1991–).

[26] Schneiders, "Hermeneutical Approach," pp. 10–12.

[27] Bradley Hanson has argued for a broadly construed "Spiritual Theology" as the best conception for the study of Christian spirituality, for example, "Spirituality as Spiritual Theology," in *Modern Christian Spirituality*, ed. Bradley C. Hanson, American Academy of Religion Studies in Religion No. 62 (Atlanta: Scholars Press, 1990), pp. 45–51.

[28] *NDCS*, p. 937.

[29] *Spirituality and Theology*, pp. 65–95, especially p. 85.

[30] Ibid., pp. 19–21.

[31] Ibid., p. 61.

ly corrective dialogue, the danger of subordinating spirituality to a deductive use of theological doctrine can be avoided. The legitimate concern of the "hermeneutical approach" for appropriate integration of elements from non-Christian sources (which has been present since the very foundation of the tradition, after all) is best met, I believe, by the dialogical approach to interfaith conversations, which eschews philosophizing about a generic "religious experience" in favor of a real dialectic between possibly complementary particularities.[32]

In this light, I propose that as dialectically conceived the theological approach to spirituality is valid at all levels, including that of graduate study in an interreligious context. While it must be itself in dialogue with the experiential through the historical and hermeneutical, and indeed through consideration of anthropological, sociological and psychological theories of human growth, spiritual theology must finally be in some sense normative for theory and practice of the Christian life, even as these also have a normative evaluative role for such theology. This is true of the discipline of Christian spirituality, both for its teaching in denominationally based professional formation programs and for the training of spiritual directors and guides.

It is not only the dogmatic tradition as a whole which is so authoritative; a systematic theology of Christian life in the Spirit is still required to make the critical correlations and judgments between the dogmatic tradition (the Gospel and the Catholic Faith) and the experiential data of the historical and hermeneutical scholarly approaches, and the pastoral practice and experience of the Church in a practice of guidance and discernment. To prescind from this dialogue with theology is to decontextualize Christian spirituality, precisely as Christian, from the dogmatic tradition that is, as Lindbeck[33] has taught us, the indispensable grammar of all legitimate Christian speech. What we have learned from the best contemporary theology and spiritual praxis is that there is not some generic "spiritual experience" which is then named in different ways by differing religious or denominational traditions. Nor is there an experience deductively derived from theological norms.[34] Rather, the great dogmatic tradition of the Gospel and

---

[32] See my "Christian Theology of Interfaith Dialogue: Defining the Emerging Fourth Option," *The Sewanee Theological Review* 40 (1997): 383–408.

[33] George A. Lindbeck, *The Nature of Doctrine: Religion and Theology in a Postliberal Age* (Philadelphia: Westminster Press, 1984).

[34] This is also much the point of McIntosh's work, see esp. pp. 112–114.

the Catholic faith is the ecclesial context in which the Christian life in the Holy Spirit can be named and claimed as part of the construction of what Nicholas Lash called a pedagogy (dare one say catechesis) of contemplative praxis.[35]

If we are to attempt a truly constructive theology of the Christian life in the Spirit construed along the lines just delineated, we still need to decide where to locate it—literally, where to begin. I offer three propositions for making such a beginning.

1) The proper subject of a theology of the Christian life is the Holy Spirit.

The characteristics, properties, virtues, moral goods and similar attributes which are at stake in a theology of the Christian life are increasingly seen by theologians as in the first instance characteristics of God. Indeed, all theology is primarily about God, even if, with Tillich,[36] we recognize that all theological symbols also have an anthropological pole. In the moral realm, for example, Owen Thomas has argued, "The essence of all Hebrew-Christian ethics is the nature of God received as a demand upon the life of humanity. Thus the highest moral calling of the Christian is imitation of the outgoing love of the holy God as it is manifest in Christ."[37] We are called to be perfect, just as our heavenly Father is perfect. In that sense, moral theology and spiritual theology alike begin with the study of such attributes of God as righteousness, holiness and love as characteristics of God manifested in Jesus Christ. A study of the Christian life would then turn to these characteristics as mediated by the indwelling of the Holy Spirit, thereby allowing humans to be "in Christ" in Paul's sense, and hence to participate in what are essentially divine attributes through the mystery of the *communicatio idiomatum*. For example, many of the

---

35 *Easter in Ordinary*, pp. 254–285.
[36] A *locus classicus* is Paul Tillich, *Systematic Theology*, three volumes in one (Chicago: University of Chicago Press, 1967), I, 131. This is as good a place as any to note again that Tillich is one theologian who shared the view argued here about the proper systemic locus for a theology of Christian life in the Spirit, even if his quasi-Trinitarianism makes it unclear whether or not the subject of Volume 3, the "Spiritual Presence," is entirely equivalent to the credal "Holy Spirit."
[37] Owen C. Thomas, *Introduction to Theology* (Wilton, Conn.: Morehouse-Barlow Co., 1983), p. 88.

classical dilemmas about Justification can be resolved when we understand humans are being called not to any righteousness of their own, but to a participation, by grace, in God's righteousness.[38]

These characteristics or virtues are not attributes of human nature, not even as *capax,* something of which we are inherently capable, apart from the "supernatural" (in Rahner's sense) presence of human being before a gracious God in human existence. This is what I believe Rahner meant by his controversial concept of "the supernatural existential."[39] In the structures of human existence, this being-in-the-presence of God as demand and *capax,* as generative of all human life, let alone specifically Christian, is always embedded and effective, but only by sheer grace and not as a property of human nature. Righteousness, for example, is not even a potentiality for human nature, apart from its being evoked in us as call and gift by God's righteousness. Hence, there is a fundamental structure of human existence that is "supernatural" in the sense of transcending nature without contradicting it. It is a property of human being, but not of human nature, precisely because it is a relational property, already mediated by the Holy Spirit even to those who are not fully "in Christ."

In this light, we can see how each of the available starting points for spiritual theology is misconceived if viewed as a natural human capacity, but becomes viable as a topic of pneumatology.

First, Christian perfection is an important concept for Christian spirituality, but it is participation in the *perichoresis* or inter-penetration of the Trinitarian life, and hence in the perfections of God, which are simple and undivided. It is therefore not possible to derive successive stages from participation in God's Righteousness (Justification) as opposed to God's Holiness (Sanctification.) As a result, there can be

---

[38]   See James D. G. Dunn and Alan M. Suggate, *The Justice of God: A Fresh Look at the Old Doctrine of Justification by Faith* (Grand Rapids: William B. Eerdmans Publishing Company, 1993), esp. pp. 31–42.

[39]   "Concerning the Relationship of Nature and Grace," *Theological Investigations,* I, pp. 297–317; "The Eternal Significance of the Humanity of Jesus for our Relationship with God," *TI,* III, pp. 35–46 links the concept indelibly to the Incarnation. Rahner's own clearest short statement of the concept and the issues it addresses is the section "III. The Existential: B. Theological" in *Sacramentum Mundi: An Encyclopedia of Theology* (New York: Herder and Herder, 1968) II, pp. 306–307. For an excellent analysis of this view of human being as defined by a *telos* it cannot fulfill by natural capacity but only by deifying grace, notably in Augustine, Luther, and de Lubac, see David S. Yeago, "Martin Luther on Grace, Law, and Moral Life: Prolegomena to an Ecumenical Discussion of *Veritatis Splendor,*" *The Thomist* 62 (1998): 163–191, esp. pp. 164–174.

no question of moving from commandments to counsels in a simplistic way, and no sense that perfection involves supererogation. Indeed, while we may have some reason for distinguishing various moments in its impact on us, we have learned from recent theology that the great movement from creation to redemption to eschatological fulfillment is all one movement in God.[40] The movements in ourselves, often construed as the classic *ordo salutis,* or order of salvation, are thus not divided, but are conceptually distinguishable from our side, as long as we understand we do not complete the process of justification and *then* begin a process of sanctification and perfection. The end of this supernatural perfection is not within the capacity of human nature but is itself gift, even if universal because all humans are defined in their existence by the invitation to relationship with God. As noted, I believe this is what Rahner intends in his concept of the supernatural existential. That is, Christian perfection is as surely and as integrally related to human being through presenting it with the *telos* for which it has no natural *capax* as is the call to moral obligation and justification. Indeed, it is one movement of the Spirit by which this being-in-the-presence of God is mediated to all persons. Thus, there can be no theology of Christian perfection either apart from or subordinate to moral theology.

Secondly, from what has already been said, and the critique of stage-theory by Karl Rahner already cited, it is clear that a spiritual theology as a law-like ascent through stages of growth defined in normative terms is also no longer possible. It is especially true that we must follow Rahner in asserting that there can be no conflation of the three classic Dionysian stages with those of Beginner, Proficient and Perfect without a hopeless disregard for the complexities of human life as the context in which spiritual growth occurs.[41] Nevertheless, a certain wisdom in the tradition about this threefold rhythm continues to haunt us. We can bring this wisdom together with a contemporary appreciation of the human complexity by envisioning three great tidal currents or rhythms in the Spirit's *Missio*—the Trinitarian rhythm of

---

[40]   The *locus classicus* is Karl Rahner, "The Order of Redemption within the Order of Creation," *The Christian Commitment: Essays in Pastoral Theology* (New York: Sheed and Ward, 1963), pp. 38–74. See also the third section of this essay for implications for a theology of the Christian life. John Macquarrie, *Principles of Christian Theology* (2nd ed.) (New York: Charles Scribner's Sons, 1977), pp. 268–69, makes the same point.

[41]   "Reflections on the Problem of the Gradual Ascent to Christian Perfection."

the *Missio Dei* from the viewpoint of the Spirit to be discussed below, as it affects the community and individual members of it. These concurrent currents, however unchangeably shaped by the *Missio Spiritus*, take a unique local form at every bay or inlet of land on which they impinge—the realities of human difference. Envisioning the process in this manner allows us to sustain the classic threefold rhythm, but as derivative of the divine agent, leaving the complexity of human life intact. It also respects Luther's great insight of *simul justus et peccator*; because the three tides are always concurrent, one does not abandon the need for repentance as one grows in the Spirit.

Thirdly, self-transcendence has been proposed as a kind of inclusivist tag to give an anthropological definition to spirituality transcending religious boundaries.[42] A careful tracing back of this notion reveals roots in the theology of David Tracy, and earlier, Bernard Lonergan.[43] While this emphasis on self-transcendence as a human characteristic is useful for anthropological generalization and inclusivity, it can ignore the Christian "fact" that our self-transcendence is an element of the supernatural existential, and is, in fact, evoked in us first by God's self-transcendence, as both Lonergan and Tracy realized.[44] Human self-transcendence is ultimately dependent upon being in the presence of God's self-transcendence, as Rahner so carefully argues, grounding this human self-transcendence in the self-communication of God.[45] But, of course, for Rahner, God's self-communication is the heart of the Trinitarian processions and *perichoresis*. Thus human self-transcendence is not a property of human nature, character, or *capax*, in isolation from God, but a characteristic of human existence

---

[42] Bernard McGinn gives a helpful summary of the approach and of the literature which reflects this position, including Joann Wolski Conn and, to some degree and at one point, Sandra Schneiders, in his "The Letter and the Spirit," pp. 5–6.

[43] Bernard J. F. Lonergan, S.J., *Method in Theology* (New York: Herder and Herder, 1972); see the index entry for self-transcendence, pp. 399–400. See also David Tracy, *Blessed Rage for Order, the New Pluralism in Theology* (New York: Seabury Press, 1975), p. 11, for example, and *The Analogical Imagination: Christian Theology and the Culture of Pluralism* (New York: Crossroad, 1981), pp. 429–438.

[44] Lonergan, *Method*, pp. 116, 243; Tracy, *Analogical Imagination*, p. 432.

[45] One can watch Rahner develop this so carefully in *Foundations of Christian Faith: An Introduction to the Idea of Christianity*, trans. Wm. V. Dych (New York: Seabury/Crossroad, 1978), first in "Man as Transcendent Being," pp. 31–35, then in "Man's Relation to His Transcendent Ground," pp. 75–81, and then finally in the full-blown doctrine of the "supernatural existential" in Chapter 4, "Man as the Event of God's Free and Forgiving Self-Communication," pp. 116–138.

evoked by the proximity of God's self-transcendence, which is the Trinitarian *perichoresis*.[46] Human self-transcendence, then, is a property of human character or human being precisely as a characteristic of God mediated to humans by the Holy Spirit. Once again, we see how a contemporary starting point for spiritual theology that has severe problems comes into proper focus when located in pneumatology. Indeed, we can now see the relevance of the second constructive proposal:

2) *The primary object of study for a spiritual theology is the Trinitarian movement of the Holy Spirit in the* Missio Spiritus.

There is a rhythm and dynamism in the spiritual life that is more than just a religious view on human growth and development. As we have seen, efforts to describe this rhythm, which appears to be threefold, in terms of a law-like ascent of the human spirit in its growth, are no longer viable. I have already suggested a shift in metaphor—what we are dealing with are consistent tidal currents of the Spirit's movement, making an impact on the variegated shore of the human historical reality in a complex of flows and eddies. The situation becomes theologically clear, and capable of some organization in a new spiritual theology, if we understand that the threefold rhythm observed since Neoplatonic times is not a law-like description of human growth, but the concurrent impact on the complex human reality of the tidal movement of the *Missio Spiritus*. This *Missio* has its own Trinitarian shape as the Spirit first cooperates in the missions of the Father and the Son, and then, with their cooperation, pursues her own proper mission. Envisioning the situation in this manner requires us to give up the classical Western insistence that the external acts of the Blessed Trinity are entirely undivided and indivisible, and accept the "Cappadocian correction" proposed so effectively by Robert Jenson, that the missions of the Trinitarian persons in the divine economy are one, yet distinguishable, in the very sense that their mutuality of action reflects the Trinitarian *perichoresis* of the immanent Trinity.[47]

---

[46] Mark McIntosh's critique of the purely anthropological approach is strikingly similar to the one just given. *Mystical Theology*, pp. 19–23.

[47] *Systematic Theology*, I, pp. 110–114. On all that follows see also Yves Congar, *I Believe in the Holy Spirit*, especially Vol. 1, "The Holy Spirit in the Economy."

The first attempt to describe this Trinitarian mission of the Spirit which follows is heavily indebted to Jenson's own display of the Trinitarian rhythms of the Father as originating, the Spirit as perfecting, and the Son as mediating between origination and perfection, but does not follow his account in detail.

First, the Patrological mission of the Spirit is, then, the Spirit's role in supporting the Father/Mother's[48] *Missio* of Creation alongside the Word/Wisdom. This mission begins with the Spirit "hovering" over the Creation, and most especially the Spirit's role as "Giver of Life." But the *Missio* of Origination does not stop there, proceeding as it does to its culmination in the calling of Israel, the summoning of the priestly people under the Covenant. What shape that might have taken in the absence of fall and sin is mere speculation, but that it would have occurred I am fully convinced. Here the Spirit's role as breath of life includes the anointing of prophets, priests and kings as the officers of the covenant people. The resonance invoked in the human reality is, I believe, best called conversion, though perhaps it might have had another name in the absence of sin. The principal theological virtue (as gift of the Spirit) associated with this resonance is faith.

Secondly, the Christological mission of the Spirit is in support of the Word/Wisdom carrying out the Father/Mother's mandate for mediation of salvation and illumination. Alasdair Heron has given a particularly nuanced account of the intricate dance of the Word/Wisdom and the Spirit in the incarnation and life of Jesus.[49] He traces it from the hovering of the Spirit over Mary at the Annunciation through the anointing of Jesus as Messiah (and hence to all three Messianic offices), to Jesus' sending of the Spirit as "another advocate" at Pentecost, issuing in the birth of *Ecclesia* as the new Israel under New Covenant, as inauguration and sacrament of the coming Commonwealth of God. If the Spirit is primarily life as gift in the first *Missio*, here the Spirit is primarily fire and light, leading to the tradition that baptism is "the Illumination." This is clearly seen in the mystery of Transfiguration, which is the resonance I believe this *Missio* of the

---

[48]   Unlike Jenson, I believe we best "translate" "Abba" as Jesus' proper name for the First Person of the Trinity in this bi-gendered fashion, and the Second Person as "Word/Wisdom." It would require another essay to say why.

[49]   *The Holy Spirit* (Philadelphia: Westminster Press, 1983).

Spirit raises in us—the gift of the light, which is the Word/Wisdom and shone forth in Jesus' own Transfiguration, given us in person to illuminate us and the whole world with divine glory.[50] The Spirit's gift of virtue in this resonance is hope.

Thirdly, there is the pneumatological *Missio* proper: The Father/Mother and Word/Wisdom support the Holy Spirit in her proper mission as eschatological perfecting gift. This includes everything in the third paragraph of the creeds—the continuation of prophecy, the assembling of the Church and its final perfecting as the communion of saints in eternal life, as the four eschatological notes of the Church (One, Holy, Catholic, and Apostolic) find fulfillment in the unity of the human race in God's perfect Commonwealth of justice and peace. Here is also found the Spirit's role not just in the ecclesial sacraments, but in the sacramental consecration of the entire material cosmos, as consistently envisioned by the Eastern Orthodox tradition. In this *Missio* the Spirit is engaged in both *henosis* and *theosis*, the forging of all true relationships of unity with God, and her calling all the redeemed elect into final participation in the Trinitarian *perichoresis*, the dynamic meaning of *theosis*—"being made God." The resonance raised in us by this *Missio* is glorification/theosis, perhaps best described by anticipation in St. John of the Cross's great "The Living Flame of Love." The gift of theological virtue in this resonance is love itself, the proper name of the Third Person. The Spirit which is life in the Father/Mother's *Missio* and light in the Word/Wisdom's is properly love in her own.

> *The proper systematic locus for a spiritual theology is, therefore, pneumatology. Specifically, spiritual theology is to pneumatology as soteriology is to Christology.*

The Western theological tradition must be corrected and expanded by adding a locus proper to the Holy Spirit herself. As a perspective on the person of the Spirit within the Trinitarian Godhead this will be pneumatology. As spiritual theology it will be analogous to soteriology in the theological locus of Christology, and thus an account of the entire role of the Spirit in the divine economy, one element of which will

---

[50] I still find the most provocative work on the subject to be Arthur Michael Ramsey, *The Glory of God and the Transfiguration of Christ* (London and New York: Longmans, Green and Co., 1949).

be a unified theology of the Christian life. The parallels are nearly exact. Contemporary theology sees Christology and soteriology (doctrines of the person and work of Christ) as distinguishable but inseparable, and tends to do "Christology from below" by starting with soteriology and working up to a view of Christ's person, rather than beginning with the dogmas of Chalcedon and deductively "working down." We arrive back at the divinity of Christ and the *homoousion* of the Word by noticing that in his *Missio*, Jesus the Word/Wisdom does what only God can do. Ethical and spiritual implications for Christian life are drawn from the character of Jesus/Word/Wisdom by the *imitatio Christi*.

Similarly, a restored pneumatology in a contemporary mode would begin with spiritual theology as the impact on the Christian life of the character of the Spirit in her proper *Missio*. From this vantage, the traditional "moral" perspective will be on the given virtues as conducive to ethical choices that build up the Commonwealth and edify Christian character for choices of the Good in all areas of life.[51] The traditional "spiritual" perspective will be the giving of these virtues and other movements of the concurrent tides of the Spirit as they affect the complex shore of the human reality, drawing it into the Trinitarian *perichoresis* and glory. Of course, part of the Gospel is that in the end these two terminal images, Commonwealth and Beatific Vision, are the same, just as in the end the *imitatio Christi* merges with following the Spirit wherever it blows, and to be in Christ and in the Spirit are one and the same.[52] With the *Missio* of the Spirit thus fully described as the work of the Spirit, we can then do "pneumatology from below" by constructing pneumatology proper as the doctrine of the Spirit's person, by noticing that in her *Missio* the Spirit is doing what only God can do. Take, for example, the classic teaching on "the Dominion of Charity." A reflection on the theological virtue of love as response to the great commandments in the moral realm will move directly into the classical spiritual perspective of love as the source of

---

[51] For an important book in the current explosion in moral theology of a focus on character and virtue ethics, see Stanley Hauerwas, *Character and the Christian Life: A Study in Theological Ethics* (San Antonio: Trinity University Press, 1975). For a different but compatible view of the convergence of moral and spiritual theology see Philip Sheldrake, *Befriending our Desires* (Notre Dame, Ind.: Ave Maria Press, 1994.)

[52] And I cannot resist the conclusion of each of Jenson's two volumes, that this will be a deep praise of God's beauty in a perfect society of song.

mystical union and *theosis* as gifts of the Spirit flowing from the virtue of love as gift. It will conclude by noticing this can only be so if the indwelling Spirit is love *in propria persona,* love as that which God essentially is, and hence the Spirit must also be fully God.

Once we have the discipline of spiritual theology properly located in this manner, with its primary subject matter so delineated, we may now begin the discipline again in a manner which will preserve the wisdom buried in the old syllabus without being subject to its errors. Indeed, it becomes, as a study of the Trinitarian rhythms of the Spirit's *Missio* and its impact on the complexities of human life, the very foundation of pneumatology proper and hence, with "Christology from below," of the revival of Trinitarian thought as a whole. In partnership with moral theology, it forms also a practical theology of the Christian life that does not require perfection as supererogation. It also does not demand a simplistic view of human spiritual growth, since the classical threefold rhythm now derives from the Trinitarian structure of the Spirit's *Missio* and not from an inner-human law-like dynamic. This proposal, I believe, thus makes it possible to make a new start in spiritual theology that avoids the errors of the earlier works while preserving their pastoral wisdom. It demands that we make such a start as the foundation of a restored pneumatology and as one of the experiential grounds for a restored Trinitarianism.

It comes then to this: only a restored locus of pneumatology can offer a new beginning for spiritual theology; but only a newly begun spiritual theology can ground the content of a restored pneumatology. It is time to begin.[53]

---

[53] Subsequent to submission of this essay, I have become aware that Rowan Williams advocates a similar approach; see "Word and Spirit" in *On Christian Theology* (Oxford and Malden, Mass.: Blackwell Publishers, 2000), pp. 107–127, esp. p. 123.

Gratia: Grace and Gratitude

Fifty Unmodern Theses as
Prolegomena to Pneumatology

CHARLES HEFLING*

> *The organic wholeness of the Christian faith is at once the joy of*
> *believers and the despair of those who wish to think and write of*
> *it. Each member of the body of Christian doctrine is so closely*
> *interwoven with the rest that it seems almost impossible to treat of*
> *one part without a discussion of the whole* (Leonard Hodgson).
>
> *All things cooperate for good to those who love God* (Rom. 8:28).

Any value these theses may have, they have as an ensemble. Individually, they are too sharp-edged and crayon-colored. The shading and
detail that should be there are not, and as a result they wear a look of
certainty and sureness. I am painfully aware of how intricate and important the philosophical debates are that I have omitted, and how
thin some of the theological ice is that I have skated over. But to stop
and give all this its due would be never to get started. As it is, the theses may, taken together, succeed in conveying a single point of view
that is cogent and comprehensible on the whole; and there may be
some value in that, even though the component parts need to be elab-
orated and qualified.

The point of view rests on three "methodological" assumptions.
First, that a "systematic" pneumatology will aim at *understanding,*
that is, at insight that sheds light on what Christians have said and believed, and what they might now believe and say, about the Holy Spirit. *Second,* that one way to promote an understanding of any theological statement is to consider it—and perhaps adjust it—in relation to
other statements, theological and otherwise. *Third,* and perhaps most
importantly, that before the question of how to understand the Holy
Spirit can be addressed there are a number of other "systematic"

* Charles Hefling is Professor of Systematic Theology at Boston College, Chest-
nut Hill, Massachusetts. He is grateful to Bruce Morrill, S.J. and Jeremy Wilkins for
their godly conversation and the help it gave him in writing this article.

questions that it would be a good idea to answer, at least in a preliminary way. It is true, of course, that every Christian belief is related to all the others; but pneumatology in particular would seem to be a zone of theology that can hardly be entered except by an indirect route. That in itself tells us something about the Spirit—a point I shall return to in concluding.

Not least among the defects of the theses is their lack of citations that acknowledge indebtedness or draw comparisons and contrasts. One such mention may be included, though, by way of introduction. In a pair of reviews of recent books on the Trinity, Bruce Marshall offers two critical observations that chime with the position these theses set out. He observes, first, that in recent years there has grown up a "research program" which sets the "current Trinitarian agenda" for many if not all theologians. Among its assumptions is that "plausible Trinitarian theology has to start with the 'economic' Trinity (roughly, God as He acts in the history of salvation) rather than the 'immanent' Trinity (roughly, God apart from the history of salvation)." Theology might, Marshall hints, be better off without much of this program. His second observation is that "Even a modest familiarity with the Scholastic tradition"—modern and baroque as well as medieval— "may lead one to wonder how many of the proposals offered as needed Trinitarian novelties . . . have already been scrutinized, and perhaps found wanting."[1]

This second observation is one that Anglicans, especially, might do well to ponder. We are accustomed to supposing that theology shut down after Augustine and the Council of Chalcedon, and did not really start up again till Charles Gore and *Lux Mundi*. But if Hooker has anything to teach us, it may be that to jump back over the millennium between the Reformation and the Fathers is like jumping off one's own shadow. The more judicious procedure is Hooker's: to accept with gratitude the tradition that has made us who we have in fact become, and to go forward from there without resentment.

Gratitude is a theme of the theses, and the context in which they are appearing in print prompts a final preliminary comment. The essays gathered here include one that was written by my first teacher of theology, the late Charles Price, and another that is dedicated to him. The keynote of his whole ministry, not least though not only his teach-

---

[1] Bruce D. Marshall, "Briefly Noted," *First Things* 108 (December 2000): 59, 60.

ing, was thanks. That, more than anything else, is what I learned about from him, especially from the public prayers he composed and arranged and spoke. I am pretty sure he would not have agreed with everything I am presenting here, but I should like to present it in grateful remembrance of his gratefulness.

1. As in Christology, so in pneumatology there is a "way up" and a "way down." From observing the moon's phases, we reason "upwards" to their *causa essendi*, the sphericity of the moon. From knowledge that the moon is a sphere, we can reason "downwards" and explain why the phases, the *causa cognoscendi*, are as we observe them. Corresponding to a *causa essendi* in Christology and pneumatology alike is the Holy Trinity. What corresponds to a *causa cognoscendi* is the trinification of the world, by which mortals are taken into the life of the only God there is: the Father, the Son, and the Holy Spirit. The better we come to understand either, the better we understand the other. Like Christology, pneumatology is a two-way street, and the theological traffic always moves in both directions.

2. This is not exactly to say there is an "immanent" and an "economic" Trinity. John Milbank is right; there *is* only an "immanent" Trinity, in which men and women participate. What the New Testament has to say on the matter is that God has sent his Son and his Spirit. We may call this the divine "economy," but it is not a trinity. It is two sendings, two "missions."

3. Almost the whole of Christian systematics is comprised in setting out in orderly fashion what there is to say about the missions of the Son and the Spirit and the trinification of humanity. "Almost," because trinification is not the only way in which what is not God participates in God, not the only relationship of finite to infinite. To *be* finite is to be related to God. The name of that relationship is creation.

4. Creation is not the "economic" role of the Father. Rather it is *to* the Father that humans, "already" created, are being ordered by their participation together with the Son and the Spirit who have been sent to a created universe that "already" exists.

5. If "*all* that is, seen and unseen" is truly God's creation, then even less-than-human things, to which the Son and the Spirit have not been

sent directly, can nevertheless be construed *as* related to God. It is true that to separate "rational" from "revealed" theology was and is a mistake. It is true that the God of the philosophers is not all that the God of Abraham, Isaac and Jacob is. It does not follow that there should be no treatment *de Deo uno* whatever, or that the God of Abraham, Isaac and Jacob is in no way whatever known to the philosophers. It all depends on which philosopher. The point of a philosophical theism that articulates the finite-infinite relationship need not be to put Christianity on a non-religious basis. It can be to indicate just how *other* God is, by defining second-order statements that govern, at one remove, what we say about God. The rules of such a theological grammar have an "apophatic" function: they regulate speech, not by saying what God is (for that we do not know), but by saying what God is not.

6. Rather than "economic Trinity," it would be better to speak of divine gift. But creation is "already" a gift; to be created is to be gifted, and everything that is not God is a creature. Hence a gift *from* God that is not—because it is even more than—creation has to be a gift that *is* God, a divine *self*-gift. Such are the missions of the Son and the Spirit.

7. One reason for the neglect of the Holy Spirit in theology is a tendency (especially since Hegel) to subsume all divine self-giving under Christology. Anglican theologians have been especially inclined in this direction, as in their different ways were Barth and Rahner. The reasons for the tendency, in turn, have much to do with how we choose the terms for conceiving God and how we structure the grammar for using them. Barth and Rahner have this much in common: they conceive God as an absolute subject. But while the Incarnation is certainly a divine self-gift, it is not the only one. "Hypostatic *union*" is the name of one participation by created reality in the Trinity, namely the participation of Christ's humanity. There are two others, two other divine self-gifts and two other participations. There is the eschatological self-gift of union with the Father, the "beatific vision of God" (thesis 4). And meanwhile there is the self-gift of the Spirit, who, as well as the Son, has been sent.

8. On the other hand, pneumatology cannot declare itself independent from Christology. What we are able to understand about any of

God's self-gifts will, presumably, help us understand the others. About one of them—what it might be to "see God face to face"—we understand nothing in this life, since we do not and cannot know what it is to be God (thesis 5). But about the Incarnation we do understand at least a little. What we say about the gift of the Spirit will need to take account of both similarity and dissimilarity to the gift of the Son. Pneumatology and Christology will go forward *pari passu*.

9. God is not an absolute subject. God are three subjects. But what it means to speak of God as "three," or to say that the three are "subjects," needs to be determined so as to conform with the grammatical protocols that apply to "God." Let "subject," then, be defined for the moment in a purely anticipatory sense: a subject is what there are three of in God. As for "three," there are different ways to use the word. Three apples are three as items that are materially distinct and so can be counted by pointing to one, another, and a third. Three ideas are distinct inasmuch as understanding any one of them is different from understanding either of the others. Now, in God there is nothing to count, and a positive idea of the Son or of the Spirit is no more ours, in this life, than an understanding of the Father. We can, however, on New Testament grounds, truly assert that the Father *is not* the Son, the Son *is not* the Spirit, and the Spirit *is not* the Father. These three negative judgments extend the "apophatic" character of theological grammar (thesis 5). They give us no information, exactly. They mean only that the Father is an *identity* in the restrictive sense with respect to the Son and the Spirit, and similarly with each of the others.

10. Another negative judgment is possible. Whatever the Father may be, in a positive sense, it is no different from what the Son or the Spirit is. "For that which we believe of the glory of the Father, the same we believe of the Son, and of the Holy Ghost, without any difference or inequality," as the (original) Book of Common Prayer would have it said on Trinity Sunday. This formula amounts to a further rule of Trinitarian grammar: whatever we say positively about one of these identities, we should say about the others as well. Thus the formula brings into liturgy Athanasius's own gloss on *homoousios*, "consubstantial," which is similarly a rule of speech: whatever is said about the Father is said about the Son, except that the Son *is not* the Father. And both these grammatical prescriptions are summed up and applied in the creed that goes by Athanasius's name. "Such as the Father is, such is

the Son, and such the Holy Ghost," where "such" means uncreated, incomprehensible, eternal, almighty—in a word, God.

11. Negative judgments posit distinctions. They do not, of themselves, specify what *kind* of distinctions they posit. If we want to keep away from tritheism, then in God the distinctions between the three identities are not absolute, because God, by the rules of theological grammar, is simple. If we want to keep away from modalism, then the distinctions are not relative either; at least not relative to something other than God. For in that case we would be saying that something other than God constitutes the Father as Father, the Son as Son, the Spirit as Spirit. That too is a blunder of theological grammar, because it would be saying that the Father or the Son or the Spirit is not Creator, not uncreated but a creature, not infinite but finite—in a word, not God.

12. There remains the possibility of distinctions between three divine identities which are not absolute and not relative to creation, but which are relative to each other. This again is Christian orthodoxy as the Athanasian Creed formulates it. Two of the three are *of*. Each is *from*; and the *from* is not the same for both. The name referring to the Son's being *from* is generation or being begotten; the name referring to the Spirit's is proceeding or (preferably, to avoid ambiguity) spiration, being "breathed." We may leave in abeyance, at this point, the question *"from* which?" and with it the dispute over *filioque*. Important as it is, that dispute is not the same as whether there is a difference between the Son's "fromness" and the Spirit's.

13. Turning from the Trinity to the divine self-gift that is the Incarnation (thesis 8), the Son not only is "such as the Father is," *homoousios* or consubstantial or "one in being" with the Father, but also is such as we are, consubstantial with us. The Son is an identity in the restrictive sense with respect to the Father and the Spirit, but *not* an identity in the restrictive sense with respect to some "rational creature," or however else we may define the species we belong to. For the Son belongs to it too. He became an individual member of that species, a particular first-century Jewish carpenter. Otherwise stated, that the Son is not the Father or the Spirit is true; that the Son is not Jesus is *not* true. That is one way that the mission and gift of the Son differs from the mission and gift of the Spirit.

14. The preceding five theses are not so much "systematic" theology as doctrine. They belong to the catholic faith as formulated in the Athanasian Creed. We no longer use that hymn in worship, which is perhaps a pity; but its contents, construed in the minimal, heuristic, "grammatical" way that theses 9–13 set out, do not go beyond the affirmations of the Nicene Creed, which we do use. How it might be possible to *understand* what in the creed we declare to be true is a different question. Systematic theology concerns itself with that question—not with conjectural speculation or totalitarian system-building. The Trinitarian and Christological dogmas orient language towards a mystery, mostly by saying what should *not* be said. Suppose, then, that we follow all their heuristic anticipations and honor all the grammatical rules. How are we to form a positive conception of the Trinity about which our speech is thus regulated? The general answer is: analogically.

15. An analogical conception of the Trinity can never be more than hypothetical. It does not preclude revision or exclude alternatives. Still, some analogies are better than others. By "better" is meant, among other things, that the analogy is taken from realities, among those which we do know positively, that we judge to be most like God, and that it illuminates and explains the prescriptive judgments that constitute theological and Trinitarian "grammar."

16. What an analogy needs to shed light on, first of all, is the distinctions because of which we speak of Father, Son and Spirit as three (thesis 12) while asserting that there is but one God.

17. The best, though not the only, analogy for the Trinity will be psychological. The reason: among created things it is *mens*, soul, *psuchê* that bears the least faint resemblance to God. The chief characteristic of a psychological analogy is that it cannot be imagined, and that is one thing that makes it a good analogy. You can break the leaves off a shamrock, or dam a wellspring and cut off "living water" from its source. These are indeed Trinitarian analogies, but they are material—intrinsically conditioned by space and time. Acts and operations of human consciousness, insofar as they are not so conditioned by space and time, are more like the God who, in the words of the first of the Thirty-Nine Articles of Religion, is "without body, parts, or passions." In discourse other than systematic theology, to be sure, there may be

good pedagogical or political reasons for using material analogies. But "good" in such cases is defined by some other end than the pupose of systematic theology, which is *fides quaerens intellectum*, "faith seeking understanding" (thesis 14).

18. There is a much-discussed way of understanding the Trinity which would have it that two of the three in God bond with each other, and that the nexus of their mutual love is a third. It is commonly called "the Augustinian psychological analogy"—about as apt a name as "Holy Roman Empire." In the first place, it is not uniquely Augustinian. By one count Augustine has more than twenty analogies for the Trinity. In the second place, it is not all that psychological. What it has love uniting is not two other psychological states or acts but a lover and a beloved. In the third place, therefore, it is not much of an analogy. It assumes that lover and beloved are, and that they are distinct, before their loving unites them. There is no explanation of "generation," which alone distinguishes the Son from the Father (theses 12, 16). It would be more accurate to say, on this analogy, that God is like a psychosocial community of two individuals. Hence the binitarianism so prevalent in Western theology.

19. Not that love as psychological analogue is a mistake. Humans in love are humans at their best, their most human. If to be human is to be created in the image of God, human loving will show that image most clearly. A consistently psychological analogy based on love, however, will have to introduce differentiation, and that for two reasons. On the one hand, love is various. English has only a single word, but its meaning is not univocal. On the other hand, the New Testament associates not only the Spirit with divine love but also the Son; and in 1 John 4:8 ("God is love") *ho theos* is the Father.

20. Love is "existential," a state of one's whole being that integrates thought and feeling. It is a conscious state characterized by two sorts of conscious activities, which have a certain internal order. They are (1) approving, affirming, valuing, yea-saying or benediction, and (2) delighting, rejoicing, thanksgiving. Someone who is "in" love recognizes or discerns or grasps the evident goodness of someone or something—the beloved. Inasmuch as the discernment is not abstract, the lover (1) inwardly and soundlessly "pronounces" the affirming, evaluative judgment which expresses that the beloved *is* indeed good. And

inasmuch as this silent benediction is wholehearted, the lover (2) rests content, delighting in and thankful for the goodness he or she has discovered and come to know.

21. Such a state of being in love, though it certainly has feeling as a component, is not unthinking or stupid. "Reasons of the heart" are not unreasonable. To evaluate the evidence for the goodness of X takes discerning intelligence; otherwise, judging and affirming are arbitrary. That is infatuation, not love. The affirming judgment that X truly *is* good emerges *because of* intelligent discernment; otherwise it is untrue. That is delusion, not love. And thankfulness for the known goodness of X emerges *because of* having made up one's mind that X is good and so to be loved; otherwise it is mendacious. That is hypocrisy, not love.

22. Such is the basic analogy. It regards love of any good, and so is not limited to any single kind of love, whether romantic, aesthetic, filial, platonic, patriotic, conjugal, or what have you. The intimacy of two human beings is a particular and perhaps privileged instance, but not the only one. As many as there are real goods to love, so many are the potential realizations of the *imago Dei*. Moreover, unless it can be shown that women and men love in essentially different ways, the psychological analogy has the advantage that its basic terms are not gender-specific.

23. The basic analogy, however, is only a basis. It is not (yet) an analogy for three identities, or for that matter three of anything. It is an analogy for two emergings or emanations: (1) the springing to light of an expression or "word" that bespeaks a recognized goodness, and (2) the blossoming of thankful delight on account of the goodness expressly known. What these are analogous *to*, in God, are the two divine "processions," generation and spiration.

24. The analogies are suitable, not only because the psychological activities involved are in themselves non-material, but because in both cases what emerges is neither a change nor an effect (thesis 15). This is one point at which the distinction between creation and divine self-gift (thesis 5) comes into operation. An effect is other than its cause. What God causes is not God, namely the created universe (thesis 29). The Son, however, is *not* made or created, and neither is the Spirit

(thesis 10). In the analogy, being in love does not *cause* judgments of value, though such judgments emerge *because* someone in love can and does discern the evidence for the goodness of what is therefore lovable. Nor are such judgments the *cause* of thankfulness, though thanksgiving emerges *because* goodness is recognized and expressed. Nor, finally, do approving and thanking change the state of being in love. They *are* being in love.

25. Thus, analogically speaking, we may say there are two emergings or emanations in God, which hereafter will be termed benediction and thanksgiving. It follows that God is "related to" God in three ways: (1) There is a relation of the uttering source to the uttered word of benediction. In God, the speaking of goodness is completely honest, holds nothing back. Call this relation, then, *sincerity*. (2) There is a relation of affirmation to its source, the relation of the word spoken to the speaking that speaks it. In God, the utterance corresponds completely and truthfully to the goodness discerned and grasped. Call this relation, then, *fidelity*. And (3) there is a relation of delighted contentment to the event of speaking, to the speaker and the spoken. In God, the good honestly approved and truthfully expressed is enjoyed, rested in, relished in its completeness. Call this relation, then, *gratitude*.

26. Sincerity, fidelity and gratitude are modalities of love, conceived as a dynamic state of being. Each of them, in its own way, is the essence of being-in-love. Analogically speaking, then, it is *by* these relations of sincerity, fidelity and gratitude that God is being-in-love. But in keeping with one of the rules of theological grammar there is no difference in God (as there is in everything else) between "what" and "by which." That by which God is, and what God is, are identical. So in God sincerity *is* being-in-love; that is, it is God. In God, fidelity *is* being-in-love; so is gratitude. That is, each is God.

27. The analogy under construction is psychological in the sense that it takes its terms and their relations from a "phenomenological" account of conscious activities. By conscious is meant that activities of mind and heart such as these not only make us aware of someone or something other, but also make us aware of ourselves *as* aware of the other. Hence being in love is a conscious state because benediction and thanksgiving are conscious acts (thesis 20). For the same reason, the relations here termed sincerity, fidelity and gratitude are also con-

scious. Each, differently, is a conscious being-in-love. But to be a conscious being-in-love, to be consciously loving, is to be in the psychological sense of the term a *subject*. That is the sense in which, analogically speaking, there are three subjects in God or, better, three subjects who are God.

28. "Consciousness" and "subject" are reciprocally defining terms. A subject, in the psychological sense, is the subject *of* consciousness. A human being, unconscious under anesthesia, is still a human being, still an identity, but he or she is not experiencing, thinking or loving anything or anyone, and so is not a subject. In us, subjectivity is a variable, with a minimum in dreaming and a maximum in loving (thesis 19). Divine subjectivity does not vary; divine consciousness is always active, always loving, and of that consciousness there are three subjects. There is one divine act of love, one grasp of unlimited goodness; and there are three identities that repeat this love non-identically, three that share the state of being in love but "be" in it differently. God the Father is conscious love in a way that is analogous to the way human being-in-love manifests itself in affirmation, in uttered benediction. God the Son is conscious love in a way analogous to the way a truthful expression of approval depends on the self-manifesting love that utters it. God the Spirit is conscious love in a way analogous to the way gratitude for what is good depends on goodness expressly manifested. The Trinity is not—or not only—three modes of loving. The Trinity is three who are in love.

29. A certain amount of obscurity involved in talk about an "economic" Trinity may be cleared up by attention to the "*ad extra* rule." This is yet another "grammatical" protocol, which applies to statements that relate the created world to God and especially to statements about divine "agency." We need not think in terms of causal agency, but if we do then God is "first cause" but not an item in any causal series. By creating the universe God fulfills, all at once, the conditions for everything that exists to exist and everything that occurs to occur, including the existence of any causal series and the occurrence of any result. In other words, God affects the parts by effecting the whole. This is just a slightly more philosophical way of saying that creation is not necessary but contingent—a gift (thesis 6). Now, everything we say about God we say about each of the three who are God (thesis 10). So Father, Son and Spirit are the Creator. No finite being or event, precisely as finite, is any more the effect of Father or Son or Spirit than it is of any of the

others. The same reasoning applies to everything God "does." That is why to invoke Creator, Redeemer and Sanctifier is to invoke the one God three times, but not to invoke the Trinity.

30. The *ad extra* rule applies to both the Son and the Spirit as "agent." It need not apply to either as *gift*. In the same way that it is not true to say God created such-and-such unless such-and-such really exists, so too it would not be true that the Son and the Spirit are given unless their being given makes some real difference in the existing world (thesis 1).

31. As in God there are two divine subjects who proceed but do not proceed in the same way, so in the world there are two divine subjects who are shared with the human race, but who are not shared in the same way. The Son is the subject of divine consciousness analogous to the faithfulness of an approving word of judgment uttered because of intelligent discernment. As such the Son is distinct from the Father and the Spirit, and as such the Son is given. The Spirit is the subject of divine consciousness analogous to gratitude for love sincerely manifesting itself and faithfully expressed. As such the Spirit is distinct from the Father and the Son, and as such the Spirit is given.

32. Far from excluding a social analogy, the psychological analogy here proposed includes what advocates of a social analogy rightly stress: intersubjective order. Divine subjects are subjects by the relations that they are (thesis 26). God, then, is entirely relational, a community of subjects constituted by their relations—by sincerity, fidelity and gratitude. As the Son and the Spirit, with the Father, constitute a community of love, so they are sent by the Father to establish and nurture an ordered good which, like God, consists of many subjects, and of which they themselves are constituents. Otherwise stated, human participation in God is participation in relations that are divine, namely the fidelity that is divine love and the gratitude that is divine love (theses 26, 28). It is in this connection that "economy" is most appropriately used—as a metaphor for an orderly, relational, intersubjective good. It is not, of course, the only authorized metaphor. Others are "kingdom," "household" and "city."

33. The *efficacious* metaphor—the sacrament—of the world's trinification is worship. Worship, like God, is benediction and thanksgiving.

To worship is to be blessed by blessing, to be made thankful by thanking. This is, and is to be, the completion of the image of God, the purpose of being a conscious subject, the end that humans (and angels) were made *for*—"to glorify God and enjoy him for ever." In time, this eschatological end is common prayer, *leitourgia*. Principally, it is *eucharistia*, blessing and giving thanks *to* God the Father *through* Jesus Christ *in* the Holy Spirit. Eucharist is the "economic" Trinity *par excellence*.

34. In eucharistic *leitourgia*, the *ergon* or operation that makes worshipers a *laos* is a cooperation. As God gives us "our selves, our souls and bodies"[2] so that we might worship, so God gives himself, his Spirit and his Word, in order that we might worship in spirit and truth. Eucharist, as a participation in God's own fidelity and gratitude (thesis 32), is "divine service," something men and women do as selves, and at the same time gift, something they receive as selves.

35. Eucharist is received as gift in two ways that correspond to the ways in which the two divine subjects who cooperate in worship are given. Eucharist is at once an "outward" and an "inward" communication. It is given outwardly, "objectively," through bodily words and gestures, physical bread and wine. It is given inwardly, "subjectively," in "hearts on high," *sursum corda*. Given in one way, it is *through* Christ, in that "Christ is the language which we speak to God."[3] Given in the other way, it is *in* the Spirit. There is no dichotomy, but there is a difference. Eucharistically conceived, the ways in which the Son and the Spirit are given is the difference between visible and invisible, outer and inner, *ex auditu* and *ex infusione*, or mediated and immediate.

36. A divine subject is always immediate in the sense that God never *is* a means. God does *use* means; every "secondary cause" is a finite means by which the world is divinely ordered (thesis 29). In God's gift of God that was the Father's gift of the Son, a divine subject *became* a "secondary cause." This is to say that the divine self-gift was mediated through the human existence, the meaningful words and deeds, of the mediator, Jesus of Nazareth (thesis 13). *What* was mediated was the

---

2   Eucharistic Prayers 1 and 2, BCP, pp. 336, 342.

3   C. H. Sisson, "The Usk," in *In the Trojan Ditch: Collected Poems and Translations* (Cheadle, Cheshire, U. K.: Carcanet Press, 1974), p. 33.

conscious Word of benediction which eternally expresses approval of divine goodness and which, in time, continues to be mediated in Christian speech.

37. God never *is* a means; God does *use* means; but God does not *always* use means. In God's gift of God that is the mission of the Spirit, "God's love has been poured into our hearts through the Holy Spirit which has been given to us" (Rom. 5:5). This love is the gratitude that eternally delights in the uttered expression of divine goodness and that, in time, draws the subjects of human consciousness towards their divine origin and end (theses 4, 7, 33).

38. Pneumatology is an orderly account of this drawing. If it is true that the Spirit is really given, there is some reality within the created world because of which that statement *is* true (thesis 30). But the Spirit is not another Son, not another mediator; and the reality that is the Spirit's activity *ad extra* will be given and received not mediately but immediately. The relevant data, that is, will be experiential, "subjective" in the sense of belonging to one's own subjectivity. To know the gift of the Spirit is to know oneself as gifted. It is a matter of "introspection" in the sense of coming to awareness and understanding of one's own conscious states and activities. Discerning the Spirit takes place in "discernment of spirits."

39. One thing that pneumatology will therefore take into account is "religious experience." Neither the "liberal" account, however, nor the "cultural-linguistic" alternative will serve. Their common drawback is that each posits a starting point or an *a priori*. Either language (including religious language) provides labels for experiences that are independently prior to them, or else language is independently prior and determines in advance what sort of experience (including religious experience) can be had. This either/or, however, is abstract. Religious experience is conscious—it makes a subject self-present as present to her or his world (thesis 28)—but its being conscious is not the same as its being attended to, much less its being understood and known. Attending, distinguishing, naming, conceiving and affirming one's conscious experience does depend on language. Equally, however, the available languages are many; they may be more or less accurate; inaccuracy can be noticed, and the language refined. The process, like the process of self-knowing generally, is concrete, dy-

namic, and historical. Categories applicable to conceptual logic are not the most useful.

40. The reciprocal interdependence of "inner," conscious experience and the meaning mediated by "outward," embodied signs is the counterpart of the gifts, respectively, of the Spirit and the incarnate Word, of love bestowed and love avowed (thesis 35). It is because of the "outer" word of Christian *kerygma* that we can recognize and name the gift of the Spirit and know what accepting such a gift implies. It is because of the "indwelling" Spirit that we can welcome, accept and assent to the meanings and values mediated in preaching and teaching, in Scripture and liturgy, and in the "secondary incarnations" that are the saints.

41. As "religiously" experienced, the gift of the Spirit is anonymous and incognito. To name it means selecting from the available terms and images, modifying and combining them by the criterion of one's own conscious self-presence. There is no other way. Subject to the same criterion, then, pneumatologically relevant experience can be described as finding oneself in a condition of "universal willingness," of "absolute dependence," of "ultimate concern," of "consolation without a cause," of *complacentia boni*, resting in the good that is.

42. Such experience is difficult to articulate because it inverts a "normal" order. We are accustomed to knowing the objects of our love before we love them. There is ordinarily some cognitional apprehension; then comes affective response. In fact it is this "normal" order that the Trinitarian analogy constructed in theses 20–22 has followed. Religious experience, however, is response ("consolation," "concern," "willingness") that is not restricted to any apprehended object. Its quality is the quality of gratitude, the presence of a beloved in the lover; but in this gratitude the beloved is not restricted to *some*one or *some*thing that excludes anyone or anything else. It is "universal," "ultimate," "absolute," or, in the biblical phrase, "with *all* one's heart, soul, mind, and strength." Yet *for* what or *to* whom one is grateful, dependent, willing, concerned—that is not given.

43. The development and refinement of such a "phenomenological" account would seem to provide a point of departure both for a Christian (that is, Trinitarian) theological treatment of religion and for the

"wider ecumenism" of dialogue with "non-Christians." As long as religion is conceived of as primarily cognitive, the question at the fore will be how true religion is to be distinguished from false. A positive evaluation of religions other than Christianity will therefore involve ascertaining a minimum of cognitive truths. Such was the "natural religion" of the eighteenth century. If, however, the cognitive aspects of Christianity, its teachings as linguistically formulated, are associated with the sending of the Word, and the affective, interior aspects with the gift of the Spirit (theses 35–37), it becomes possible to attribute to the same Spirit those positive aspects of other religions which constitute the experiential infrastructure of their spirituality. On such a position, Frederick Crowe's term "anonymous Spiritan" is better than "anonymous Christian." But if the term is not to be used condescendingly, it must take its meaning, not from a set of theses, but from the self-giving of dialogue among people who are—what is rare—both experienced in and articulate about the gratitude that is worship.

44. Distinguishing the gifts of Son and Spirit as mediated and immediate implies a certain rearrangement of Christian doctrines. It is customary to think that the Father first sent the Son and afterward sent the Spirit. But the past-tense verb is appropriate to the mission of the Son because that gift is mediated by created realities. Insofar as he was a member of the human species, Christ began to be and began to be given. That is one of the limitations entailed in his *kenôsis*. The giving of the Spirit is not thus limited. It can be—and is—always and everywhere. If it was because "God so loved the world that he gave his only Son" (John 3:16), that love was real not only in God but in the world. On the present position, the Father's love for humankind, as bestowed, is the Spirit as gift. So the Father gives the Spirit and "then," that is in the fullness of time, avowed his love, once for all, by giving the Son.

45. In the traditional "system" of Christian theological *topoi*, pneumatology should include and inform the doctrine of grace, and in particular "sanctifying" grace as "elevating" and grace as "cooperative."

46. The multivalent word "grace" means at least the following: the favor that A has towards B ("to be in someone's good graces"); a gift bestowed on B by A (a "gratuity"); and B's thanks to A on account of A's gift ("grace" at meals). The Father's love for humankind is divine

grace in the first sense; the Spirit he has sent is divine grace in the second sense; and the unrestricted, conscious gratitude here associated with the term "religious experience" should be identified with divine grace in the third sense.

47. Previous theses give the basic reason why grace *is* grace—why it is gracious, a gift rather than something due or something owed. The reason is that to be no longer a child or a servant but a friend of God does not belong to any finite creature, precisely because creatures are finite. Friends have everything in common; they share one life. But in order to share in divine life it would be necessary to be, in some fashion, infinite. To love God above everything else is "natural" to humans, in the sense that it is within our capacity; but to love God unrestrictedly, with God's own love, with "the love of God poured into our hearts by the gift of the Holy Spirit," is in the primary sense of the word "supernatural." Hence the metaphor of "elevating" grace.

48. Intimacy with God is beyond our capacity. It is also, contingently, beyond our deserving. Humankind is not only finite but "fallen." To love someone is to wish, will, want, desire what that other wishes, wills, wants, desires. The human condition, as it actually exists, is that we do not will what God wills and that we are impotent to change ourselves in this regard. To change ourselves would be to reorient our self-constituting, to begin to become other than what we have been becoming. Such a change is not impossible in principle. Concretely and objectively, however, the probabilities are infinitesimal. Reversing those probabilities is not the reason why the Spirit is given; the gift of the Spirit is defined, not by human need, but by divine generosity. It is, nevertheless, because the Spirit is given that those probabilities are reversed. *Gratia elevans*, the grace that "elevates," is also *gratia sanans*, grace that heals. Forgiveness of sins is a special case of trinification, so to say.

49. Pneumatology will nonetheless be concerned with *conversion*. The "phenomenological" data on spirituality are data for a theology of the Spirit (thesis 38), and spirituality has a dimension of its own. It is not reducible to morals or politics, any more than liturgical worship is reducible to aesthetics. Still, spirituality does include all one's relations to oneself and others, and it is in those relations that human subjects are drawn by the Father "out of error into truth, out of sin into

righteousness, out of death into life."[4] Conversion is principally the immediate gratitude that has "love, joy, peace, patience, kindness, generosity, faithfulness, gentleness, and self-control" as its fruits (Gal. 5:22). But the same gratitude that registers as "contemplative" delight in the good that *is* also invites repentance for the good that should be but is not, and "active" concern for the good that is not but should be.

50. As the gift of the Word took effect "not by conversion of the Godhead into flesh, but by taking of the manhood into God," so the gift of the Spirit takes effect not by invasion of "sacred" abnormality but by opening up of self-constituting human subjects to their own self-transcendence. Rowan Williams remarks that the spirituality of working out a "Son-like" life, rather than episodic or idiosyncratic occurrences, "specifies" the activity of the Spirit. Stated in terms of the foregoing theses, this is to say that the criterion of Christian self-transcendence, and of Christian conversion, is fidelity to the Father—the criterion, that is, of the relation which in God is the Son and which in these last days has been sent to be incarnate in one human life and death (thesis 26). Christian spirituality, then, is *imitatio Christi*. It has the eucharistic "shape" of the paschal mystery.

These theses were offered as prolegomena, and the reader who has made his or her way through them might well ask what sort of pneumatology they turn out to be prolegomena *to*. But an even more pertinent question would be whether the theses lead up to *any* sort of tract or treatise concerned with the Holy Spirit and nothing else. The absence, or the thinness, of such a treatment of pneumatology in its own right is not infrequently a ground for criticizing theological systems. Such a criticism, however, is perhaps open to critique itself. Slicing the theological pie into manageable wedges, adjacent but self-contained, is sometimes convenient. But if there is a conclusion to be drawn from the foregoing theses, it would seem to be that pneumatology ought not to be a distinct department of theological understanding, so much as an integrator of other departments.

This is not to say that pneumatology has no content of its own. It is to say that the "office" or "work" of the Holy Spirit, the operation of this divine subject as distinct from the Father and the Word, is *cooperation*. What there is to say about the Spirit, consequently, will be

---

[4] Eucharistic Prayer B, BCP, p. 368.

said while speaking of something else as well. The theses themselves have already alluded to a number of standard headings within Christian systematics—grace, sacraments, soteriology, eschatology. They might, indeed should, have mentioned ecclesiology also. The Church is called "temple of the Holy Spirit" or "Spirit-filled community." If these are not just rhetorical flourishes, it would seem that they name, concretely, what the Spirit enables people to do, as one body, on behalf of humankind—namely, "to make prayers, and supplications, and to give thanks for all,"[5] and to be an efficacious sign, within the world of human antagonism, of the eschatological city of peace, citizenship in which the Spirit offers to everyone.

To make the same point in a different way, the "disappearance" of pneumatology *per se* into other topics of theological discourse might be construed as a sign of the way the Spirit, in Vladimir Lossky's phrase, "effaces himself" as a divine subject before the human subjects in whom he operates and with whom he cooperates. The otherness of this "other" is in no way extrinsic, in no way over-against, in no way rivalrous. It is purely gift. And whereas the gift of the Word now has the face of Mary's son, the "face" of the Spirit is still in the making, for it will be the diversified face of the whole communion of saints, each in the fullness of his or her particular identity, united in common gratitude expressed through common fidelity to one Father.

---

[5]   The Prayers of the People, The Holy Eucharist, Rite I, BCP, p. 329.

The Spirit in the Blood

PAUL F. M. ZAHL*

> *When he comes, he will convince the world of*
> *sin and of righteousness and of judgment* (John 16:8).

This short essay is an exploration of the relation between the Holy Spirit as entity or quantity and the Holy Spirit as justifying action. What is the relation between Jesus Christ as forensic Justifier of the human race and the identity of Christ as Spirit within the Trinity? Classically expressed, what is the relation between the Spirit and the Son in the core work of salvation, which is the justifying, substituting Atonement of Christ Jesus on the Cross?

I write as an Anglican theologian of the Cross, who understands the Atonement, or God for us, as *prior* in theology to the Incarnation, or God with us. While it is obvious that God's Incarnation preceded His Atonement in *history*, it is also obvious in theological reflection that the Incarnation is a deduction from the Atonement: for "It is only God who can forgive sins" (Mark 2:7; Luke 5:21). If He has in fact achieved our forgiveness in respect to His action, then He must be divine in respect to His being.

I write as an Anglican theologian whose lens or focus on the biblical revelation is the Atonement rather than the Incarnation. Therefore the person of the Holy Spirit has got to be linked to the *act* of God on the Cross at least to the same extent that the Holy Spirit/Comforter is linked to the *presence* of God in experience.

In the New Testament, there is no more direct a declaration of the role of the Spirit in the justifying work of salvation than John 16:8. This word from the farewell discourses of Jesus describes the Holy Spirit as the One who will convince or convict the waiting, mourning world of sin, righteousness and judgment. Verses 9, 10 and 11, which appear to explain this threefold action, are hard, even obscure verses. But they are vital for this theme.

* Paul F. M. Zahl is Dean of the Cathedral Church of the Advent in Birmingham, Alabama.

The Holy Spirit convicts the world of sin "because they do not believe in me" (John 16:9). Sin is the opposite of faith. The Spirit exposes the appalling and evenly distributed self-deception of our belief in ourselves. It does the pre-evangelistic work of wearing down and also unmasking the idols of false truth and false constructions of truth which human beings manufacture in the billions. The Spirit is Truth's Spirit. Without this Truth, we are all characters on the journey towards Step One of the famous Twelve Steps. When, on the other hand, our faith in the false gods of human rationalization and contrivance is confronted by their true terminus, which is the death of Christ on the Cross, the false gods are toppled and shattered. Great is their fall.

The Holy Spirit places the human person in front of the Crucified God and compares his or her dismal performance as imagined subject of his/her destiny with the terminus to which belief in oneself inevitably leads. That terminus is condemnation and death. Thus Luther's celebrated dictum in his commentary on Psalm 51:

> The proper subject of theology is man guilty of sin and condemned, and God the Justifier and Savior of man the sinner. Whatever is asked or discussed in theology outside this subject, is error and poison.

The work of the Holy Spirit that places the human person before the Crucified God is evoked memorably in Oscar Wilde's story for children entitled "The Selfish Giant." Wilde, whose *The Picture of Dorian Gray* is *the* Romantic parable of substitutionary guilt in the light of Original Sin, tells the tale of a mean reclusive giant who refuses to allow children to play in his walled garden. He does, however, rescue a little boy who is being bullied. Later, years later, still enclosed within the inverted shroud of his own hard-heartedness, inside his locked and walled garden, the giant spies the same little boy playing alone in the garden. The boy shows the giant his hands, red with nail prints. He shows the giant his feet, scarlet with the same scars. "Who hath done this?" asks the giant, appalled. "These are the wounds of love," replies the boy. Selfishness is routed by the moving, transforming effect of the "glorious scars" (Charles Wesley). The giant dies in his sleep that night, covered in a blanket of white blossoms.

We could say that the Holy Spirit's convicting the world of sin is the same as the alien work of God, the love of God revealed to us through the wrecking ball of human catastrophe. This alien work of God is also the *usus theologicus* of the Law. That is to say, conviction of our true state before God, which is dismal, evasive, and guilty, is what the Law, theologically understood, is all about. The "wounds of love" pierce the heart, as in "Depart from me, for I am a sinful man" (Luke 5:8).

The Holy Spirit uses the Law as its characteristic instrument to shatter the universal sinful posture of desperateness and self-assertion. The crucified child in Oscar Wilde's parable is the sharpest possible illustration of the convicting power of pentecostal and also accusatory love. My case rests. The Holy Spirit convicts the world of sin.

The Holy Spirit convicts the world of righteousness "because I go to the Father" (John 16:10). In the presence of Christ's absence, which is the entire sum of human time and history after the Ascension, the human being no longer knows what goodness really is. The Law convicts of sin, but without the Spirit of Christ, the Decalogue, which is the biblical Law in its proper sense, is no different from the natural law of Aristotle. It does not point the accused to the specific and unique grace of Christ as Savior. The Law applied, however, by the Holy Spirit in the physical absence of Christ directs the human being to the proper, sufficient, concrete object of hope, the expiation by His blood (Romans 3:25).

The Spirit mediates the Law in its theological use to a world that now exists in the physical absence of Christ. The Spirit as convictor is the unmasking Persona of Christ who exists Himself *in absentia*. The triple office of the Comforter as declared in John 16:8 comprises the hammer of God in relation to human sin.

Christ's ministry *here* was heartbreaking to all the stony types who found themselves riveted by His words and His persona. When He ascended to the Father (John 20:17), the divine and cosmic question became: "Who will go for us?" (Isaiah 6:8). Who will break the stony hearts now? John's answer to that question is the Spirit as Emmanuel. Who else could be sufficient to convict the world of righteousness?

The Holy Spirit convicts the world of judgment "because the ruler of this world is judged" (John 16:11). This verse suggests a "classic" theology of the Atonement, by which Satan has been cast aside as the world's puppet master because he was judged in the place of Jesus on the Cross. Golgotha's judgment is not only the nailing of our own sins to the tree (Colossians 2:14, 15; 1 Peter 2:24); it is the shedding and final extinction of Satan's lifeblood.

The "classic" understanding of the Atonement, which seminarians have for decades been drilled into associating with the Swedish Lutheran Gustav Aulén, is definitely limited in its effectiveness in the pulpit. That is to say, it *sounds* better than it preaches, for it speaks of a past victory that comes across to the hearer as abstract. What good is it to announce that the ruler of this world is judged when he appears still to be so active and effective in human experience? This is always the challenge of Christian preaching: how to bring the "already" into the "not yet." As a Sunday-to-Sunday preacher in the same pulpit year after year, I believe it is true to say that the substitutionary model of preaching the Cross gets through more readily to most hearers than the classic model. An example of this in media-culture would be the long sermon at the end of Robert Duvall's 1996 film *The Apostle*.

Despite one's own skepticism concerning the classic model and its inadequacies for getting through to everyday people who are preoccupied with their problems in the present, there is no denying that the "classic" theme is found in John's Gospel. What we can say to redeem it for pastoral/homiletic use is that the power vanquished in 16:11 is Satan and we are therefore in the world of equally classic Pentecostalism. Our brothers and sisters in the Church of God in Christ, for example, that astonishingly potent denomination with immense crossover from the black community to the white community, receive a big assist through this verse. The Spirit convicts the world of judgment, because the ruler of this world is judged.

To summarize thus far, the Holy Spirit participates in the salvation wrought by Christ on the Cross, by *exposing* the deception of unfaith, by *applying* for our good the standards of the Law in the physical absence of the One who fulfilled it in life and death, and by *assuring* us of Satan's dethronement as ruler of the world.

In historical theology, the Spirit has been conceived to be an emotional and gift-giving force field of praise and thanksgiving, as in Pentecostalism. Or the Spirit has been conceived to be authentication (unseen) of the instruments of water and of bread and wine in the two sacraments, as in various forms of Catholicism. Or the Spirit has been conceived to be the inspirer of the Word, Scripture's Word, to the hearers, as in Reformation Protestantism. The Spirit also has been conceived to be the mediator of Christ's earthly presence through the icon, as in orthodoxy.

Each of these conceptions of the Spirit creates an ecclesiology, and probably all visible representations of Christianity fall under one or another of these categories. Most expressions of Anglicanism fall under the second or the third, depending on whether one is more protestant or more catholic by temperament or nurture.

What I think we need to get away from, or rather what we need to *broaden out*, is the attempt to represent the Holy Spirit as a quantity or entity, the attempt to understand the Spirit objectively. We need to transpose to our conception of the Holy Spirit Bultmann's famous objection to the concept of the Word as *thing* or measurable unit. The Holy Spirit is first an action before it is an entity.

There is nothing one-sided or strange about affirming the Holy Spirit's presence in the world first as an action before it is an entity, or rather, an action in the place of an entity. This is always the way with love. It is a regard, a conclusion about ourselves from an outside entity, as in "she loves me, she loves me not, *she loves me*," which establishes every relationship we ever know. I can gaze at the beloved all I want, but nothing can *happen* until the beloved wants me. No relationship that is two-sided—and all relationships have got to be two-sided to endure—is entity-adoration. Rather, all relationships are grounded in a mutual action of some degree. This is manifestly true in experience. Therefore Christian thinkers should not be surprised if the Holy Spirit is described in John's Gospel in terms of action rather than in terms of entity.

The greater question, methodologically speaking, is whether biblical theology is first and foremost *ethical* or whether it is first and foremost *ontological*. Is the Spirit's witness to Christ initially a statement concerning the forgiveness of sins or is it a statement concerning the God who was found in human form? To put this existentially or, better, pastorally: Is the Spirit's witness to Christ a praise for the conscience unstressed or is it an acclamation of Emmanuel, God with us? Naturally, it is both these things. Yet it is initially a statement concerning the conscience in the light of the Law. "This is a true saying, and worthy of all to be received, that Christ Jesus came into the world to save sinners" (1 Timothy 1:15—a Comfortable Word!).

The ethical moment is the human moment. The human being is human in respect to his or her inescapable moral responsibility. Original Sin, which is universally debilitating, compounds the problem of responsibility, because it paralyzes the will's freedom while at the same time assuming the will's accountability. This creates the absolute dilemma for everyone who has ever lived, which Paul described in Romans 7:7–8 and 3:21–26. It is the hammerlock of supreme moral demand in relation to the all-paralyzing toxin of sickened human nature that forces the Christian affirmation to be *ab initio* an ethical deliverance. Thus the core work of the Holy Spirit is to establish Christ's ministry to the moral theme in human history objectively understood and in personal/individual history subjectively understood. Thus the Spirit applies the Blood to the lintel of the heart!

The Holy Spirit convinces and convicts. The Holy Spirit acts to make concrete, specific and individual the universally required and completed achievement of atoning Justification on the Cross. The Holy Spirit reminds us that the devil is a liar (Bishop T. D. Jakes' refrain!)[1] and is no longer in charge. Thus the Holy Spirit is *informing, mediating, individualizing,* and *de-mythologizing.* Christ's Spirit is destructive of all unbelief that is rooted in false belief.

Is the Spirit solely relational? John 16 does not go quite that far. Is the Spirit quantifiable? John 16 does not think of the Spirit objectively. Is the Spirit sanctifying? Yes, if by "sanctifying" we mean the personalizing within the human personality of Christ's objective accomplishment.

Is the Holy Spirit active in salvation? Yes. The Third Person of the Trinity is a doer!

---

[1] T. D. Jakes is a leader in Black American Pentecostalism who is seen and heard by millions of people. Consistently he links "The Blood" (of the Cross) with the "Anointing" (of the Spirit).

Justification and the Holy Spirit

REGINALD H. FULLER*

Over half a century ago the well-known Anglican liturgiologist Gregory Dix reminded us that the Reformation was not all about incense,
vestments, or other externals—the Lutherans anyhow kept most of
those things—but about the doctrine of justification. In a nutshell, the
issue was whether God's righteousness is imputed (thus the Lutherans) or imparted (thus Rome). The Reformers could appeal to the Old
Testament and Hebrew background of the relevant terms, righteousness and justification, and to Paul's argument of Romans 4:6–12,
which is based in part on Psalm 32:2, "Happy are those to whom the
Lord imputes no iniquity." Rome could base its argument, at least in
part, on the literal meaning of the Latin *justificare*, meaning literally
to *make* rather than *declare* righteous. While the Reformation understanding is exegetically correct as far as it goes, it often has had unfortunate consequences in practice. Luther maintained, correctly
enough, that the message of justification by the grace of God, made
available through the saving act of God in Christ and received by faith,
is the heart and soul of the gospel, the doctrine by which the Church
stands or falls (*articulus tantis vel cadentis ecclesiae*). He was even exegetically correct, though questionably paraphrasing, when he added
the little word *allein* to his translation of Romans 3:28, despite its absence from the Greek: "Thus we hold that the human being becomes
righteous without the works of the law through faith *alone*" (my translation from the German, emphasis added). Our Anglican Reformers
agreed with Luther on this point:

> We are accounted righteous before God, only for the merit of our
> Lord and Savior Jesus Christ, by Faith and not for our works or
> deserving. Wherefore, that we are justified by Faith *only*, is a

---

* Reginald H. Fuller was Molly Laird Downs Professor of New Testament at Virginia Theological Seminary, and served as President of the Society of New Testament
Studies. He dedicates this article to his friend and colleague, Charles P. Price, priest
and doctor of the Church, who died on October 13, 1999, the day the first draft of this
article was completed. *Requiescat in pace*.

129

> most wholesome Doctrine, and very full of comfort (Article XI of
> the Articles of Religion, emphasis added).

There can be no doubt that Anglicans/Episcopalians are committed
to the Reformation position. But in other contexts this crucial Reformation doctrine can have questionable consequences. It has been
used, for instance, though not by Luther himself, by the more radical
Reformers, to downplay the necessity of the sacraments, to give them
a purely symbolic significance, or to abandon them altogether. This is
what happened with the Socinians, the Quakers, and the Salvation
Army.

Justification by faith only can also be interpreted in such a way as
to neglect the importance of good works in Christian life. In fact, one
sixteenth-century Lutheran theologian went so far as to assert that
good works were harmful for salvation (!). Perhaps that was merely a
piece of rhetoric for a particular situation, and not meant to be taken
as a general truth. A third effect, particularly evident in seventeenth-
century Lutheran orthodoxy, was an excessive concentration on right
doctrine (*rechte Lehre*), to the neglect of devotional life and of moral
effort. Despite the legitimate reaction in German pietism, some of the
consequences of this neglect have persisted to this very day. Bishop
Stephen Neil, probably the only Anglican to have held a professorship
in a German theological faculty, once remarked that his students there
never seemed to say their prayers. I can vouch for that from my own
experience in the Evangelical Stift (Seminary) in Tübingen just before
World War II. It led me to coin the expression *Biergartentheologie*
(beer garden theology). There seemed to be little appreciation for the
principle *lex orandi lex credendi* (what you pray determines what you
believe). This impression was reinforced for me some years later while
lecturing at the Ecumenical Institute of Bossey to an international
conference for students. I was invited as an Anglican to conduct a
quiet day. The students from the Reformed traditions welcomed what
for them was a new experience, but the German Lutherans protested.
Keeping silence all day was looking for justification by the works of the
law! While pietism, whether in its German or Anglo-Saxon forms (Anglican Evangelicalism and Methodism), rightly insisted that justification, or conversion as they preferred to call it, must be followed by
lifelong growth in sanctification or holiness of life, popular piety has
concentrated too much on the initial moment of conversion. It often
seems to get no further than the beginning of the Christian life. Some
readers may remember the story of the Victorian bishop of Durham,

Brooke Foss Westcott. One day, when he was still a professor at Cambridge, he was traveling by train to London when a Salvation Army lass got into the carriage at Hitchin. Taking her seat opposite him, she asked him: "Are you saved?" To which he replied, "Do you mean *sō theis, sōzomenos,* or *sōthēsomenos*?" (saved at some moment in the past, in the process of growing into salvation, or hoping for salvation at the Last Day). There is more to the Christian life than its initial moment.

In his Anglican days John Henry Newman proposed a middle way of interpreting the doctrine of justification, seeking to do justice to the truth in both Protestant and Catholic positions while avoiding their pitfalls. Justification, he agreed with Luther, begins when God imputes to the believer the righteousness of Christ. God grants his grace to the believer as a free gift, consequent upon Christ's redeeming work, through the operation of the Holy Ghost, and it is appropriated by faith alone. Thus far Luther is correct. But that is not all. Justification initiates a process in which the Holy Ghost enables the believers to perform good works. This growth reaches its completion at the Last Day. Thus righteousness, initially imputed, is increasingly imparted, and results in good works. This is the truth in the Catholic position. Moreover "faith alone" does not eliminate the sacraments, for it is through baptism that righteousness is initially imputed, and through the eucharist that it is increasingly imparted. Believers, however, must cooperate with the Holy Spirit in performing good works: they cannot do them by their own unaided effort. Thus the Catholic view follows St. Augustine. Here Newman supports his argument with three quotations from the Pauline writings:

> Work out your own salvation with fear and trembling; for it is God who is at work in you, enabling you both to will and to work for his good pleasure (Phil. 2:12–13).

> The fruit of the Spirit is love, joy, peace, kindness, generosity, faithfulness (Gal. 5:22).

> For by grace you have been saved through faith, and this is not your own doing; it is the gift of God—not the result of works, so that no one may boast. For we are what he has made us, created in Christ Jesus for good works, which God prepared beforehand to be our way of life (Eph. 2:8–9).

Newman argued that when Paul speaks of "works" without qualification he always means the works of the law, works done before justifi-

cation. These are the works that according to Article XIII do not justify but "have the nature of sin." That is to say, they are done while we
are under the wrath of God, still unreconciled to God. When Paul
speaks of works done after justification he calls them *good* works.
Today we would need to qualify this. It is the deutero-Pauline letters,
rather than Paul himself, which speak of good works in connection
with justification or salvation (Eph. 2:10; 1 Tim. 2:10, 3:1, 5:10). This is
not a departure from Paul's own teaching. The deutero-Pauline writers could safely use language that Paul, faced with the Judaizing controversy, could not; he preferred to speak about the fruit of the Spirit.
Newman recognizes that in the new life in the Spirit the believers frequently fall into sin and need to repent. This is the truth of Luther's
simul justus et peccator (at once righteous and a sinner). It does not
mean that we remain morally no better than we were before we were
justified, and that Christ's righteousness continues to be only externally imputed. The Christian life is a process of becoming what we are, of
participating in the righteousness of Christ initially imputed to us.

We may add that Newman's argument may also suggest a correct
understanding of Luther's *pecca fortiter* (sin boldly). It does not mean,
"Go on sinning as much as you like, God will forgive you anyhow."
Rather, it means that when you have done your best through the grace
of God and with the assistance of the Holy Spirit and nevertheless
have failed, God will still forgive you through Jesus Christ if you truly
repent. As Bonhoeffer states, *pecca fortiter* comes as good news only
after we have borne the heat and burden of the day.

Newman's treatment of justification reflects the structure of
Paul's letter to the Romans, the closest Paul ever came to a systematic
presentation of his theology. Paul does not stop at chapter 5. After presenting his doctrine of justification, he proceeds to talk of baptism
(chapter 6), of the new life in the Spirit (chapter 8), and of the good
works expected of those who are justified by faith (chapters 12–15).

In the bilateral dialogues which have taken place since Vatican II,
Newman's attempts to reconcile Catholicism and the Reformation
over the doctrine of justification have borne remarkable fruit. This can
be seen in the report of the Lutheran-Catholic Consultation in the
USA of 1985, in the ARCIC-II document *Salvation in the Church*
(1987), and the Lutheran-Catholic Joint Declaration on the Doctrine
of Justification of 1999. The last of these documents is particularly significant, for it is the only one of the three documents that has been officially accepted by the participating churches, and it removes the

anathemas pronounced by each side in the age of the Reformation. This document was officially signed by representatives of the Roman Catholic Church and the Lutheran World Federation at Augsburg, Germany, on October 31, 1999. Both date and place of this event are significant: Augsburg, the place of the Augsburg Confession in 1529, and October 31, the anniversary of Luther's 95 theses, which launched the Reformation in 1517. The central statement in this Joint Declaration is found in paragraph 15:

> Together we confess that by grace alone, in faith in Christ's saving work, and not because of any merit on our part, we are accepted by God and receive the Holy Spirit, who renews our hearts while equipping us to do good works.

Earlier, in paragraph 11, the Joint Declaration had affirmed that justification occurs through the reception of the Holy Spirit in baptism, and that baptism in turn incorporates the believer into the one body. In paragraph 12 it interprets Luther's *simul justus et peccator* exactly as Newman had done (see above).

The renewed emphasis on the role of the Holy Spirit in justification should have further desirable consequences. The pietistic concentration on the moment of conversion has often led to an excessive individualism. The Church, however, does not come into being when the justified or converted get together and say: "Let us share our experience." It is significant that the Acts of the Apostles speaks of the first convert as "being added" through baptism (Acts 2:41). You can't add something to nothing, so baptism is the means by which converts are brought into an already existing community by the justifying act of God (divine passive). In this context, the divine activity is expressed through the passive voice which reverently avoids naming God as the agent of the saving activity.

The recognition of the Spirit's role in justification also calls attention to another important truth, namely the eschatological aspect of justification. As Paul puts it, the Holy Spirit is the *arrabōn* (down payment) and *aparchē* (first fruits) of a salvation which will not be consummated until the parousia. This is true of all the soteriological images employed in the New Testament: justification, reconciliation, regeneration, redemption and salvation. That was the point of Brooke Foss Westcott's reply to the question, "Are you saved?" Here too is the solution to the apparent contradiction between Paul, who asserts that we are justified by faith (alone), apart from the works of the law, and James, who asserts that we are justified by works and not by faith only. Paul and James are speaking of justification in two different senses— Paul about what happens in baptism, James about what happens at the Last Judgment. They are also speaking about "works" in different senses, Paul of works done before justification, James of works done after what Paul calls the fruit of the Spirit. In this connection Protestants have been a little reluctant to speak about "rewards." Rightly understood, there is a place for such language, and even Paul did not shrink from it on occasion (1 Cor. 3:14; cf. Col. 3:24). This is recognized by ARCIC-II in *Salvation and the Church*:

> The works of the righteous performed in Christian freedom and in the love of God which the Holy Spirit gives us are the object of God's commendation and receive his reward (Matt. 6.4; 2 Tim. 4.8; Heb. 10.35, 11.6). In accordance with God's promise, those who have responded to the grace of God and consequently borne fruit for the Kingdom, will be granted a place in that Kingdom when it comes at Christ's appearing. They will be one with the society of the redeemed and rejoicing in the vision of God. This reward is a gift depending wholly on divine grace. It is in this perspective that the language of "merit" must be understood, so that we can say with Augustine: "When God crowns our merits it is his own gift that he crowns" (paragraph 23).

The promised reward is not external to our own good works or granted to merits accumulated by our achievement, but the consummation of the new life of the Holy Spirit. The righteousness of Christ, initially imputed to the believers by the Spirit in baptism and received by faith alone, continues to bear fruit in good works through the operation of that same Spirit, and is thus imparted to us. Thus it reaches fulfillment in final salvation at the Last Day.

Now that both the Episcopal Church and the ELCA have accepted the revised form of the Concordat and as of January 6, 2001, have entered into full communion, both parties will bring gifts to enrich each other. Our Lutheran brothers and sisters should help us rediscover the centrality of justification by grace through faith alone, a doctrine which seems to have played little part in Anglican thinking since the time of Newman. It is notable, for instance, that LED I was content to list "justification by grace through faith" by title as "one of the fundamentals of Church doctrine on which both partners were agreed." We, for our part, might help our Lutheran friends to realize the importance of growth in holiness through prayer and devotion. Then let us hope that we Lutherans and Episcopalians may bear fruit in good works together, including those social concerns so dear to us today. We may then be reminded by our Lutheran friends to beware of the ever-present temptation to self-righteousness. The doctrine of justification by grace through faith alone will then help us to see these concerns, not as our own achievement or merit, but precisely as the fruit of the Spirit. In this way the doctrine of justification may become for all of us an *articulus stantis ecclesiae*, an article by which both Episcopalians and Lutherans stand in the power of the Holy Spirit.

A Clarification on the *Filioque*?

GEORGE H. TAVARD*

That the doctrine of the *filioque* and its uncanonical insertion in the Latin creed present serious obstacles to the reconciliation of churches has long been clear. It was manifest in the twelfth and the fifteenth centuries when the Orthodox people and patriarchs rejected the compromise that had been suggested by the Second Council of Lyon and the Council of Florence. It has also been clear in the modern ecumenical movement since the Orthodox churches began to take part in the Commission on Faith and Order, in the 1920s. The conversations that have taken place since the formation of the World Council of Churches in 1948, and especially since the end of Vatican Council II in 1965, have confirmed not only that the *filioque* presents a major problem, but also that the problem is not about to vanish. On the one hand the very life of the Orthodox churches is tied, if not directly to a denial of the Augustinian doctrine that the Spirit proceeds "from the Father and from the Son as from one principle," at least to the affirmation that the Spirit eternally originates from the Father alone. On the other hand, the Western churches and theologies generally have seen no sufficient reason to abandon the insight of St. Augustine, even if some of them are willing to remove the *filioque* from their official creed.

On July 6, 1982, the Joint International Commission for Theological Dialogue between the Roman Catholic Church and the Orthodox Church alluded to the problem of the *filioque*. Without examining the question at length, it formulated a basic consensus:

> We can already say together that this Spirit, which proceeds from the Father as the sole source in the Trinity (John 15:26) and which has become the Spirit of our sonship (Rom. 8:15) since he is also the Spirit of the Son (Gal. 4:6), is communicated to us par-

---

* George H. Tavard is a Roman Catholic theologian. He lectures at seminaries and universities across the United States and Canada.

ticularly in the Eucharist by this Son upon whom he reposes in time and in eternity (John 1:32).[1]

The reference to the eucharist evidently raises a secondary question regarding the experience of the Trinity in the sacrament. If one leaves this aside, the chief point is strictly Trinitarian. The Christian faith confesses the Father as the "sole source in the Trinity," that is, as the sole origin of the Second and the Third Persons.

When Ecumenical Patriarch Bartholomew I paid a visit to Pope John Paul II in June of 1995, the pope expressed the wish, inserted in a homily, that

> the traditional doctrine of the *Filioque*, present in the liturgical version of the Latin Credo [be clarified] in order to highlight its full harmony with what the Ecumenical Council of Constantinople of 381 confesses in its creed: the Father as the source of the whole Trinity, the one origin both of the Son and of the Holy Spirit.[2]

In response to this desire, the Pontifical Council for Promoting Christian Unity issued a Clarification that was printed in the daily paper of Vatican City, *Osservatore Romano*, on September 13, 1995, under the title, "The Greek and the Latin Traditions regarding the Procession of the Holy Spirit."[3] As included in the *Information Bulletin*, this document is introduced by a short statement, in which one is informed that, as printed in *Osservatore Romano*, the text was "accompanied by three stars." The meaning of three stars in this context is not explained, although in journalistic convention it often implies that the anonymous source of the text is highly authoritative. Whatever three stars convey to the usual reader of the newspaper, however, this journalistic device has no standing in canon law.

In fact, it is not only the authorship, but also the canonical authority of the document, that are not clear. The text indeed declares: "We are presenting here the authentic doctrinal meaning of the *Filioque*. . . . We are giving this authoritative interpretation. . . . ," *we*

---

[1] *Information Service of the Secretariat for Promoting Christian Unity*, n. 49, 1982 II/III, p. 108).

[2] Quoted in *Information Service. . .* , n. 89, 1995 II/III, p. 88.

[3] *Information Bulletin of the PCPCU*, n. 89, 1995 II/III, pp. 88–92. The text is available as a short pamphlet, *The Greek and Latin Traditions about the Procession of the Holy Spirit*, London: CTS Publications, 1995.

being the Pontifical Council. In any case, the document is intended to contribute to a theological reflection at the highest level.

Five points stand out. Firstly, the symbol of the First Council of Constantinople is normative for the whole Church in its unaltered form, notably in the confession that the Spirit takes his origin (*ekporeuomenon*) from the Father. It is part of the Christian faith that "the Father alone is the principle without principle of the two other persons." The monarchy of the Father is common to the Greek and the Latin patristic traditions. For this reason the Roman Catholic Church has refused to put an equivalent of the *filioque* in the Greek text of the Creed, "even in its liturgical use by Latins." The only such use of the Greek symbol of faith is, I believe, in some of the papal liturgies. Because of this scarcity of use, most of the Western world is probably unaware of this restraint in the liturgical formulation of the *filioque*. It is nonetheless significant.

Secondly, the Orthodox formulation of Trinitarian doctrine is qualified by a number of the Greek Fathers, with the addition that the (*ekporeusis* of the Holy Spirit passes "through the Son" *dia tou huiou*). This, the Clarification specifies, "is the basis that must serve for the continuation of the current theological dialogue between Catholic and Orthodox."[4]

Thirdly, adopting a more normative tone, the Clarification turns to the Latin doctrine of the *filioque*. This "must be understood and presented by the Catholic Church in such a way that it cannot appear to contradict the Monarchy of the Father, nor the fact that he is the sole origin . . . of the (*ekporeusis*) of the Spirit." The *filioque* tradition, according to which the Spirit "proceeds eternally from the Father and the Son," goes back to the early Latin Fathers.

Fourthly, it was unfortunate that "a false equivalence was created" when it was assumed in the Middle Ages, on the basis of the Vulgate translation of John 15:26, that the Latin emphasis contradicted the Greek teaching. In reality—and this is the new point of the Clarification—*ekporeutai* in John does not mean *procedere*. The Greek term is very specific, and refers only to the Father being the sole source of the other persons, while the Latin word is broader, and designates "the communication of the consubstantial divinity from the Father to the Son and from the Father, through and with the Son, to the Holy Spirit." At this point three elaborate footnotes ground this

---

[4]   Ibid., p. 89.

statement in several texts of the Latin Fathers. For the Latins, the original credal formula, translated as *ex Patre procedentem,* "could only suppose an implicit *filioque* which would later be made explicit in their liturgical version of the Symbol." It is in this context of non-contradiction between the Greek and the Latin views that one should understand the Trinitarian doctrines of the Fourth Council of the Lateran (1215) and the Second Council of Lyon (1274). These doctrines were in harmony with reflections on the Trinity that had been made by St. Maxim the Confessor: the Spirit does not proceed from the divine substance, but from the Persons of the Father and the Son as from one principle.

Fifthly, the Orthodox teaching is said to imply that the Spirit "comes from" the Father as from his one and only principle (this being the *ekporeusis*), and that he nonetheless comes from the Father through the Son (this being the *processio*). The Clarification notes that this was the point of the Council of Florence, which saw an equivalence between the Latin formula, *Spiritus Sanctus ex Patre Filioque,* and a formula that is common to East and West, *Spiritus Sanctus ex Patre per Filium.*[5] Admittedly, the Second Council of Lyon, in 1274, had not mentioned this equivalence when it affirmed that the Spirit proceeds *ex Patre et Filio . . . tanquam ex uno principio . . . unica spiratione.*[6] This formulation, however, should be read in light of the previous doctrine of the Fourth Council of the Lateran (1215): "It is the Father who generates, the Son who is begotten, the Spirit who proceeds."[7] In any case, the *Catechism of the Catholic Church,* issued in 1992, is clear on the contemporary doctrine: "The eternal order of the divine Persons in their consubstantial communion implies that the Father, as the principle without principle, is the first origin of the Spirit, but also that as Father of the only Son he is with the Son the single principle from which the Spirit proceeds."[8] The sense of this statement clearly rests on the acceptability of the distinction, and the complementarity that is implied between being "the first origin" of the Spirit and being "the single principle" from which the Spirit proceeds. The Clarification sums up the question as follows:

---

[5]   Decree for the Greeks, 6 July 1439 (DS. 1300).

[6]   DS. 1300.

[7]   DS. 804.

[8]   *Catechism of the Catholic Church,* n. 248. The English translation came out in 1994.

Just as the Father is characterized as Father by the Son he generates, so does the Spirit, by taking his origin from the Father, characterize the Father in the manner of the Trinity in relation to the
Son and characterize the Son in the manner of the Trinity in his
relation to the Father: in the fullness of the Trinitarian mystery
they are Father and Son in the Holy Spirit.

This summary would obviously be clearer if it contained an exegesis of "in the manner of the Trinity."

I do not think that historical or doctrinal difficulty can be ascribed
to the first three points. Concerning the fourth point, the distinction
between *ekporeusis* and *processio* that is proposed may well prove to
mark a breakthrough in the conversations between the Catholic and
the Orthodox churches, for if *processio* and *ekporeusis* indeed refer to
different aspects of the mystery of the Trinity, then the two doctrines
of East and West may well be mutually compatible. Whether they are
or not will depend on whatever assessment is agreed upon as to the
implications of the distinction.

The fifth point, however, does raise unexpected difficulties. First
of all, it implies that in a certain sense Spirithood is logically antecedent to Filiation and even to Fatherhood. But this would seem to
question the Trinitarian order as it appears in the creed. Admittedly,
the point must be balanced with the explanation, given in the Clarification, that in another sense it is Filiation that is antecedent, and in a
third sense it is Fatherhood that is antecedent. This is precisely the
point of these lines:

> The Father only generates the Son by breathing (*proballein*)
> through him the Holy Spirit, and the Son is only begotten by the
> Father insofar as the spiration (*probole*) passes through him. The
> Father is Father of the One Son by being by him and through him
> the origin of the Holy Spirit.

At this point a footnote gives historical backing to the proposal as
it refers to the middle position of the Spirit between the First and the
Second Person in the theologies of Gregory Nazianzen and of Thomas
Aquinas. More systematically, the text tries to avoid the logical consequence of the anteriority of the Spirit to the Son by pointing to the
function of the Son, who "characterizes as Father the Father from
whom the Spirit takes his origin, according to the Trinitarian order."

"According to the Trinitarian order" must be equivalent to the
previous formula, "in the manner of the Trinity." It is difficult, howev-

er, to determine the exact order or manner that is invoked here. It seems to be neither the order of the Persons in the Creed of Constantinople, nor an order of priority between Essence and Persons. The monarchy having been clearly affirmed at the start, it should be an order in which the Father is indeed the sole source. In this case, however, the Father must be the source of all his own properties, and then one cannot qualify the amplitude of this source by adding that the Father gains a character or characteristic from the Son who is born of him and from the Spirit who proceeds from him. If each Person to some extent characterizes the others in their very specificity, it is logically antecedent to the distinctive characteristic it gives them. In this case the Trinity would include a priority—in some sense—of each Person over the other two. If, however, this is the intended meaning of the "Trinitarian order" or the "manner of the Trinity," it brings up a new problem. For then the Trinity need not start with the "only source in the Trinity," the Father, but it may start equally with each Person. The "order of the Trinity" is then constantly shifting, the Persons taking turns to be First, or perhaps each being First in three different perspectives. If this is so, however, a new question is raised in regard to the Father's monarchy.

I take it that these passages of the Clarification draw on the circumincession (total reciprocal mutuality) or *perichoresis* of the three Persons to escape the dilemma of the *filioque*. This, however, causes a new problem. For if circumincession is primary, then the specificity of each Person is conditioned by it, and it is difficult to maintain the monarchy of the Father, unless the capacity for circumincession was understood to be an attribute of the divine *ousia* and, as such, equally to belong to each Person. This in turn would evoke the mostly forgotten Trinitarian theology of Gottschalk,[9] who in the middle of the ninth century argued, against archbishop Hincmar, that, like *unitas*, *deitas* is *trina* because it is an attribute of the three Persons. The Clarification shows no awareness of it, although *trina deitas* was included in the confession of faith of Pope Pelagius I in 557.[10]

---

[9]   George H. Tavard, *Trina Deitas: The Controversy between Hincmar and Gottschalk* (Milwaukee: Marquette University Press, 1996).

[10]   The *Fides Pelagii* is part of the letter *Humani generis*, addressed to the Merovingian king Childebert I. Tavard, *Trina Deitas*, p. 57, n. 101. The *Fides Pelagii* is echoed without acknowledgement in *The Catechism of the Catholic Church* (New York: Doubleday, 1995): "The Trinity is One . . . (n. 253). The divine Unity is Triune (n. 254)." This translation, however, obscures the parallel by its substitution of "triune"

On another point further reflection is needed than appears in the Clarification. Quite properly the text asks, "What is this Trinitarian character that the person of the Holy Spirit brings to the very relationship between the Father and the Son?" The answer derives from the theology of mission: "It is the original role of the Spirit in the economy with regard to the mission and work of the Son." Now, granted that the temporal missions of the Son and of the Spirit follow the character of their eternal Personhoods, it is difficult to see how the temporal mission, retroactively, as it were, can affect the eternal relationships of which it has to be the faithful image. The movement of the economy follows the order of creation; it goes from the eternal to the temporal. The reverse movement, from the temporal to the eternal, has validity in regard to human knowledge of the Three Persons, not in the ontological order of the divine mystery.

An additional difficulty is raised by Thomas Aquinas's doctrine that divine personhood is constituted by the originating relationship of each Person (*S. Th.*, I, q.28, a.2; q.29, a.4). The eternal Word is Son because he is Filiation from the Father. Likewise, the Spirit is constituted as Person by its joint relationship of origin to the Father and the Son, that is, by its procession *ab utroque*: *Processio (est) persona Sancti Spiritus procedentis* (I, q.30, a.2 ad 2). But if the procession *ab utroque* is not the ultimate origin of the Spirit, this origin being in the Father alone, then the Spirit is the Third Person by virtue of its *ekporeusis*, its sole relation of origin to the Father, and not by its *processio ab utroque*. One should then ask what, if anything, its relation to the Father and the Son as its joint principle adds to the Spirit, who is already constituted as Person by its only source, the Father. But if *processio* adds nothing, then it would seem that recourse to Ockham's razor would be appropriate: *Entia non sunt multiplicanda sine necessitate*. In this case, however, the doctrine of the *filioque* would become superfluous.

The assertion that the Eastern and the Western Trinitarian traditions are not mutually incompatible may be correct. If each tradition derives from the Fathers of the Church, then the churches of East and West have the task of discovering the compatibility of their doctrines. Any suggestion in this direction deserves the closest attention.

---

for "trine," since "triune" is an artificial compound that refers at the same time to unity and to trinity.

I have not read any reactions to "The Greek and Latin Traditions regarding the Procession of the Holy Spirit" on the part of Orthodox theologians, and it is too soon to know how the dialogue between the two churches will deal with the question. I do hope that the Clarification will bring the Orthodox and the Catholic traditions closer together. The distinction that is made between *ekporeusis* and *processio ab utroque* suggests that both the Eastern and the Western doctrines may be regarded as correct, though more complementary than identical. This should be regarded as an advance. Nonetheless, the Clarification raises questions regarding the order of the divine Persons and the monarchy of the Father[11] that will deserve critical review on both sides of the historical debate.

In any case, whether or not the Clarification succeeds in allaying the Orthodox impression that Latin theology has not given the proper place to the Holy Spirit, the problem of the *filioque* will not be entirely solved until agreement is also reached on the implications of pneumatological doctrine regarding the structures of the Church and the papal primacy.

---

[11] Although this may not be a major point, one may wonder why, except in some patristic quotations, the Clarification never designates the Second Person as the *Logos* of God, but always as the Son.

Some Notes on *Filioque*

CHARLES P. PRICE*

At the Minneapolis General Convention of 1976, a lay deputy moved to end debate on whether or not to omit the phrase "and the Son" from the text of the Nicene Creed in the *Proposed Book of Common Prayer* with the following speech: "The Father incomprehensible, the Son incomprehensible, the Spirit incomprehensible. Let's vote."

It is a remarkable fact that after nearly fourteen centuries, during which it has troubled the Church repeatedly, *filioque* remains an ecumenical stumbling block. The phrase has acquired along the way an unhappy freight of theological pride and acrimony and has served as the scapegoat for political controversies with which it had nothing to do. This paper is written to untangle and clarify the historical and theological problems of *filioque*, and to elicit a response from Anglican theologians.

Certain parallels suggest themselves between *filioque* and *homoousios*.[1] For one thing both words served as the focus for both a theological debate and a power struggle. Such a situation is never far from a faith based on incarnation, since God has entrusted to mortal and sinful men and women the ministry of reconciliation. Theology cannot simply be divorced from power, and these instances are simply salient examples of a general state of affairs. Nevertheless we have to try to sort out theological from political considerations both to understand what has happened in either case and to decide on appropriate action in the case of *filioque*. For another thing, words are frail carriers of truth, especially when they have to describe deity. Even Athanasius was able to recognize that the word *homoousios* had certain liabilities. It had, for example, been condemned by the Synod of Antioch in 268 as the word used by Paul of Samosata to elaborate his monarchian idea of the relation of the Son to the Father. Athanasius also recognized

---

* Charles P. Price taught theology and liturgics at Virginia Theological Seminary, where he held the William Meade chair in Systematic Theology.
[1] Cf. Terrence R. O'Connor, S.J., "*Homoousios* and *Filioque*," *Downside Review* 83, 1965, pp. 1–19.

that the word *homoiousios* might be used in an Orthodox sense.[2] Similarly, *filioque,* as we shall see, has liabilities as have its alternatives; and alternatives may be recognized as also communicating the truth. From a strictly theoretical point of view, *there is no real virtue in the word as such, or its omission,* as surely and necessarily expressing the truth about God. In this case, as always, one must simply do the best one can with the words and the traditions available, and acknowledge at the end, as at the beginning, incomprehensible mystery.

The discussion of the relation of Son to Spirit prior to the insertion of filioque *in the Nicaeno-Constantinopolitan Creed by the Council of Toledo in 589.*

Scripture can be cited to support any Trinitarian heresy, and it is difficult to prove conclusively from the New Testament even the Trinitarian structure of God. There is some clear witness to binitarianism. "The Lord is the Spirit,"[3] for example. The binitarian strain in early literature is well known.[4]

As far as the relation of Spirit to Father is concerned, the clearest word, picked up in the original text of the Nicaeno-Constantinopolitan Creed is John's: "But when your Advocate has come, whom I will send you from the Father—the Spirit of truth that issues from the Father—he will bear witness to me."[5] This scriptural passage has continued the essential vocabulary to the relationship of Spirit to Trinity. The Spirit *proceeds* from the Father.

On the other hand, the Son is certainly involved in the sending of the Spirit, as that passage itself indicates, and as the breathing of the Spirit upon the community gathered in the Upper Room confirms. At least as far as the activity of God in his dealings with humanity (the economy) is concerned, Scripture testifies that the Son dispenses the Spirit.[6] Moreover, the Spirit is often identified as the Spirit of Christ, or the Spirit of Jesus.[7] The Spirit is received by mortals on earth through the Son and has the character of the Son.

---

[2] *De synodia seu de fide Orientalium* 68, 81. Pl. 10, 525, 534; cited in O'Connor.

[3] 2 Cor. 3:17.

[4] Cf., e.g., H. A. Wolfson, *The Philosophy of the Church Fathers,* 2nd ed., Harvard, 1964, pp. 155–167; pp. 183–191.

[5] John 15:26 (NEB).

[6] John 15:26; John 20:22.

[7] See, e.g., Rom. 8:9, Gal. 4:6, Phil. 1:19, etc.

We must acknowledge that these texts do not give us enough grounds for deciding whether there is a difference between God in himself, an immanent Trinity, and this economy. Consequently, whether a distinction can or must be made between the *procession* of the Spirit from the Father and his *sending* by and through the Son must be more carefully examined later. The issue, of course, is crucial in the resolution of the question between East and West regarding *filioque*.

The difficulty of the ancient Church in arriving at a satisfactory account of the understanding of the Spirit's role both in creation and in the life of God is well known, as is the length of time it took to make a distinction between economic and immanent Trinity. It is not always easy to interpret ancient texts on the basis of this fourth-century distinction.

Aside from the Augustinian "thunderclap" in Athenagoras,[8] there was a decided inclination to downplay the Spirit in pre-Nicene thought. Justin Martyr, for example, assigned "third rank to the Spirit of prophecy." The Spirit's role in prophecy and the inspiration of Scripture was well understood, but Origen limits the Spirit to the inspiration of the saints.[9] Elsewhere the Spirit and Wisdom were sometimes identified.[10]

There was little speculation about the relation of Spirit to the Son in the Trinity. Tertullian, it is true, in his Orthodox days, understood that the Spirit proceeded through the Son.[11] Certain Gnostics represented the Spirit and the Son (Wisdom and Logos) as a syzygy, a dialectically related pair both emanating from the Father.[12]

With the Nicene resolution against the Arian subordination of the Son, the tendency to subordinate the Spirit was intensified. The teaching of Eunomius and Macedonius applied to the Spirit Arius's teaching regarding the Son. If the Son was now to be thought consubstantial with the Father then the felt necessity to provide an intermediate step between the divine and the created order was expressed through subordination of the Spirit. This teaching prompted further

---

[8] "Let no one count it absurd that God should have a Son. . . . The Son is the Word of God the Father, both in thought (*idea*) and also in working; from him and through him all things had their beginning, the Father and the Son being One. The Son is in the Father and the Father in the Son by the unity and power of the Spirit" (Leg. 10).

[9] Justin, *I Apol.* ch. 13; Origen, *De Princ.* Bk. 1, ch. 3.5.

[10] Theophilus, *Ad. Autol.* II, 15, 18, Irenaeus, *Adv. Haer.* IV, 20. cf. Wolfson, pp. 245–247.

[11] *Adv. Prax.* Chap. 4.

[12] Wolfson, pp. 515 ff.

speculation on the relation of Spirit within the Trinity, with an eye to establishing the consubstantiality of the Father, Son and Spirit. *Such developments took place in both East and West.*

One finds in Victorinus, for example, the following exegesis of John 7:38:

> Jesus is the well from which the rivers of the Spirit flow. As the Son is in the bosom of the Father (*in gremio*) so the Spirit proceeds from the bosom of the Son (*procedit a ventre Filii*): the three are consubstantial, and they are one God.[13]

Gregory of Nyssa says,

> One says of the Holy Spirit that he is of the Father and one testifies also that he is of the Son (*ek tou Huiou*), the Spirit which is also of God being also the Spirit which is of Christ.[14]

Basil, in *De Spiritu Sancto*:

> One Form, so to say, united in the invariableness of the Godhead, is beheld in God the Father and in God the Only-begotten. For the Son is in the Father and the Father in the Son, since such as is the latter, such is the former, and such as is the former, such is the latter; and herein is the Unity. So that according to the distinction of Persons, both are one and one, and according to the community of Nature one. How, then, if one and one, are there not two Gods? Because we speak of a king and a king's image, and not of two kings. The majesty is not cloven in two nor the glory divided. . . .

> One, moreover, is the Holy Spirit, and we speak of Him singly, conjoined as he is to the One Father through the One Son (*dia*. . .) and through Himself completing the adorable and blessed Trinity. Of him the intimate relationship to the Father and Son is sufficiently declared by the fact of His not being ranked in the plurality of the creation. . . .[15]

Epiphanius is quite explicit: "The Father always was, and the Spirit proceeds from the Father and the Son" (Ancoratus 75), and

---

[13] Pl. 8 col. 1044, cited in Claude Gerest, *Une querelle de plusieurs siècles: le Filioque*, Verbum Caro, 76, 1965; pp. 39–56.

[14] Illtrd. Orat. On Lord's Prayer, P. G. 44, col. 1120, ibid.

[15] *De Spir. Sanc.* 18.45. PNF(2). 8, p. 28.

Ephraem, "The Father is the Begotten, the Son the Begotten from the bosom of the Father, the Holy Spirit, He that proceedeth from the Father and the Son" (*Hymnus de defunctis et trinitate* 11). In the fifth century, long after Augustine, Cyril of Alexandria wrote, "the Holy Spirit . . . proceeds both from the Father and the Son" (Theo. de trin. 34).[16]

Theodoret commented, "If Cyril said of the Spirit that he is proper to the Son in the sense that he is consubstantial and proceeds from the Father, then we are in agreement with him. But if on the contrary, it is in the sense that the Spirit draws his substance from the Son or through the Son, then we reject this expression as blasphemy and impiety" (PG 76 col. 132).

Cyril conceded to Theodoret the desired interpretation.

It seems difficult not to agree with Claude Gerest in asking whether the Greeks had not reached in their own way a position very close to *filioque*. Karl Barth, commenting on similar evidence, concludes, "It (the Creed) might refrain from saying that (*filioque*) *because there was at that time, even among Greek theologians, no opposition to the material content of that addition.*"[17] Latin scholastic theologians in the thirteenth century thought in complete good faith that the two traditions agreed on the procession *ab utroque*,[18] and at the Council of Florence in 1439, a majority of the Greek theologians, including the saintly patriarch Joseph who died during the proceedings, held that *filioque* was not contrary to Orthodox faith.

> I will never change or vary the doctrine handed down from our fathers but will abide in it till my last breath. But since the Latins, not of themselves but from the Holy Scriptures, explain the Procession of the Holy Spirit as being also from the Son, I agree with them and I give my judgment that this "through" gives to the Son to be cause of the Holy Spirit. I both unite with them and am in communion with them.[19]

---

16 Gerest.

17 Karl Barth, *Church Dogmatics*, T. and T. Clark, 1955; I/1, p. 546 (italics mine).

18 Cf. Aquinas, *Contra Errores Graecorum*, cited in Gerest, p. 42.

19 Quoted in Gill, J., *The Council of Florence*, Cambridge, 1959, p. 260. Gill continues, "When the Partriarch finished speaking there was general accord that the Holy Spirit proceeds from the Father and Son as from one principle and one substance, that he proceeds through the Son as of like nature and substance, that he proceeds from the Father and Son as from one spiration and procession."

But we get ahead of ourselves. Between the fifth and the fifteenth century lie not only a thousand years of political controversy but also the towering figure of St. Augustine, whose *De Trinitate* has shaped Western thought on the subject so decisively.

From one point of view it might be said that Augustine simply presses the position taken by Basil to a logical and not very far distant conclusion. Like Basil, Augustine is interested in establishing the consubstantiality of the three personae, and he begins with the hard-won results of the Arian struggle: the absolute substantial identity of Father and Son. The personae are distinguished by their difference in origin: the Father unbegotten, the Son begotten, the Spirit proceeding. But the Father and the Son have everything in common except the principle of differentiation. Otherwise they would not be consubstantial. Basil said as much in the passage already quoted. But if "the Father has in Himself that the Holy Spirit should proceed from Him, so has He given to the Son that the same Holy Spirit should proceed from Him. . . ."[20] The Spirit of both necessarily proceeds from both. And what is at issue here is plainly the immanent and not simply the economic Trinity.

The problem of double causality is not lost on Augustine. The Father is uncaused cause, for Augustine as much as for any of the Greeks. Nevertheless, the community of Father and Son requires Augustine to recognize some element of causality in the relation of Son to Spirit. He therefore concludes, "the Holy Spirit proceeds from the Father principally (*principaliter*), the Father giving the procession without any interval time, yet in common (*communiter*) from both [Father and Son]."[21] Whether this is really a solution to the problem or only a recognition of it may not be clear. Nevertheless, Augustine does not allow himself to be accused of providing for two causes or two spirations of the Spirit.

There is another consequence of this point of view which Augustine presses: namely, it is not altogether perspicuous to allow the expression "proceeds through the Son." For "the Holy Spirit does not

---

[20] Augustine, *De Trin.* 15.26.47 PNF(1) 3, p. 225.
[21] Ibid., p. 225. Cf. 5.14.15, "It must be admitted that the Father and the Son are a Beginning (*principium* or *arché*) of the Holy Spirit, not two Beginnings; but as the Father and Son are one God, and one Creator, and one Lord, relatively to the creature, so are they one Beginning relatively to the Holy Spirit."

proceed from the Father into the Son, and from the Son proceed to sanctify the creature, but proceeds at once from both."[22]

Augustine's emphasis on the co-eternity of the three Persons in this connection, and on the fact of the occurrence of the double procession *out of time* seems to represent a step beyond the Greek fathers. John MacIntyre's study of the Holy Spirit in patristic thought concludes that the most complete intra-trinitarian statement the Greek fathers were willing to make would be that

> the Holy Spirit is by nature (that is from eternity) identical in essence with the Father and the Son; secondly, that the relation in which He stands to the Father is not that of Sonship. . . . Thirdly, that He is produced *after* the Son, being therefore third in order in the Trinity; fourthly, that He has the Father as His cause or origin.[23]

Augustine would concur absolutely with the first two points, would disagree with the third, and modify the fourth, as we have seen. Yet in these two latter issues, Augustine's developments do not contradict, but simply carry further, the line of thought pursued in the East.

From a second point of view, however, Augustine represents a radical departure from previous thought, both Eastern and Western, and it is this feature of his work on the Trinity which gives rise to considerable criticism from Orthodox theologians. This departure is the use of the psychological analogies: mind, the knowledge mind has of itself, and the love by which it loves itself and its knowledge; or, memory, understanding, and will; or, bodily object, its image in the mind, and the will which unites them; etc., etc. The elaborations are manifold and ingenious. But they are not based on Scripture (though Augustine does not introduce them until he has thoroughly examined the Scriptural evidence for the Trinity; he has no intention of contradicting Scripture). These analogies have the effect of establishing an analogy between the substance of Godhead and an individual human person, rather than between the hypostases and three human persons. Augustine uses human analysis to represent the inner life of the Trinity. Prior theology uses human analogies to represent the several persons of the Trinity (e.g., king and king's image).

---

[22] Ibid. 15.27.48, p. 226.

[23] John McIntyre, "The Holy Spirit in Greek Patristic Thought," *Scottish Journal of Theol.* 7, 1954, pp. 353–375.

It would doubtless be easy to overstress the significance of this difference, since both kinds of analogies break down. On the one hand, the biblical language of Father and Son invites personal analogies to the several hypostases, although all the Greeks are absolutely clear in the end that they do not mean to establish three Gods. On the other hand, biblical language depicts the one God in a personal way. The effort, particularly after Nicaea, to understand the substance of God in personal terms and the hypostases in terms of the ways a person has of being a person seems both natural and inevitable, despite the fact, to which Greek critics continually call attention, that to define the hypostases or personae as inner relations depersonalizes them and may seem to exalt the common essence over the several hypostases.

Filioque *as a Bone of Contention between Latin and Eastern Christianity*

As is well known, the creed promulgated by the Council of Nicaea in 325 ended abruptly with the phrase, "I believe in the Holy Spirit." Although anathemas followed against any who disagreed with the faith so formulated, there was no prohibition against altering the creed at a future council. The Council of Constantinople did in fact add to the creed, which it published with all the familiar clauses pertaining to the Spirit. This was regarded as legitimate, and the creeds of Nicaea and Constantinople were regarded as identical.

The third Council, at Ephesus, did prohibit any further alterations in the creed. "The holy Synod enacted that it was lawful for no one to put forward, that is to write or compose, another faith than that defined by the Holy Fathers congregated in the Holy Spirit in Nicaea. Those who dared either to compose or to proffer or put forward another faith . . . if they were bishops or clerics should be alienated, bishops from the episcopacy and clerics from the clergy; but if laymen, they should be under anathema."[24] The Council of Chalcedon repeated a slightly altered and intensified version of this prohibition and the sixth Council followed the fourth.

Cyril of Alexandria wrote, "We prohibit any change whatever in the creed of Faith drawn up by the holy Nicene Fathers. We do not

---

[24]   Mansi 4, 1362 D; cited in Gill, p. 149.

allow ourselves, or any one else, to change or omit one word or syllable in that Creed."[25]

In view of these rigorous strictures against alterations in the Creed, it is worth noting that important as the term *theotokos* became in defining Orthodoxy against the Nestorians, it was never added to the Creed.

It is also worth noting that because the Council of Ephesus did not recognize the primacy of the Roman pontiff with sufficient vigor, it was for a long time not held in as high esteem in the West as were others. In the West, new creeds were in fact produced.

Procession of the Spirit *ab utroque* was used in the West after Augustine to discriminate and defend Orthodoxy from Arianism, which was rampant among Germanic invaders. In 447, the Bishop of Palentia (Valencia?) composed a confession of faith using *filioque*, and at about the same time *Quicunque vult* appeared, with its phrase, "*Spiritus sanctus a Patre et Filio, non factus nec creatus, sed procedens.*"

In 589 the Synod of Toledo ordered "the insertion," just about the time, as O'Connor suggestively observes, that the Creed began to be used in the Mass.[26] It was in the aftermath of the conversion of the Visigothic king, Recared, to Orthodoxy. The twenty-three anathemas of this Council bespeak a violent reaction against Arian Christianity.[27] The introduction of the phrase produced shock waves in Eastern churches, which by that time regarded the prohibitions against alteration or addition with utmost seriousness. It was, however, not the first local council to make such an addition, as will be seen below.

The matter was not formally debated, however, between East and West until 649. The issue at that time was monothelitism. The emperor advocated that doctrine and tried to impose it on the Church. The pope came out in support of the Orthodox position, agreeing with the majority of Eastern opinion. The emperor's party tried to discredit this support by bringing up the matter of *filioque*. At this point, Maximus the Confessor, then the most significant Eastern theological voice, in order to claim the pope's support as truly Orthodox, made a conciliatory statement about *filioque*. He wrote:

---

[25]   Binii Council, v. 1, par. 2, p. 430, cited in Ostroumoff, Ivan N., *The History of the Council of Florence*, Boston, 1971, p. 68.

[26]   O'Connor, p. 9.

[27]   Gerest, p. 45.

The Western theologians have begun with the testimony of Latin fathers and Cyril of Alexandria where they agree. They have thus demonstrated that they do not hold the Son to be the cause of the Spirit, for they know that the Father alone is cause of both Son and Spirit—the one by generation and the other procession. They show only that the Spirit proceeds through the Son, indicating thereby conjunction and perfect likeness of substance.[28]

The debate did not materialize. One notices that Maximus did not represent the full weight that Augustine and his successors put on the procession from (as opposed to through) the Son (*supra*); and it must be observed that although the pope supported *filioque* at this time, it had not been introduced into the recitation of the Creed in Rome itself. It was a provincial practice in the West.

During the reign of Charlemagne, the relations between Eastern and Western churches worsened measurably. The root of the matter, of course, was presumably the reestablishment of the Roman Empire in the West without Byzantine authorization. But *filioque* was involved in the tension, and became the focus for bitter disagreement.

The decisions of the Seventh Council—Nicaea II—were not to Charlemagne's liking. Regarding himself as defender of the faith, he sought to call its orthodoxy into question. His theologians discovered the letter sent by Tarasius "to the Patriarchs" at the end of the Council, which makes a sharp distinction between *through* the Son and procession *from* the Son. This was attacked by the Synod of Centilly (787) as a *subtraction* from Orthodox faith. At this point Pope Hadrian I defended the doctrine of procession through the Son against Charlemagne. *Filioque* still appears a provincial concern, not a matter *stantis ac cadentis ecclesiae* at Rome.[29]

Nevertheless, when Charlemagne in 794 requested permission to include *filioque* in the recitation of the Creed at Mass in the royal chapel at Aachen, Pope Leo III granted it. Consequently, a few years later, traveling Frankish monks observed the practice, admired it, and instituted it in their monastery on the Mount of Olives in Jerusalem. Since there was much visiting back and forth to the Holy City, then as now, "the insertion" caused a major scandal. The patriarch and pope both became involved. The pope's response was illuminating and

---

28   Ep. Ad Maruinum, P. G. 91 col. 136, cited in Gerest, p. 46.
29   Cf. O'Connor; Gerest.

characteristic: he assured the monks of their Orthodoxy on the one hand, and withdrew his permission to use it in the Creed, "out of love and solicitude for the orthodox faith,"[30] on the other hand.

Charlemagne balked. A French council asked the pope to make "the insertion" universal. Leo refused, and set up two silver tablets in Old St. Peter's with the text of the Nicene Creed inscribed in Greek and Latin *without the insertion*. Nevertheless his prohibitions had little effect in Gaul. A "hands-off" policy ensued.

At the end of the ninth century (867) the Patriarch Photius spoke of Frankish missionaries in Bulgaria as "execrable men who blasphemed the Spirit," because of their use of *filioque*. In what Bulgakov refers to as "latinism reversed,"[31] Photius, holding that the Franks were teaching two *archai*, two causes, two aspirations, began to talk about procession from the Father only, and to deny *any* involvement of the Son, even *through* the Son.[32]

It is clear that so far in this story, "the insertion" has been pushed by Western Emperors, denied by the Greeks, and acknowledged as Orthodox by the popes, though not included in their version of the Creed. In 1014, however, Benedict VIII succumbed to the urging of Henry II and introduced *filioque* to the use of Rome. Neither at this time, however, nor subsequently, was there any effort to impose *filioque* on Catholics of the Eastern Rite. "There is not some kind of basic unconditional need that the *filioque* be inserted in the creed."[33] It was thought to be a matter of product and local or occasional necessity.

Eastern and Western churches were separated decisively in 1054. In the disputes which led up to the schism, *filioque* played a minor role. Rome's refusal to acknowledge the bishop of Constantinople as Ecumenical Patriarch, the subservience of popes to emperors, even the use of unleavened bread in the eucharist and the discipline of clergy figured more prominently. On the other hand, Humbert, the papal legate, like the Frankish theologians at Charlemagne's court nearly three hundred years before, thought that the Greeks had *dropped* *filioque* from the original text of the Creed, out of some survival of macedonianism.

---

[30] Gerest.
[31] Bulgakov, "Le Paraclet," cited in Gerest, p. 48.
[32] O'Connor.
[33] Ibid., p. 13.

After the Great Schism, of course, positions hardened on both sides, including the position on *filioque*. There have been two subsequent attempts to compose differences, both prompted by the desire and need of Eastern emperors to gain Western assistance against the Turks. One occurred in the thirteenth century (Lyon, 1274) and one in the fifteenth (Ferrara-Florence, 1438–9).

At Lyon, a small Greek delegation under the control of the emperor, Michael Paeleologus, accepted the Latin formulation virtually without theological debate, and agreed to make "the insertion." "The Holy Spirit proceeds from the Father and the Son," ran the formula subscribed in the Lyon cathedral in July, "not as from the two principles (*archai*) and through two spirations," but one. It was the Augustinian doctrine. When the Creed was chanted with the insertion in both liturgical languages, the Bishop of Nicaea obviously kept his mouth closed!

The agreement was unpopular in the East, and did not survive the death of the emperor in 1282.

The Council of Florence (1438–9) was also preoccupied with political concerns. Now the Turks were at the very gates of Constantinople. First at Ferrara and later at Florence, fourteen months were spent in discussing the procession of the Spirit, more time than was devoted to any other issue! Participants on both sides seem to have been better informed than on earlier occasions when the matter was discussed. As previously indicated, the Greek delegation was divided, and the military needs of the Emperor unquestionably led him to press for a resolution. The final decree of the Council, *Laetentur caeli*, was a victory for *filioque*. Nevertheless the Greeks were not required to add "the insertion," and some attempt was made to recognize that both sides were trying to express an important truth:

> The testimony of sacred scripture and many authorities in the Holy Doctrines of east and west were presented: some of them said that the Holy Spirit proceeds from the Father and the Son, some from the Father through the Son—all having in view the same understanding under different words. The Greeks assert that when they say the Holy Spirit proceeds from the Father, they do not mean that they exclude the Son; but because it seems to them, as they say, that the Latins assert the Holy Spirit proceeds from the Father and the Son as from two principles and two spirations, they have therefore abstained from saying that the Holy Spirit proceeds from the Father and the Son. The Latins indeed

affirm that they do not mean to say that the Holy Spirit proceeds from the father and the Son in such a way as to exclude the Father as the *fount* and principle of the whole Godhead, of the Son as well as of the Spirit; or that when the Holy Spirit proceeds from the Son, that the Son does not have [receive] from the Father; or that they posit two principles or two spirations but in such a way as to assert one principle and a unique spiration of the Holy Spirit. And since one and the same sense of truth is elicited from all of these expressions, they agree and consent unanimously in the same sacred sense and meaning written down and pleasing to God.[34]

This agreement, too, was unpopular in the East; and after the Turks captured Constantinople despite Western assistance (never very whole-hearted) the antifilioquist party gained control of the Eastern Church, and the concordat was repudiated.

Anglican-Orthodox Conversations: Filioque *Since 1874*

In his review of the history leading to the Moscow Agreed Statement of 1976, Colin Davey points out that genuine scholarly dialogue between Anglicans and Orthodox has been going on since the end of the First World War and the Lambeth Conference of 1920.[35] Prior to that time there was "still more than enough ignorance about each other on both sides."[36]

Nevertheless, about fifty years earlier, in 1874, a remarkable though unofficial conference was held in Bonn, among Old Catholics, German Evangelicals, Anglicans (English and American), Scottish Presbyterians, and a member of the French Reformed Church. Delegates simply responded to a general invitation, published in the newspapers, issued by the Old Catholic theologian J. von Döllinger to those interested in "a renewed common confession of those main Christian doctrines which form the sum of the articles of faith fixed by the original and undivided Church,"[37] and intercommunion and "confederation" of churches on that basis.

---

[34] *Laetentur caeli*, cited in Gill, p. 413 (translation mine).

[35] *Anglican-Orthodox Dialogue*, ed. Archimandrite Kallistos Ware and the Reverend Colin Davey, SPCK, 1977, pp. 4–14.

[36] Ibid., p. 4.

[37] Report of the Proceedings of the Reunion Conference held in Bonn between the 10th and 16th of August, 1875, trans. H. P. Liddon, London, 1876, p. liii.

The statement of this conference regarding *filioque* is basically an acceptance of the language of John of Damascus, who uses the formula "through" the Son, although Article 4 of the statement on the Spirit reads, "The Holy Ghost is the Image of the Son Who is the Image of the Father, issuing out of the Father and resting in the Word as the power radiating from him."

H. P. Liddon of Oxford Movement fame, a participant, observed that the Orientals had come to the conference espousing the position of procession from the Father *alone*, the Photian position, but had conceded during the discussions that

> There was a certain "intermediate relation . . . on the part of the Son in the eternal production or procession of the Spirit."

> Although they used the term *eklampsis* (*shining forth*) to describe this relation, but not *ekporeusis* (*procession*) (since this would imply a distinct cause), it was hard to see when applied to this subject matter that the expressions were distinguishable.

> They finally assented to Damascus's language, "the Holy Ghost proceeds from the Father through the Son" (Article 3 of the Agreement).

The Bishop of Winchester, unable to attend the Conference, wrote to Döllinger to express first that "the addition" should not have been made without the consent of a General Council, but second, quoting the passages from Epiphanius and Cyril which we have already cited, that it was not in error. "We, therefore, do not see how we can acknowledge that it is wrong so to speak, though we admit that the *filioque* was an unjustifiable addition to a Catholic symbol without Catholic assent."[38]

Liddon's report produced a long response by E. B. Pusey, perhaps the most exhaustive review of the subject in English.[39] It is an extended defense of *filioque*. "It would be a happy employment of the closing years of one's life to understand our Western language, and to induce

---

[38]   Ibid., p. 139.
[39]   Pusey, E. B., *On the Clause "And the Son,"* Oxford and New York, 1876.

some (*especially our brethren in the United States*) to pause in their eagerness to sacrifice our old expression of belief, under a mistaken idea that so they will promote unity."[40]

Two features of Pusey's survey claim attention. First, beyond the multiplication of texts from early Fathers, both Eastern and Western, in which the phrase *ek tou huiou* (*from the Son*) appears, he cites the Creed of the Council of Selencia and Ctesiphon (410), which claims to be based on the Creed of Nicaea. The clause regarding the Spirit runs,

> And we confess the living Holy Spirit, the living Paraclete. Who is from the Father and the Son, in One Trinity, in one Essence, in one Will, in harmony with the faith of the 318 bishops, which was in the city of Nicea.[41]

He also quotes liturgical texts from both Nestorian and Eutychian sources which express the Double Procession. These were all locally official texts well before the Second Council of Toledo.

The second point of interest in Pusey's discussion is his review of confessions of faith in Spain prior to 589. Stemming mostly from the Athanasian Creed and from "the rule of the Catholic Faith against all heresies . . . which the Bishops of Tarragona, Carthagena, Lusitania, and Boetia, made. . . ." (ca. 400), all had phrases expressing the Double Procession.[42]

Pusey uses these lines of argument to say in the first place that the Council of Toledo did not intend a novel addition, but "supposed that the *filioque* had dropped by mistake out of the Latin translation of the Nicene Creed, to which alone they probably had access in Spain at the time";[43] and in the second place, local councils in the East made additions as much as in the West. There may have been arrogance and the high-handed use of power in the relation between Oriental and Occidental churches, but it does not extend to the insertion of "the addition" into the Creed at Toledo in 589.

The Range of Orthodox Opinion Regarding Filioque

---

[40] Ibid., p. 2 (italics mine).
[41] Ibid., p. 158. There is apparently doubt about the authenticity of the records of the Council, which Pusey attempts to quiet.
[42] Ibid., pp. 50 ff.
[43] Ibid., p. 64.

Although there is complete agreement among the Orthodox that "the insertion" is an unwarranted intrusion into the text of the ecumenical creed, there is apparently no universal rejection of *filioque* doctrine. "Possibly a majority of the Orthodox," O'Connor asserts, "maintain the position of Photius, 'proceeding from the Father *only*.'" This view, of course, was not the only view of the early Fathers; and, as we have seen, was itself a polemical formulation, designed to contradict the *filioque* of the West. Others use the patristic formula, "from the Father through the Son," although today this phrase is usually interpreted as having to do with the temporal mission of the Spirit. Some regard the issue as open. Some absolve *filioque* from error.[44]

Vladimir Lossky may be taken as an example of the extreme *ex Patre solo*. He regards *filioque* as a doctrine that puts the general in the Godhead before the personal and emphasizes the essence (substance) more than the hypostases (personae). By linking Spirit to Word as it does, it limits the activity of the Spirit to the initiative of the Word. From this original error flow all the distortions of Western Catholicism—its legalism, its institutionalism, its literalism regarding Scripture. In Orthodoxy, he argues, "procession and generation mutually condition each other. That is why sacrament and inspiration, institution and event, the economy of the Son and the economy of the Spirit condition each other in reciprocal service."[45]

Sergius Bulgakov, on the other hand, while recognizing that "the insertion" was unwarranted, nevertheless held that the welfare of the Church requires that *filioque* be allowed as a possible understanding of the Trinity. He wanted to get over the representation of the Trinity in terms of causality, which was the ground for the original criticism of *filioque*. Once one accepts that the three personae are "given" and need no causal explanation, the *filioque* controversy becomes imaginary. The three persons must be seen "in their subject existence, independent from nature. They must not be seen as 'proceeding from one another,' but as 'independently related to one another.'"[46]

The essence of the Trinity is the self-revelation of the Father through the revealing hypostases of Word and Spirit. Thus the monar-

---

[44]   Cf. O'Connor, p. 18.

[45]   Lossky, V., *Théologie Mystique de l'Eglise de l'Orient*, Aubier, 1944, p. 60. Cited in Gerest, p. 53.

[46]   Graves, C., *The Holy Spirit in the Theology of Sergius Bulgakov*, Geneva, 1970, p. 176.

chy of the Father is preserved. The Spirit proceeds from the Father, but goes to the Son, and "is the Love Itself between Father and Son." In this sense the *filioque* is true, as is also the *dia* (through). In fact, "all of the above phrases are acceptable (*filioque*, *dia* [through], and *ek monon tou Patron* [from the Father alone]) as long as they are held as 'theologoumena' rather than as exclusive statements of the Faith."[47]

Theological Reflections and Conclusions

From the Second Council of Toledo in 589 until Henry II persuaded Benedict VIII to insert *filioque* into the text of the Creed used at Mass in Rome in 1014, the position of the Popes was that *filioque* expressed an Orthodox understanding of the relation of the Spirit to the Father and the Son and that it should not be added to the creed of the Roman Church. That position seems to me to be the unexceptionable one, and my regrets about *filioque* are connected with the pope's decision in 1014—even more than the local decision of the Council of Toledo, especially in view of the appearance of *filioque* in other local conciliar creeds.

It is striking testimony to the power of liturgical use that the widespread acceptance of *filioque* was associated with its recitation at Mass, a practice just beginning in the sixth century, notably in Franco-German churches. It did not become part of the Mass at Rome until the eleventh century.[48] The Roman rite was not enforced in the whole of Western Europe until Charlemagne's time. He, in Frankish Europe, apparently faced widespread use of *filioque*,[49] liked it, and persuaded the pope to permit its use in the royal chapel. The case of *filioque* might be called a prime instance of *lex orandi lex credendi*.

Until the bitter controversies between Eastern and Western Churches began in the ninth century (extending at least to the fall of Constantinople in the fifteenth century), there is every indication that all the formulas—"from the Father," "from the Father and the Son," "from the Father through the Son"—were recognized in both East and West. The Judgment of the Council of Florence is surely just: "All [texts] bore the same meaning, though expressed differently."

---

[47]   Ibid., p. 174.
[48]   Klauser, T., *A Short History of the Western Liturgy*, Oxford, 1979, pp. 64, 77.
[49]   It appeared in the English council of Hatfield in 680, presided over by the Greek Archbishop of Canterbury, Theodore of Tarsus.

The Photian doctrine, *ek Patrou monou* (from the Father alone), if taken to exclude the Son in the eternal procession of the Spirit, raises—at least for Westerners—acute epistemological difficulties. For if, as both Eastern and Western theology agree and as biblical texts specify, the temporal mission of the Spirit is from the Father and the Son, what are the grounds for asserting a different procession in the eternal and immanent life of God? God in his revelation in Christ reveals fully and wholly God in his inward life. We have no other knowledge of it. To affirm that the economy involves the Spirit from or through the Son, and the immanent life of God involves the Spirit in procession from the Father only, implies a source of knowledge separate and distinct from God's revelation of himself in Christ. This objection to the Photian doctrine is raised by both Pusey[50] and Barth.[51] Pusey and Barth between them include a broad spectrum of Western thought. Yet there has apparently been no modern Eastern attempt to address this problem. Lossky simply ignores it.[52]

On the other hand, the suggestion of Donald Berry[53] and Claude Gerest,[54] that *filioque* could be used by contemporary theology to improve or emphasize the assertion that the Holy Spirit is the Spirit of Jesus Christ, misses the Orthodox insistence that the *mission* of the Son *is* through or even from the Spirit. There is no contention on that score. But *filioque* does not express this aspect of Christian doctrine. If Western theology at this late date were to use *filioque* to mean "the assertion that the Holy Spirit is the Spirit of Christ,"[55] it would compound confusion a hundred times over. In Gerest's paper, the suggestion occurs at the very end and is not developed. In Berry's paper, there is a recognition at the beginning that, for Western theologians, "the double procession of the Holy Spirit [is the] ontological ground

---

[50]   Pusey, p. 174, "[They] conceive of God existing otherwise than He has revealed Himself."

[51]   Barth, pp. 549–550; e.g., "The Eastern doctrine . . . reads off its pronouncements upon the being of God 'antecedently in Himself' not from revelation; it does not adhere to the order of the divine modes of existence which according to its own admission is valid in the realm of revelation, but it reaches out beyond revelation, in order to arrive at a quite different picture of God 'antecedently in Himself.' At this point, quite apart from the result, we must at once record dissent."

[52]   Cf. Berry, Donald L., *"Filioque* and the Church," *Journal of Ecumenical Studies* 5, 1968, p. 541.

[53]   Berry, p. 543.

[54]   Gerest, p. 54.

[55]   Berry, p. 535.

for the assurance that the Holy Spirit really introduces us to that revelation of God which is Revelation and not to some theophany which
has nothing to do with the self-revealing and redeeming God who was
in his fullness in Jesus Christ."[56] That point, of course, is precisely
Pusey's and Barth's. On the other hand, the body of the paper concerns *filioque* in relation to God's manifestation in Christ.

For example, "We have seen that, for Western theologians, to
speak of the Holy Spirit as the Spirit of Jesus Christ is the means
by which Christian faith claims that Christ is, in fact, *seen*."[57] Or again,
"In order to say that the Holy Spirit is the Spirit of Jesus Christ,
we were concerned to show the manner in which the Holy Spirit
manifests Jesus Christ to the Church."[58] He concludes, "When the
filioque is used to point to the inseparability of the Holy Spirit and the
Son in some such fashion and for such purpose as we have outlined in
this essay, then it would appear that nothing is being asserted that
Eastern theologians would deny."[59] This use would give *filioque* an entirely new context and meaning and would miss the whole point of the
argument.

The criticism that Occidental Christianity is distorted by its legalism, institutionalism and literalism may be true, and certainly needs to
be heeded carefully. Nevertheless it seems doubtful that blame for
these developments can be laid at the door of *filioque*. It seems much
more likely that one deals here with the cultural inheritance of the
Roman Empire. To say that *filioque* "limits the activity of the Spirit to
the initiative of the Word" sounds, at least to Western ears, not like
criticism but strong affirmation. Is not the realm of the Spirit inseparable from that of the Word?

One hastens to add that Word *can* be understood in the West in a
too purely mechanical and literalistic way, as the orthodox critic here
seems to have done. In scriptural terms, however, Word is dynamic as
well as cognitive, living as well as intellectual; and there is no access to
God apart from the Word. "No one comes to the Father but by me"
(John 14:6).

---

[56] Ibid., p. 542, citing John McIntyre, "The Holy Spirit in Greek Patristic
Thought," *SJT*, VII, 1954, pp. 353–375.
[57] Ibid., p. 546.
[58] Ibid., p. 551.
[59] Ibid., p. 554.

The criticism that *filioque* rests on an understanding of Godhead which puts the general before the personal and emphasizes essence more than hypostases (substance more than personae) needs to be sorted out on two levels. In the first place, orthodox Trinitarian doctrine cannot afford to emphasize either substance at the expense of personae or personae at the expense of substance. Adequate doctrine must put essence and hypostasis on the same level of reality and importance. To the extent that Western theology does not emphasize substance more than personae, Eastern theology serves as an important corrective. But this judgment essentially has nothing to do with *filioque*. As we have seen, East and West had come a long way together in understanding and expressing the inner relation of Son and Spirit before the issue was clouded by polemic and political controversies.

But in the second place, the Eastern contention that Western Trinitarian thought deals with the personae as abstraction rests, as we have seen, on the Augustinian psychological analogies. One does not need to affirm the permanent validity of Augustine's particular use of memory, understanding and will to recognize the importance of being able to treat the Trinity—the One—as the analogue of person. It is God, the blessed Trinity, to whom we pray. If so, the consequence is that the hypostases, Father, Son and Spirit, do become inner relations. Barth's phrase is better, however: "God's ways of being God." If one applies the analogy of person to the hypostases, they become something like "self as subject," "self as object," and "self as self-related whole." To such expressions, we must admit, the biblical images, Father, Son and Spirit correspond rather poorly.

On the other hand, if we retain the personal analogy for the hypostases (personae), the biblical expressions Father, Son and Spirit correspond rather well. But one then seems to have three personalities on one's hands, and the *unity* of God becomes abstract.

What we are dealing with, to be sure, is the inadequacy of any analogy to deal with the mystery of God. We somehow have to recognize the force of personal analogy as it pertains *both* to the essence of God *and* to the three personae. Eastern and Western theology are doubtless colored by their respective emphases on one over the other, and in this respect too, should recognize in each other complementary illuminations of one reality. But here again, *filioque* is not essentially involved.

We need to state what has been agreed at least since the Council of Florence, and what Augustine himself stipulated. To affirm that the Spirit proceeds from the Father and the Son does not affirm two causes or two spirations. We are not likely to do better than Augustine's distinction that the Spirit proceeds from the Father *principaliter* (as from an *arché*), and from the Father and the Son together *communiter*, since Father and Son are consubstantial.

Bulgakov's proposal to eliminate all talk of causality, and to recognize the personae as givens, "seen in their subject existence, independent from nature," seems to surrender too much. God is known as God by being *arché* (John 1:1). Besides, such a proposal would destroy any applicability of the personal analogy. Bulgakov is surely right, however, in insisting that all the expressions which describe the relation of Spirit to Father and Son are acceptable as *theologoumena*, none exclusively adequate as dogma. But then, no words are.

Adam, Eve, and Seth:
Pneumatological Reflections on an Unusual Image in Gregory of Nazianzus's "Fifth Theological Oration"

ALEXANDER GOLITZIN*

I have been asked to contribute to this volume primarily, I suspect, in order to serve as the voice of the Christian East. While it is perhaps a little odd for a California boy, and coming thus from the uttermost West, to present himself as an "Oriental," I nonetheless welcome this opportunity to speak on behalf of an entire Christian universe of theological discourse which, up until recent centuries at least, took shape independently of the Western (Roman Catholic and Protestant) traditions, and, in particular, with no input whatsoever from the great Father of Western theology, Augustine of Hippo. It is, of course, St. Augustine's elaboration and defense of the double procession of the Holy Spirit from the Father and the Son which, long after the saint's death (his writings were not translated into Greek until the end of the thirteenth century), provoked heated controversy between medieval Greek and Latin theologians. No single issue between Christian East and West, including the debate over the nature of papal primacy, has led to such an outpouring of polemic as the Western *filioque*. Indeed, it continues to the present day.

I have no particular wish to dive into this sea of ink, and have so far in my life happily avoided even wading on its shores. Few things so depress the spirit (and occlude the Spirit!) as this seemingly endless controversial literature which, beginning with the Carolingian divines of the late eighth century, now boasts a history of over 1200 years—with no end to it in sight. What I do want to do, however, is offer a very modest suggestion as to why, aside from the more abstruse realms of divine causation, such as the quarrel over one or two sources of origin

* Alexander Golitzin, hieromonk (priest-monk) of the Orthodox Church of America, is Associate Professor in the Department of Theology at Marquette University, Milwaukee, Wisconsin.

in the Trinity, or over the more rarified heights of Augustine's analogy of the intellect (*mens*) for the mutual relations of the Three, Eastern Christians reacted so viscerally, almost instinctively, against the Spirit as proceeding from the Father and Son. To be sure, there were and are lots of other factors in play: the ancient linkage between the *filioque* and the legitimacy or illegitimacy of the Carolingian and Byzantine empires, or of papal primacy once the popes had committed themselves to the credal addition, or simply the very human reality of an underdog East asserting itself against the ever more massive material, intellectual, and institutional might of the West. None of these interests me, at least for the purposes of this essay. What does, though, is the very long, indeed unbroken tradition of Eastern Christian spirituality, and especially the great role played in it by the thought and practice of early Christian Syria, whose Jewish roots are well known and are lately coming under increasing scholarly investigation. One instance of this influence, only now beginning to be perceived, is that of the Cappadocian Fathers—Basil the Great, Gregory Nazianzus, and Gregory of Nyssa—whose own influence on Eastern pneumatology and triadology is universally admitted and standard fare in the manuals.

This is a vast subject, so for the purposes of one necessarily brief essay allow me to focus on a single passage from the writings of the middle Cappadocian, Gregory Nazianzus, called "the Theologian" in the East out of gratitude for his enormously influential and successful *Five Theological Orations*, given in defense of Trinitarian doctrine in Constantinople just prior to the Ecumenical Council of 381. The passage in question comes about a third of the way through Gregory's fifth oration, "On the Spirit." He is struggling to explain the difference between the procession (*ekporeusis*) of the Spirit and the generation (*gennesis*) of the Son, in order to avoid the twin absurdities of the Son and Spirit as brothers, on the one hand, or the Father as "grandfather" on the other. This is, of course, the point where Augustine's analogies in *De trinitate* came into play: the Spirit as "love" and "gift" linking "Lover" (Father) and "Beloved" (the Son), or the analogy of the intellect, with will (Spirit) as flowing from memory (Father) and intelligence (Son). Gregory does something quite different and even a little shocking:

> What was Adam? A creature of God. What, then, was Eve? A fragment of the creature. And what was Seth? The begotten of both. Does it, then, seem to you that creature and fragment and

begotten are the same thing? Of course not. But were not these persons consubstantial? Of course they were.

He interjects the caution that his scriptural image is not intended to "attribute creation or fraction or any property of the body to the Godhead," but then goes on to explain

> the meaning of all this. For is not the one an offspring, and the other a something else of the One? Did not Eve and Seth come from the one Adam? And were they both begotten by him? No . . . yet the two were one and the same thing . . . both were human beings.

"Will you then," he addresses his opponents, "give up your contention against the Spirit, that He must be altogether begotten, or else cannot be consubstantial, or God?"[1] He has demonstrated, through the illustration of Eve's beginning, a mode of origin that is not begetting, but a "something else of the One."

Gregory does not pursue this analogy beyond what I have quoted here, and as far as I know it appears in Greek patristic literature only this once. Perhaps this is why it has not been taken up and examined in detail by the scholarly literature, though I claim no encyclopedic knowledge of the latter. This neglect may be understandable, in that the mental picture which rises unbidden and unwelcome, yet inescapably, from Gregory's image is weird, to say the least, if not positively blasphemous—thus, doubtless, his caution against attributing "any property of the body to the Godhead." On the one hand, he has certainly come up with a very concrete mode of origin that is not begetting, but that very concreteness, on the other hand, cannot avoid giving rise to a certain theological queasiness. I am reminded of nothing so much as my first-grade primer featuring the adventures of Daddy and Mommy, Dick and Jane, and their dog Spot. True, Jane and Spot are missing from Gregory's picture, but the Trinity as nuclear family is otherwise quite complete, and even, we might say, in its limitation to only three ecologically à la mode as well: Adam (the Father), Eve (the Spirit), and their child, Seth (the Son). The now uneasy reader might also recall at this point Mormon teaching about Mr. and Mrs.

---

[1] "On the Spirit" 11, from *Christology of the Later Fathers*, trans. E. R. Hardy (London: SCM Press; Philadelphia: Westminster Press, 1954), p. 200.

God, though I seem to recall that the Mormons do not particularly identify the Spirit with Herself, Whom in any case they generally keep pretty much under wraps.

St. Gregory is certainly not a Mormon, but he is, I submit, drawing here on ancient traditions which were especially lively in early Syriac-speaking Christianity and which continue to run—not so openly, but still very deeply—in the wider Christian world east of the Adriatic. These derive first of all from the simple, grammatical fact that spirit or breath, *ruach*, is a feminine noun in both Hebrew and Aramaic/Syriac. To this we may add, second, the Synoptic accounts of Christ's baptism at the Jordan and, third, St. Luke's narrative of the Lord's nativity, in particular the words of Gabriel addressed to the Virgin: "The Holy Spirit will come upon you, and the Power of the Most High will overshadow [*episkiasei*] you; therefore the child to be born of you will be called holy, the Son of God" (Luke 1:35), words which are reflected indeed in the Niceno-Constantinopolitanum: "made flesh of the Holy Spirit and the Virgin Mary." As Susan Harvey has recently pointed out with great thoroughness and theological restraint, the grammatical use of the feminine for the Spirit remains normative in Syriac Christian literature through the fourth century.[2] The Gospel story of Christ's baptism and the resting of the Spirit upon Him appears to have been not only central to the earliest Syrian baptismal ordinals, but as well their primary source for the theology of baptism and the Christian life—to the exclusion, for example, of the Pauline notion of sharing in Christ's death (Rom. 6), which only later, sometime in the late fourth century, finds its way into the rite. Likewise, the feast of Epiphany in the East celebrates the baptism at the Jordan and continues to enjoy a more notable prestige (at least judging from the texts and hymns assigned to it) than Christmas, which only later, in imitation of the West, came to be commemorated on its own separate date (save in the case of the Armenians, who have never adopted the Western practice).[3] To this list I would add the well-known matter of the

---

[2] S. A. Harvey, "Feminine Imagery for the Divine: The Holy Spirit, the *Odes of Solomon*, and Early Syriac Tradition," *St. Vladimir's Theological Quarterly* 37.2–3 (1993), pp. 111–139.

[3] See, e.g., J. A. Jungman, *The Early Liturgy to the Time of Gregory the Great*, trans. F. A. Brunner (Notre Dame: University of Notre Dame Press, 1959), pp. 266–277. On the Holy Spirit in Syrian liturgy more intensively, see Sebastian P. Brock, *The Holy Spirit in the Syrian Baptismal Tradition* (Poona, India: 1979).

Eastern *epiklesis*, itself a source of considerable medieval debate between Greek and Latin theologians over the moment of the eucharistic consecration, i.e., whether the latter takes place at the recitation of the dominical words, *hoc est corpus meum*, or at the conclusion of the prayer for the Spirit to "make this bread the body of Your Christ." The great Syriac poet and preacher, Jacob of Serug (+521), catches nearly all of these echoes in a few lines from his verse homily "On the Chariot that Ezekiel the Prophet Saw," commenting here on Ezek. 10:6–7 as an image of the eucharist:

It is not the priest [typified by the prophet's "angel in white linen"] who is sent to sacrifice the Only[-Begotten],
And lift Him up, Who is the sacrifice for sins, before His Father.
Rather, the Holy Spirit comes down from the Father,
And descending overshadows [*šr'*] and dwells [*škn*] within the bread and makes it the body.
And it is He Who makes it kindled pearls of flame,
And Who will clothe those who are betrothed to Him with riches.[4]

True, Jacob is no longer saying "she" for the Spirit, but nearly everything else—the baptismal narratives and theology, together with Luke 1:35's echo of Exodus 40:34, and the note of transfiguration in the clothing "with riches"—is fully present and accounted for in this image of the eucharistic consecration.

St. Gregory's use of Adam, Eve, and Seth—the "nuclear family"—has even more specific echoes in earlier and even contemporary fourth-century literature. The Holy Spirit as "Mother" of Christ appears, for example, in the fragments we possess of the Semitic *Gospel to the Hebrews*,[5] while the "family" shows up complete in the strange and beautiful "Hymn of the Pearl," thought by an earlier generation of scholars to be wholly Gnostic in character, but recognized

---

[4] *Homiliae selectae Mar Jacobi Sarugensis*, ed. P. Bedjan (Paris: 1908), Vol. 4: 597, lines 8–13. I find it interesting that Jacob uses the verb *škn* here for the action of the Spirit, but the same root as noun, *šekinto* (equivalent to the Rabbinic *Šekinah*), appears exclusively elsewhere in reference to the Son—see 569:21, 570:13, and 602:20. Thus the Spirit in "abiding" or "dwelling" in the bread of the eucharist makes present the "Abiding" or "Dwelling" of God among us which is Christ, the Immanuel. Here thus I would myself discern an echo of the Nativity narratives in both Luke and Matthew—and perhaps of John 1:14 as well.

[5] See W. Schneemelcher, ed., *New Testament Apocrypha*, 2nd ed., trans. R. McL. Wilson (Cambridge: Lutterworth Press; Louisville, Ky.: Westminster/John Knox Press, 1991), Vol. 1: 177, and relatedly, A. F. J. Klijn, *Jewish-Christian Gospel Tradition* (Leiden: E. J. Brill, 1992), pp. 39–40, 52–55.

more recently as an essentially Semitic-Christian composition.[6] Placed in the mouth of the Apostle in the mid-third-century *Acts of Thomas*, a work advocating typically fierce—even heretically encratite (though *not* Gnostic)—Syrian asceticism, the "Hymn" describes the descent and return of the soul. It concludes with the speaker's being clothed with the "robe of light," an ancient Jewish and Christian motif (and recall Jacob just above),[7] which in context is clearly intended to signify both transfiguration and the mystical ascent to the heavenly throne, two more themes with roots in ancient Jewish literature and Eastern Christian spiritual writings.[8] What particularly catches my eye for our purposes here are a few lines from midway through the poem. The speaker tells of a letter sent to him in "Egypt" (the fallen world) from his "parents" in heaven, and then quotes it:

> From thy Father, the king of kings,
> And thy Mother, the mistress of the East,
> And from thy brother, our other Son,
> To thee, our son in Egypt, greeting!
> Awake, and rise up from sleep![9]

Here we have the by now familiar Trinitarian formula: the Father, the Mother (the Holy Spirit, as appears elsewhere in the *Acts of Thomas*), and the Son, Christ our "brother." Neither is this formula a one-time-only business, nor is it confined to a text of an admittedly still debated nature and provenance. We find exactly the same formulation in the

---

[6] In Schneemelcher, *New Testament Apocrypha*, Vol. II: 380–385. Note that H. Drijvers's introduction to the "Hymn," pp. 330–333, barely breathes the word "Gnostic," whereas G. Bornkam's introduction in the first edition thirty years before can speak of nothing else. The scholarship has shifted one hundred eighty degrees in the space of a generation, and for once it is for the better.

[7] See S. P. Brock, "Clothing Metaphors as a Means of Theological Expression in Syriac Tradition," in *Typus, Symbol, Allegorie bei den östlichen Vätern und ihren Parallelen im Mittelalter*, ed. M. Schmidt and C. F. Geyer (Regensburg: Pustet, 1982), pp. 11–38.

[8] On these in Jewish tradition, see C. R. A. Morray-Jones, "Transformational Mysticism in the Apocalyptic-Merkabah Tradition," *Journal of Jewish Studies* 43 (1992): 1-31,, and I. Gruenwald, *Apocalyptic and Merkavah Mysticism* (Leiden: E. J. Brill, 1980); and in Christian literature, A. DeConick, *Seek to See Him: Ascent and Vision Mysticism in the Gospel of Thomas* (Leiden: E. J. Brill, 1996); J. A. McGuckin, *The Transfiguration of Christ in Scripture and Tradition* (Lewistown, N.Y.: Edwin Mellen Press, 1986); and A. Golitzin, "Temple and Throne of the Divine Glory: Purity of Heart in the Macarian Homilies," in H. Luckman and L. Kunzler, eds., *Purity of Heart in Early Ascetic and Monastic Literature: Essays in Honor of Juana Raasch, O.S.B.* (Collegeville, Minn.: Liturgical Press, 1999), pp. 107–129.

[9] *Acts of Thomas* 110:41–43, in Schneemelcher, Vol. 2: 382.

enormously influential early monastic homilies and correspondence which have come down to us under the name of St. Macarius the Great of Egypt, but which were in fact the product of an unknown Syro-Mesopotamian ascetic. In the well-known collection of *The Fifty Spiritual Homilies*, "Macarius" links the plague of darkness in Egypt with the fall of Adam:

> The veil of darkness came upon his [Adam's] soul. And from his time until the last Adam, our Lord, man did not see the true heavenly Father and the good and kind Mother, the grace of the Spirit, and the sweet and desired Brother, the Lord, and the friends and relatives, the holy angels, with whom he [Adam] had been playing and rejoicing.[10]

"Macarius" was not writing in Syriac, but in Greek. He also appears to have directly influenced the third great Cappadocian, Gregory of Nyssa, in at least one of the latter's ascetical and mystical works. Together with one of Gregory Nazianzus's disciples, Evagrius of Pontus (+399), "Macarius" indeed ranks as one of the two most important fourth-century monastic sources for later Eastern Christian spirituality and mysticism. He was not, in short and in spite of the controversy (both ancient and modern) attaching to his works, a marginal character, but was right in the midst of those figures and currents that would determine the later shape of Christian orthodoxy. Gilles Quispel and Columba Stewart have clearly demonstrated "Macarius's" other debts as well, notably to the originally Jewish-based traditions of Christian Syro-Mesopotamia, and in fact to the Syriac language itself.[11] The extent to which these same influences may have been at work in the great Cappadocians is, as I noted briefly above, only just beginning to come to light.

If my much abbreviated sampling from the early and fourth-century Syrian East has successfully demonstrated that Gregory Nazianzus was not pulling his Adam-Eve-Seth analogy out of thin air, but was rather reflecting ancient formulations of the Christian Trinity current in the surrounding region, we are still left with a couple of obvi-

---

[10]   Homily 28.4, in *Pseudo-Macarius: The Fifty Spiritual Homilies and the Great Letter*, trans. G. Maloney (New York: Paulist Press, 1992), p. 185.

[11]   G. Quispel, *Makarios, das Thomasevangelium, und das Lied von der Perle* (Leiden: E. J. Brill, 1967); C. Stewart, *"Working the Earth of the Heart": The Messalian Controversy in History, Texts, and Language to A.D. 431* (Oxford: Oxford University Press, 1991).

ous questions. First, what if anything does this archaic and to the modern Christian ear unquestionably bizarre image have to do with contemporary theological reflection on the Trinity? Second, and more specifically, what does it have to do with the issue I raised at the beginning of this little essay, the almost equally ancient but still very lively question of the *filioque* and the matter of the ecumenical dialogue between Christian East and West? I think it says quite a lot, not all of which I have time to expand on here. Suffice it to say that St. Gregory's recourse to the first human family as an illustration of the Trinity is, first of all, explicitly related to the question of the Spirit's origin, and to the difference between the latter and the generation of the Son—Eve from the side of Adam as opposed to the begetting of Seth. This is, indeed, quite as far as Gregory wants to take this or any other analogy.[12] The Spirit's procession is different from the Son's begetting, both are from the Father, and both processes are finally hidden and ineffable:

> You tell me what is the unbegottenness of the Father, and I will explain the physiology of the generation of the Son and the procession of the Spirit, and we shall both of us be stricken with madness for prying into the mystery of God. And who are we to do these things, we who cannot even see what lies at our feet . . . much less enter into the depths of God?[13]

These were the conclusions and the attitude which we find enshrined in the original form of the Niceno-Constantinopolitanum, which goes no further than a simple paraphrase of John 15:26.

The fact, however, that Western Christians have taken the matter further, beginning chiefly (though not exclusively) with Augustine, and have raised—legitimately, I think—the question of the Second Person's part in the Spirit's origin, brings us to what I, and several other Orthodox theologians before me, feel that the ancient Semitic-Christian tradition sketched above and presupposed by Gregory can contribute to the discussion. Not to put too fine a point on it, this is the so-far-unaddressed question of the Spirit's role in the generation of the Son. What the old image of the Trinity as "family" reveals, together with the Synoptic baptismal narratives and Luke's account of the Incarnation, is a different Trinitarian *taxis* or model than the one we

---

[12] See him against all analogies in "On the Spirit" 31–33, *Christology of the Later Fathers*, pp. 213–214.

[13] "On the Spirit" 8, *Christology of the Later Fathers*, pp. 198–199.

are all used to: not Father-Son-Spirit, but Father-Spirit-Son, or, and to borrow a phrase from Leonardo Boff, precisely an implied *spiri-tuque*.[14] It is this other *taxis* which I take to be effectively presupposed both by the Eastern *epiklesis* over the baptismal font and the eucharistic elements, and by the witness of the Eastern ascetico-mystical tradition, which is to say, that it has its roots in the very deepest and, I would argue, most primordial levels of Christian faith and practice as the latter have been known in the East since—well, since the beginnings of Christianity itself. Here, I think, we arrive at the real reasons—beneath and aside from the abstractions of divine *monarchia*, relations of origin, and of the properties of *ousia* and *hypostasis*, or of the purely canonical question of proper or improper additions to the ecumenical creed—for that visceral, almost instinctively negative Eastern reaction to the *filioque* which I mentioned at the beginning of this essay. In a nutshell, the *filioque* as it stands, *tout court*, offends as it were the "inner ear" of Eastern Christian faith and practice, almost exactly in the way in which we would speak of the vertigo and nausea resulting from an injury to the fluids of the body's inner ear. Put more briefly still, the *filioque* strikes us Easterns as unacceptably lopsided. If it answers to a real need to explain in intra-Trinitarian terms the Son's sending of the Spirit, it does so at the expense of the Spirit's own active role and Person. The Latter becomes entirely passive and, in our eyes, this does not in consequence account adequately for the scriptural, liturgical, and—yes—mystical data of the Tradition which witness to His (or, if the reader prefers my ancient Syrians, Her) creative and generative power.

Fr. Boris Bobrinskoy has written very recently, and Fr. Dumitru Staniloae some time ago, of the need to restore a sense of the reciprocity in the relations between the Son and Holy Spirit.[15] I would like to second that motion. As to the precise theological shape that reciprocity might take, or what formula might be found to express it adequately, I will not venture either to propose or to guess. Allow me instead to close not with my own words, but with those of a great

---

[14] L. Boff, *Trinity and Society*, trans. P. Burns (Maryknoll, N.Y.: Orbis Books, 1988), p. 205; cited in R. Del Colle, "Reflections on the *Filioque*," *Journal of Ecumenical Studies* 34.2 (1997): 211 and n. 24.

[15] D. Staniloae, *Theology and the Church*, trans. R. Barringer (Crestwood, N.Y.: St. Vladimir's Seminary Press, 1980), pp. 92–108; and B. Bobrinskoy, *The Mystery of the Trinity: Trinitarian Experience and Vision in the Biblical and Patristic Tradition*, trans. A. P. Gythiel (Crestwood, N.Y.: St. Vladimir's Seminary Press, 1999), pp. 63–77, 279–316.

Byzantine saint and mystic who wrote on the very eve of our millennial schism. St. Symeon the New Theologian (+1022) testifies here, as so often in his works, to personal transfiguration in the *visio dei*. It seems to me that his words might be taken as summing up and encapsulating the legitimate insights of both halves of the now sundered Christian *ecumene*:

> What is the "image of the heavenly man" (1 Cor. 15:49)? Listen to the divine Paul: "He is the reflection of the Glory and very stamp of the nature" and the "exact image" of God the Father (Heb. 1:3). The Son is then the icon of the Father, and the Holy Spirit the icon of the Son. Whoever, then, has seen the Son, has seen the Father, and whoever has seen the Holy Spirit, has seen the Son. As the Apostle says, "The Lord is the Spirit" (2 Cor. 3:7); and again: "The Spirit Himself intercedes for us with sighs too deep for words . . . crying 'Abba, Father!' (Rom. 8:26 and 15). He says rightly that the Lord is the Spirit when He cries "Abba, Father!", not that the Son is the Spirit—away with the thought!—but that the Son is seen and beheld in the Holy Spirit, and that never is the Son revealed without the Spirit, nor the Spirit without the Son. Instead, it is in and through the Spirit that the Son Himself cries "Abba, Father!"[16]

---

[16] *St. Symeon the New Theologian on the Mystical Life: The Ethical Discourses*, trans. A. Golitzin, here Discourse III, in Vol. I: *The Church and the Last Things* (Crestwood, N.Y.: St. Vladimir's Seminary Press, 1995), pp. 128–129.

"The Lord, the Giver of Life": A Reflection on the Theology of the Holy Spirit in the Twelfth Century

WANDA ZEMLER-CIZEWSKI*

Towards the end of the twelfth century, the Calabrian abbot Joachim of Fiore (c. 1132–1202) envisioned a Trinitarian history of humankind in three grand *status*: the age of the Law or the Father, the age of the Son and of grace, and finally, a third age yet to come, which was to be the age of the Holy Spirit.[1] As we enter the third millennium of Christian history, Joachim's prophecy may come to mind, inviting reflection on the doctrine of the Holy Spirit in the history of Christian thought and practice. Nevertheless, the flamboyant Joachim must not distract us from the many other, equally original thinkers of his time. Indeed, we may find that it is not Joachim who offers us the most fruitful of his century's resources, but instead, a handful of men and women from the older, Benedictine tradition, who sought to unfold the meaning of the Church's already centuries-old confession, "We believe in the Holy Spirit, the Lord, the Giver of Life." Quietly and without fanfare, they developed a theology of the Holy Spirit at work in creation and in the restoration of the human person, for the good of the ecclesial community as well as the personal benefit and intellectual growth of the individual. It is my intention to present in what follows a brief survey of four of these twelfth-century theologians' insights into the doctrine of the Holy Spirit, and then to conclude with a few thoughts on how their teaching might enrich Christian practice in the present.

In the early Middle Ages, it was not uncommon for children to be dedicated to a monastery by their parents or guardians, and placed there to be brought up. Both Rupert of Deutz (1075–1129) and Hildegard of Bingen (1098–1179) entered the Benedictine family by

---

* Wanda Zemler-Cizewski is Associate Professor of Theology at Marquette University, Milwaukee.

[1] See, e. g., Marjorie Reeves, *Joachim of Fiore and the Prophetic Future* (New York: Harper and Row, 1976).

this means, and proceeded to distinguish themselves as theologians and Scripture commentators. There are some striking parallels between their careers. Senior of the two, Rupert was an oblate child of the monastery of St. Laurent near Liège. Hildegard was entrusted by her parents to the aristocratic recluse, Jutta of Diessenberg, and became her successor as abbess of a convent of Benedictine nuns. Born a generation or so ahead of Hildegard, Rupert died some ten years before she began to record her visionary experiences.[2] Like Hildegard, he claimed to have been the recipient of a series of visionary encounters with the triune God, and described them in an autobiographical chapter of a commentary on the Gospel of Matthew.

Some of Rupert's visions occurred during his adolescence, while he and other monks of St. Laurent loyal to their reforming abbot were living in exile in France. Others came to him later, in his twenties, as he was deciding whether or not to be ordained to the priesthood. In those politically and personally troubled circumstances, Rupert tells us, he despaired of his life, but turned for comfort to the study of Scripture, especially the prophet Ezekiel. Finally, he invoked the Holy Spirit directly for aid and understanding. He explains:

> Even if there is one substance of the Father, Son, and Holy Spirit, one divinity and [one] inseparable operation, nevertheless, just as the proper work of the Father is the creation of humankind, and the proper work of the Son is the redemption, so the proper work of the Holy Spirit is the illumination of that same human being, the grace of revelations, and the distribution of all gifts.[3]

In the visions as Rupert describes them, the Spirit plays a prominent role, comforting him in the midst of anxiety, appearing once in the guise of a venerable, white-haired old man, and later in the shape of a mysterious globe of liquid fire, which poured itself into Rupert's bosom, filling him with a sense of peace and confidence. His prayers seem to have been abundantly answered, as his visions culminated in acceptance of a vocation to interpret the Bible for those who had no

---

[2]   See John Van Engen, *Rupert of Deutz* (Berkeley: University of California, 1983).

[3]   *"Quoniam etsi Patris et Filii et Spiritus sancti una substantia est, una divinitas et operatio inseparabilis, tamen sicut Patris proprium est opus hominis conditio, et Filii proprium opus redemptio, sic proprium est opus Spiritus sancti eiusdem hominis illuminatio revelationumque gratia et omnium gratiarum divisio."* Rupert of Deutz, *De gloria et honore filii hominis super Mattheum* 12, ed. Hrabanus Haacke, *Corpus christianorum continuatio medievalis* 9 (Turnhout: Brepols, 1979), p. 375.

books[4] as well as his decision to accept ordination to the priesthood. In this way, Rupert's personal experience of the Spirit found meaning and validation within the ecclesial community, which he felt called to serve both through scholarship and in the sacramental priesthood.

Although the door to priestly ministry was closed for Hildegard, her appropriation of her visionary experiences resembles the self-understanding achieved by Rupert. She dictated the record of her visions in a three-part collection entitled *Scivias*, probably an abbreviation of *Scite vias*, or "Know the ways [of the Lord]." In the prologue, she describes a "very great splendour," reminiscent of Rupert's globe of liquid fire, and a heavenly voice instructing her to transmit a record of the visions she had received since childhood. Like Rupert's experience, Hildegard's encounter was characterized by a sense of having been penetrated by light and fire, followed by a sudden conviction that she could understand the inner or spiritual sense of Scripture. She relates:

> It came to pass that in the eleven hundred and forty-first year of the Incarnation of God's Son, Jesus Christ, when I was forty-two years and seven months old, that the heavens were opened and a blinding light of exceptional brilliance flowed through my entire brain. And so it kindled my whole heart and breast like a flame, not burning but warming, as the sun warms anything on which its rays fall. And suddenly I grasped the underlying meaning of the books—of the Psalter, the Gospels, and other Catholic books of the Old and New Testaments—not, however, that I understood how to construe the words of the text or their division into syllables or their cases and tenses.[5]

---

4 Van Engen, pp. 342–52.

5 *"Factum est in millesimo centesimo quadragesimo primo Filii Dei Iesu Christi incarnationis anno, cum quadraginta duorum annorum septemque mensium essem, maximae coruscationis igneum lumen aperto caelo ueniens totum cerebrum meum transfudit et totum cor totumque pectus meum uelut flamma non tamen ardens sed calens ita inflammauit, ut sol rem aliquam calefacit super quam radios suos ponit. Et repente intellectum expositionis librorum, uidelicet psalterii, euangelii, et aliorum catholicorum tam ueteris quam noui Testamenti uoluminem sapiebam, non autem interpretationem uerborum textus eorum nec diuisionem syllabarum nec cognitionem casuum aut temporum habebam."* Hildegardis Scivias, Protestificatio, Adelgundis Führkötter and Angela Carlevaris, eds., in *Corpus christianorum continuatio medievalis* 43 (Turnhout: Brepols, 1978), pp. 3–4; tr. in Sabina Flanagan, ed. and trans., *Secrets of God: Writings of Hildegard of Bingen* (London: Shambhala, 1996), p. 9.

In the written record of her visions, Hildegard would begin each episode by describing what she saw, and then adding an interpretation which she claimed to have received from the heavenly voice. Often, these commentaries drew upon such familiar Scripture passages as the Genesis creation stories and the Gospel narratives of Christ's life and ministry to explain the spectacular images that presented themselves to her mind's eye.

In the voluminous correspondence that she maintained with members of the German imperial family, kings, bishops, and other notables, Hildegard drew upon her sense of prophetic insight to criticize vice and encourage virtue. She was also able to undertake numerous preaching and teaching journeys in the Rhineland and southern Germany. In this way, she was able to serve the ecclesial community through a public ministry normally forbidden to women of her day, thanks to the persuasive evidence of her visionary experiences. At the same time, she expressed her unique sense of the Creator Spirit's life-giving effect on both the cosmos at large and the *microcosmos* of the individual human person in both the prose of her visionary writings and the poetry of her liturgical music. For instance, she describes the Trinity in divine Unity by means of the metaphor of a flame:

> For the flame consists of splendid clarity and scarlet strength and fiery heat. And it has the splendid clarity so it can shine, and the scarlet strength so it can thrive, and the fiery heat so that it can burn. Therefore, by the splendid clarity understand the Father, who by paternal piety extends His light over His faithful. And in the scarlet strength that goes with it, in which the same flame shows its power, understand the Son, who assumed his body from the Virgin, in whom divinity declared its marvels; in the fiery strength recognize the Holy Spirit which hotly kindles the minds of believers.[6]

---

[6] *"Flamma enim splendida claritate et purpureo uirore ac igneo ardore consistit. Sed splendidam claritatem habet ut luceat, et purpureum uirorem ut uigeat, atque igneum ardorem ut ardeat. Unde in splendida claritate Patrem considera qui paterna pietate claritatem suam fidelibus suis expandit, et in purpureo uirore qui huic causae inest, in qua eadem flamma uirtutem suam ostendit, Filium intellege qui ex Virgine corpus assumpsit, in quo diuinitas mirabilia sua declarauit; ac in igneo ardore Spiritum sanctum perspice qui mentes credentium ardenter infundit."* Scivias 2. 2. 6, pp. 128–29; trans. in Flanagan, p. 22.

Elsewhere, she identified the Spirit as the breath connecting the Father and the Word,[7] and in relation to creatures as the living fountain that gives life to all things:

> The Living Fountain is the Spirit of God, which He himself sends in different directions in all His works, which are enlivened by it, having vitality through it just as the reflection of all things appears in water.[8]

In her hymn to the Holy Spirit, moreover, she developed a rich and complex series of images in which the Spirit is the fire from which minds are kindled, the sword that severs the effects of Adam's sin, and treasured ointment for the healing of wounded souls.[9]

The fruits of the Spirit, in Rupert's case, took the form of intense exegetical activity resulting in commentaries on the liturgy, *De divinis officiis*, and on the whole of Scripture, *De sancta Trinitate et operibus eius*. The latter work is especially interesting in that a generation or two before Joachim of Fiore, it offers a Trinitarian interpretation of earth's history, with creation week as the age of the Father, the time from Eden—and God's first words to humankind—until the incarnation of the Son, as the age of the Word, and as the age of the Holy Spirit all time from Pentecost until now. Strangely optimistic, given the troubled times in which he lived, Rupert identified the age of the Spirit as an age of scholarship and intellectual flourishing, in which knowledge of languages would aid in spreading the Gospel throughout the world.[10]

In his work on the divine office, Rupert took a similarly Trinitarian approach. As far as I have been able to ascertain, he is the first commentator on the liturgical year to offer an account of Trinity Sunday, a feast that had recently been added to the Benedictine calendar and that would eventually be included in the calendar of the whole western Church. Throughout this remarkable exposition, Rupert employs the language of Scripture, especially the Psalms, to articulate the doctrinal nuances of his Trinitarian thought. Commenting on the work of

---

[7] *Hildegardis Bingensis liber divinorum operum* 1. 1. 1–2, ed. A. Derolez and P. Dronke, in *Corpus christianorum continuatio medievalis* 92 (Turnhout: Brepols, 1996), pp. 46–50; trans. in Flanagan, pp. 62–65.

[8] Trans. in Flanagan, p. 80.

[9] "*O igne spiritus, laus tibi sit,*" in Barbara Newman ed., *Hildegard of Bingen: Symphonia* (Ithaca: Cornell Univ. Press, 1970), p. 27; trans. in Flanagan, pp. 120–22.

[10] See Van Engen, pp. 92–93.

the three Persons in creation, he embroiders upon the fabric of Proverbs 8:31 with the imagery of Psalm 148, so as to describe relations among the Persons and their created works.

> In truth it was a lovely game for God the Father to see in his Wisdom what he was about to make, first the blessed court and beautiful republic of heaven, to be distinguished by the ten orders of angels, then the visible architecture of this world, the spherical chamber of heaven, the sun and moon, the shining stars, the upper waters, the lower waters, every abyss, snow and hail, mountains and hills, and each open space on earth, the sea, and all things that are in them, whatever flies above, whatever crawls or walks below, beasts and all cattle, kings of the earth and all people . . . To see this, I say, before it came into being, was a game for God and his Wisdom, a festive game, a happy game, a delighting game. But truly, to rejoice at such things, to see all this with hilarity in greatness of heart, is the Love of Wisdom—a zealous love, a holy love—which we said earlier is the Holy Spirit.[11]

Meanwhile, all those who have received the Holy Spirit through God's grace become participants in the great game of creation, as sharers in the love between the Father and the Son.

Turning to Rupert's interpretation of the baptismal liturgy for Holy Saturday, we find an image of the Holy Spirit that is both traditional in its sources and startling in its innovative application. Just as the Spirit of God moved over the waters at the beginning of creation, so also there is a movement of the Spirit over the waters of baptism. Rupert explains the restoration of likeness to God, which had been

---

[11]   "*Ludus enim erat amabilis Deo Patri, uidere in sapientia sua, quae facturus erat, primo beatam caeli curiam pulchramque rempublicam denis angelorum ordinibus distinguendam, deinde uisibilem mundi huius architecturam, sphaericam caeli cameram solemque et lunam, lucida sidera, aquas superiores, aquas inferiores, omnes abyssos, nives atque grandines, montes et colles cunctamque terrae aream, mare et omnia, quae in eis sunt, quidquid sursum uolat, quidquid deorsum repit aut ambulat, bestias et universa pecora, reges terrae et omnes populos. . . . Haec, inquam, uidere antquam fierent, ludus erat Deo et sapientiae eius, ludus festiuus, ludus iucundus, ludus deliciosus. At uero de huiusmodi gaudere, haec omnia spectare cum hilaritate in cordis amplitudine, amor est sapientiae, amor studiosus, amor sanctus, quem supra sanctum Spiritum esse diximus.*" Rupert of Deutz, *De divinis officiis* 11. 8, ed. Hrabanus Haacke, CCCM (*Corpus christianorum continuatio medievalis*) 7 (Turnhout: Brepols, 1967), pp. 378–79; see W. Cizewski, "A Theological Feast: The Commentary by Rupert of Deutz on Trinity Sunday," *Récherches de théologie ancienne et médiévale* 55 (1988), pp. 41–52.

lost through Adam's sin, in terms of this double movement of the Spirit, using the image of the cosmic egg as a link between the two. At the beginning of creation, the Spirit first moved over the waters "like a bird, vivifying the egg with its warmth." In the sacrament of baptism, the Spirit again moves over the waters, "so that by warming them, she may regenerate into true life those who enter under her grace, spreading her wings and drawing them up, and even carrying them on her shoulders. And if it is necessary that she approach even more closely to someone, that is, if someone is prevented from approaching the waters . . . then indeed the mother of divine grace flies to him and extends her wings beyond the nest of waters."[12] The imagery seems derived, perhaps by some oral transmission we cannot trace, from eastern, specifically early Syriac descriptions of the Holy Spirit.[13]

For Rupert, the Spirit is literally both mother and father, and so also more than either. Turning to his interpretation of the feast of Pentecost for one final example from his work, we find an application of the Song of Songs to interpret the mission of the Holy Spirit. Using the same passage that Bernard of Clairvaux would later interpret in terms of the Spirit as divine kiss,[14] Rupert paints a very different picture. The impudent bride who demands a kiss is sexually immature, like so many of the little aristocratic child-brides of Rupert's day. The kiss is the incarnation, and as her bridegroom decorously kisses her through the lattice of her window, but does not fully embrace her, so also the words of Christ before his resurrection and ascension are addressed to an immature band of followers, not yet capable of bringing forth offspring to his name. For, as Rupert remarks, nobody ever made anyone pregnant with a kiss.[15] When, at last, the Spirit is sent forth on the day of Pentecost, it is as if the marriage is consummated,

---

[12] "*Ipse nunc superferetur aquis baptismi, ut ingredientes sub gratiam suam confouens in ueram regeneret uitam, 'extendens alas suas et assumens eos atque portans in humeris suis.' Et si opus est, ut amplius appropinquet alicui, id est si ab aquis arceatur aliquis . . . tunc demum aduolat mater gratia Dei suasque ultra nidum aquarum alas extendit.*" Rupert, *De divinis officiis* 7.4, p. 228.

[13] Susan A. Harvey, "Feminine Imagery for the Divine: The Holy Spirit, the Odes of Solomon, and Early Syriac Tradition," *St. Vladimir's Theological Quarterly* 37 (1993): 111–140.

[14] Bernard of Clairvaux, "*Sermo super Cantica Canticorum*" 2; trans. in *Bernard of Clairvaux: Selected Works*, ed. and trans. Gillian R. Evans (New York: Paulist, 1987), pp. 215–20.

[15] Rupert, *De divinis officiis* 10.6, p. 330.

because the Holy Spirit has the power to penetrate the souls of the Apostles so as to make them pregnant by the Word.

The image is startling to modern sensibilities, perhaps, but not unique in the twelfth century. A similar theme is developed by Peter Abelard in one of the hymns that he wrote for Héloïse and the sisters of the Paraclete, or Convent of the Holy Spirit. Describing the Spirit's life-giving powers on the first day of creation, he sings:

Aquae fovens vivificus	Warming the waters,
iam incumbebat Spiritus,	the life-giving Spirit
ut hinc aquae	lay over them long ago,
iam tunc conciperent	so that hence in those days
unde prolem	the waters might conceive,
nunc sacram parerent.[16]	whence now they may
	give birth to holy offspring.

In this bold image, the Spirit, named "Lord and Giver of Life" in the Nicene-Constantinopolitan Creed, is depicted as conjugal Lord and masculine Giver of Life, both nurturing and impregnating the material creature.

The Paraclete is best known to history as the convent established by Peter Abelard for his wife Héloïse and the community of women under her direction, but before she and her sisters received it as their permanent home, it had been Abelard's hermitage and was named by him in honor of the Holy Spirit, who comforted him, he states, amid the adversity of persecution by his theological opponents.[17] When Héloïse was granted the Paraclete, Abelard encouraged her to rededicate it as a place in which to pursue a program of biblical scholarship, devoted specifically to correction of the existing Latin text of the Bible by careful comparison with the Hebrew and Greek. In a general letter to the community, he states that Héloïse herself knows both Greek and Hebrew, and can teach the sisters the original languages of the Bible. Indeed, he goes so far as to use the word *magisterium* to describe her authority: "You have a *magisterium* in mother [Héloïse], who is able to teach you all you need."[18] Meanwhile, in a sermon for

---

[16] Peter Abelard, *Hymnarius Paraclitensis*, ed. J. Szövérffy (Albany, N.Y.: Classical Folia Editions, 1975), vol. 2, p. 22.

[17] Peter Abelard, *Historia calamitatum*, ed. J. Monfrin (Paris: Vrin, 1967), p. 95.

[18] *"Magisterium habetis in matre, quod ad omnia uobis sufficere."* Peter Abelard, Ep. 9, *Patrologia Latina* 178. 333B.

the feast of Pentecost, he urges the women of the Paraclete to seek the
assistance of the Holy Spirit in their work, since the Spirit at Pentecost
was able to give the unlettered disciples not only the interior word of
grace, but also the exterior power of languages, with which to preach
the Gospel.[19] Like Rupert, therefore, Abelard identifies the outpouring of the Holy Spirit with scholarship, especially in the study of languages. His understanding of the influence of the Spirit in the individual soul accordingly emphasizes the intellectual rather than the
affective aspect. Scholarly work under the guidance of the Spirit is described as a benefit to the women's spiritual growth, but also as a potential contribution to the whole community of the Church, insofar as
the work done by the women of the Paraclete was to supply the erudi-
tion which, in Abelard's opinion, the men of their day sadly lacked.[20]
Finally, some of his most enduring liturgical poetry (e.g., *"O quanta
qualia"*) would be composed for the Paraclete community, at Héloïse's
request.

What can we learn from these men and women of the early
twelfth century? Diverse though their experiences of the Spirit may
have been, three consistent themes recur in all. The Holy Spirit is indeed the "Lord, the Giver of Life," whose goodness pervaded creation
in the beginning, and extends through the sacramental waters to spiritual re-creation of each baptized individual. By the individual's en-
dowment with gifts of the Spirit, in turn, the community is enriched,
until at last the grace of the Holy Spirit overflows again from the
Church to the world. First, however, this is a Trinitarian pneumatology, which sees the Holy Spirit always together with the other two
Persons of the Trinity in a shared work of creation and restoration.
Second, it is scripturally based in its imagery and focus: the twelfth
century's doctrines of the Holy Spirit grew out of interpretation of
Scripture, and found the power of the Holy Spirit at work preemi-
nently in the arts of language, interpretation of Scripture, and moral
instruction based upon Scripture. Finally, the twelfth-century theologians experienced and recognized the power of the Spirit sacramen-
tally, in baptism, in ordination, in consecration to the monastic life,

---

[19] *Patrologia Latina* 178. 511D–512A; see Wanda Cizewski, *"'In saeculo quondam
cara, nunc in Christo carissima:'* Héloïse and Spiritual Formation at the Convent of
the Paraclete," *Patristic, Medieval, Renaissance Proceedings* 9 (1984): 69–76.

[20] Abelard, *Patrologia Latina* 178. 334C.

and in the divine promise of forgiveness, mediated through the sacrament of reconciliation.

What shall we skeptical moderns learn from these sources? Hildegard's fiery visions may be debunked as migraines, and few would admit experiences like Rupert's outside the psychiatrist's office. Nevertheless, a core lesson endures: the Holy Spirit is present where new life begins, not only in the material creation, but also and especially in the sacramental mediation of new, spiritual life, often where life might least be expected. Recently I stood next to a thirteen-year-old stranger who had come to live in my house some few months before, as my stepdaughter. I listened as, at her own request, she was baptized into the catholic faith, and I made the liturgical responses proper to the child's parent. In that moment, I realized that I had a child, and that we were family in the deepest possible sense. Some days later, her father, the child, and I were at Mass, and she confided to us that she felt so happy and so full of love, that she just wanted to hug everybody. Her father explained that these were the gifts of the Holy Spirit: love, joy and peace. In that moment, I was convinced that I had glimpsed the creative power of the Holy Spirit, just as Rupert of Deutz described it: new spiritual life had been born from the waters of baptism, and through the sacramental presence of the Spirit, a family had been created.

Citizenship: Re-Minded by the Holy Spirit

THOMAS HUGHSON, S.J.*

> *And finally, teach our people to rely on your strength and
> to accept their responsibilities to their fellow citizens, that they
> may elect trustworthy leaders and make wise decisions for the
> well-being of our society; that we may serve you faithfully
> in our generation and honor your holy Name.*[1]
> "For Sound Government," The Book of Common Prayer.

The above prayer trusts in an expected answer. That answer generates the question for this essay. What kind of conjunction between citizenship and discipleship might it, and a common Christian assumption of harmony between being Christian and being an American citizen, depend on? Is the conjunction theologically strong in the sense of arising from truths, values and divine influence at the core of Christianity, or weak in the sense of a permissible human adjustment to an indifferent circumstance? Can exercise (not the legal status[2]) of American citizenship mediate discipleship or does it simply attach an ethically neutral condition to it? Exploration of this question leads to undramatic results that serve to deepen appreciation of ordinary Christian lives in America. The direction of the inquiry heads toward a strong, theological basis for the conjunction between discipleship and citizenship. This represents a step beyond John Courtney Murray's argument that the natural law ethic in Catholicism—though he could have pointed to parts of natural law ethics in other churches too—found major ele-

---

* Thomas Hughson is a priest in the Society of Jesus and Associate Professor in the Department of Theology at Marquette University.
[1] From prayer 22, "For Sound Government," *The Book of Common Prayer: and Administration of the Sacraments and Other Rites and Ceremonies of the Church, According to the use of the Episcopal Church* (New York: The Seabury Press, 1979), p. 822.
[2] The legal status of American citizenship can be gained three ways: by birth in the United States (*jus soli*), whether the parents are citizens or not; by naturalization; and by descent from one or both American parents (*jus sanguinis*). See Peter H. Schuck, *Citizens, Strangers and In-Betweens: Essays on Immigration and Citizenship* (Boulder, Colo.: Westview Press, 1998), pp. 161–247.

ments of itself in the design laid down by the U.S. Constitution.[3] He argued the congruence between Catholic adherence to natural law morality and to American democracy. Here, however, the focus is on generally Christian, theological grounds for congruence, with special attention to "his own first gift to those who believe,"[4] the Holy Spirit, and to Johannine theology of the Paraclete in particular. The question can be put, does Christian discipleship, especially in light of the Third Article of the Niceno-Constantinopolitan Creed, find scope for its exercise in active American citizenship?

Members of the Episcopal Church have compiled a distinguished record of active citizenship that signifies a tradition of faith expressed, among other ways, in concern for the "well-being of our society." Most often, perhaps, that concern has issued in an exercise of citizenship that fulfills the ordinary duties of paying taxes, discussing public issues, voting for "trustworthy leaders," serving in the military, etc. Fewer, but still a remarkable number, have toiled for the "well-being of our society" in public office. Least trodden may be a path of holy indignation that has led, as with William Stringfellow, to prophetic challenge of the social and political status quo.[5] In these and other ways Episcopalians have let discipleship underwrite active citizenship.

The question, though, about discipleship and active citizenship pertains to all believers in Christ from all churches and ecclesial bodies, including my own Roman Catholic Church. The context of the question is a new attention to citizenship. Discussion of philosophical, juridical, historical, political, social, economic and ethical aspects of citizenship enjoys a new prominence.[6] Education for good citizenship has become a recognizable task. Exploring the conjunction of Christian discipleship and American citizenship has positive implications for democratic practice. Events of the recent past—for example, in-

---

[3]   John Courtney Murray, *We Hold These Truths* (New York: Sheed & Ward, 1960).

[4]   From "Holy Eucharist II: Eucharistic Prayer D," The Book of Common Prayer, p. 374.

[5]   Bill Wylie-Kellerman says that, "Theologically, Stringfellow's most significant contribution was to reappropriate the biblical language of 'principalities and powers,' opening the door for a new social critique grounded in the New Testament," in "Listen to This Man: A Parable Before the Powers," in Robert Boak Slocum, ed., *Prophet of Justice, Prophet of Life: Essays on William Stringfellow* (New York: Church Publishing Incorporated, 1997), p. 2.

[6]   See Will Kymlicka and Wayne Norman, "Return of the Citizen: A Survey of Recent Work on Citizenship Theory," *Ethics* 104 (1994): 352–381, and Gershon Shafir, ed., *The Citizenship Debates* (Minneapolis: University of Minnesota Press, 1998).

creased voter apathy, nationalist movements in Eastern Europe, failed environmental policies that depend on voluntary cooperation—"have made clear that the health and stability of a modern democracy depends [sic] not only on the justice of its 'basic structure' but also on the qualities and attitudes of its citizens."[7] To the extent that Christians gain a better grasp of how discipleship supports active citizenship, this anchors their practice of citizenship in something more solid than a putative social contract.

Admittedly, another worthwhile avenue would be to explore the mission of the Spirit in various churches that, within their overall mission, embrace a messianic social ministry on behalf of the poor and marginalized that often produces official statements and supports advocacy and lobbying on public policies. Attention to discipleship instead does not imply confinement within an individualist premise. Discipleship is as ecclesial as are the missions of Christ and the Holy Spirit.[8] Nor does focus on exercise of citizenship rather than on, for example, public advocacy of social teachings by official representatives of various churches pre-define the role of religion in society primarily as a private matter. American citizenship is a public office, not a private predilection. The adjective "public," observes Robert Wuthnow, denotes several contrasts with "private" but central among them is passage from childhood's immersion in self and family life to an adult responsibility for the good of a group or society.[9] The exercise of citizenship fulfills this kind of public office, indeed this democracy's most essential public office.

A "Public" Spirit

Still, lest a turn of attention to the indwelling Holy Spirit seem tilted toward privatized piety of a kind that readers of Wuthnow might suspect weakens the public role of religion, it will be helpful to notice at the outset that Scripture links the Spirit of God to public, often political, activity. That link, however, has not been a theological mainstay.

---

[7] Kymlicka, p. 352.

[8] The Church as a corporate whole can be conceived as a "community of disciples" without thereby dissolving the Church into a voluntary association of saved individuals. See, for example, Avery Dulles, *Models of the Church*, expanded edition (Garden City, N.Y.: Image Books, 1987).

[9] Robert Wuthnow, *Producing the Sacred: An Essay on Public Religion* (Urbana, Ill.: University of Illinois Press, 1994), p. 11. The book analyzes public expression of the sacred.

Remarks Kilian McDonnell, "[O]ne of the difficulties with the formulation of the doctrine of the Spirit is that it has been dominated either by ecclesiology . . . or by the interior life (grace)." So he has to ask, "[B]ut what about the secular order, programs of social transformation, public service, politics?"[10] And I would chime in, what about citizenship as the ordinary mode of participation in social transformation, public service and politics?

Looking to Scripture for an answer, McDonnell observes that, "[T]he tradition Jesus inherited gave the spirit of God a considerable role in the elders (Num. 11:25–29) (judicial/political), judges (Judg. 3:10; 11:29;13:25) (military); some prophets (1 Sam. 10:10; 19:23; Ezek. 2:12,22 [sic:2:1–2?]; Neh. 9:30; Zech. 7:12) (also prophetic and political); some kings (1 Sam. 11:6; 16:13–14) (political), especially the messianic king (Isa. 42:1)."[11] In reference to these activities of the divine Spirit, McDonnell points out that "Jesus appropriated this public Spirit at the beginning of his ministry (Isa. 61:1–11; Luke 4:18–19) when he characterized his messianic mission to the poor, captives and oppressed."[12] Isaiah 11:2–3 could be added to the above list of texts supporting his interpretation of the Holy Spirit as "this public Spirit."

And yet a clarification is in order. Common Christian understanding holds that Jesus' ministry, while public, was anything but political. Does McDonnell's pointing to links between the Spirit and Israel's kings (1 Sam. 11:6; 16:13–14; Isa. 11: 2–3; 42:1), and then prefacing Spirit with the term "public," skew interpretation of Jesus' public ministry toward something decidedly political? Not really, but McDonnell's phrasing indeed does imply two modifications of the common understanding. First and more remotely, there is every reason to think McDonnell presupposes the "structural separation" Jesus drew between his mission and the purpose, activity and coercive power of a

---

[10]   Kilian McDonnell, O.S.B., "Theological Presuppositions in our Preaching about the Holy Spirit," *Theological Studies* 59, 2 (June, 1998): 219–235, p. 231. This differs from Jürgen Moltmann's investigation of the impact on the sociopolitical order of the Trinitarian doctrine of God, in, for example, *The Trinity and the Kingdom*, trans. Margaret Kohl (New York: SCM Press, 1981).

[11]   McDonnell, p. 231.

[12]   McDonnell, p. 231. See Yves Congar, *I Believe in the Holy Spirit*, trans. David Smith (New York: Crossroad Publishing Company, 1997), p. 16, for the point that "a pneumatology inherited from the Old Testament and Judaism is used in the gospels." References to the Spirit in the Christian Scriptures are neither identical with nor contrary to the post-biblical affirmation of the Spirit as a distinct, divine person that informs McDonnell's reading of Scriptural texts on the Spirit.

state.[13] Jesus' messianic self-understanding, teaching and practice gave to Christianity impulses that have affected the sociopolitical order of the Christian West (Eastern and Western halves) by moving it into various modes of Church-state dualism. In this sense Jesus' public ministry had definite but eventual and indirect effects on the political order of society.

Second, it would be consistent with McDonnell's description of the Spirit as "public," with his focus on Luke 4:18–19, and with advertence to Jesus' "messianic mission to the poor, captives and oppressed," to go on to say that McDonnell indicates that Jesus appropriated a divine option for the poor that went along with the Spirit in what Jesus read from Isaiah 42. It could be said, further, that this option appropriated by Jesus, under a variety of titles and in a host of modes, generated Church ministries to widows, orphans, the destitute, prisoners, the sick, the despised, etc. If so, also this theme in Jesus' messianic self-understanding has had an impact on the public life of society and the state, not least during the past thirty years in Latin America. McDonnell keeps the door open to a link between the Spirit and contextual options for the poor that usually have implications for public policies. This is the second way Jesus' public ministry in the power of the "public Spirit" indirectly has produced differences in the sociopolitical order. McDonnell's theology of the Spirit, then, modifies but does not negate the common Christian understanding that Jesus' own ministry was public but not political.

But the whole of McDonnell's position on the Spirit as "public Spirit" exceeds the sum of such analyzed parts. Drawing attention to possible links between the Spirit and the sociopolitical order introduces an atypical perspective into consideration of Christianity's impact on society and state.[14] He remarks that the presence of the Holy

---

[13] In "Separation of Church and State," Paul J. Weber traces "structural separation" as theory to Jesus and as "part of Western political culture" to Gelasius I, Pope from 494 to 496, whose letter to Emperor Anastasius I in 494 set forth the famous, "Two there are, August Emperor, by which the world is chiefly ruled" in Robert B. Wuthnow, ed., *The Encyclopedia of Religion and Politics*, Vol. 2 (Washington, D.C.: Congressional Quarterly, Inc., 1998), pp. 684–87, p. 684. On New Testament stances toward the state, see Walter E. Pilgrim, *Uneasy Neighbors: Church and State in the New Testament* (Minneapolis: Fortress Press, 1999). On the importance of Gelasian dualism, see John Courtney Murray, *We Hold These Truths*.

[14] This is not to ignore the immense contribution of Jürgen Moltmann, but an attempt to start more from the "already" of the Incarnation and Spirit than from the "not yet" of the Kingdom to come and hope.

Spirit, and not simply Christ, Gospel and Church, has affected society and the state. His conclusion serves as a point of departure for further reflection on how the distinct mission of the Holy Spirit and the Third Article in the Creed have "ramifications for the sociopolitical order."[15] I will consider these ramifications only insofar as they occur in persons exercising their sociopolitical citizenship.

Discipleship and the Holy Spirit

What is discipleship? In the New Testament discipleship "always implies the existence of a personal attachment which shapes the whole life of the one described as *mathētēs*."[16] The widest frame of reference for the term "disciple" ("*mathētēs*") occurs in Luke-Acts and in John where it refers to anyone who believes in Christ, rather than designates only people responding to Jesus during his public ministry (e.g., Matt. 5:1 ff.). The wider meaning includes all who have come to faith after the resurrection but who had not encountered Jesus during his life and work in Israel. The disciple's main task is not so much transmitting Jesus' message but witnessing to this teacher of God, whose unique reality and not lack of labor by his disciples meant that none of them would equal him. Discipleship "shapes the whole life of the one described as *mathētēs*." This comprehensive scope logically, and in Paul's case demonstrably, includes relationships with civil society and the state. A brief discussion of a few points in Paul will precede an argument for an interpretation of the Johannine Paraclete with implications for the exercise of citizenship.

Paul was not part of the Lucan Pentecost, as he had not accompanied Jesus during his public ministry. Paul's teaching points to the Spirit entering the Church with the Resurrection of Jesus, though conceived differently from John's similar perspective. For Paul, the Spirit accompanied preaching of the Gospel and stirred a hearing that

---

¹⁵ McDonnell, p. 235.

¹⁶ K. H. Rengstorf, "*Mathētēs*," in Gerhard Kittel, ed., Geoffrey Bromley trans. and ed., *Theological Dictionary of the New Testament*, Vol. 4 (Grand Rapids, Mich.: Wm. B. Eerdmans Publishing Co., 1967), pp. 415–61, p. 441. Discipleship differed from apprenticeship to a Hellenistic philosopher or a *talmid's* devotion to his rabbi especially in the fact that disciples of Christ had no possibility of equaling his wisdom. See also D. Muller, "Disciple," in Colin Brown, general ed., *The New International Dictionary of New Testament Theology* (Grand Rapids, Mich.: Zondervan Publishing Co., 1975), pp. 483–90, p. 483; and M. J. Wilkins, "Disciples," in Joel B. Green and Scot McKnight, eds., *Dictionary of Jesus and the Gospels* (Downer's Grove, Ill.: Intervarsity Press, 1992), pp. 176–82; and M. J. Wilkins, "Discipleship," pp. 182–189.

was an awakening to faith. Faith led to baptism, which brought the Spirit into the believer's life in a definitive way, there to make possible praying, "Abba, Father" and professing that "Jesus is Lord." Faith and baptism initiated a prolonged conversion from the lingering influence of the "flesh," or human existence organized by a principle of resistance to God, Christ and Spirit. This entailed renewal of the mind and so of deliberation prior to decision and action. The Spirit enabled followers of Christ to put on the "mind of Christ" (Phil. 2:5–11). The Spirit re-minded them by helping them to "set their minds on things of the Spirit," (Rom. 8:5b). Their conversion remained ever subject to the possibility of minor and major regression, so Paul urged an intentional re-orientation to open disciples' lives in all aspects to the influence of the Holy Spirit: "Do not be conformed to this world but be transformed by the renewal of your mind. . . ." The first result will be a new habit of mind, "that you may prove what is the will of God, what is good and acceptable and perfect" (Rom. 12:2). This habit of mind was comprehensive, seeking the will of God in all areas of life, relations with the political order included.

If Paul's own self-understanding and way of acting with a mind renewed by the Spirit served as a standard for other Christians living in the Roman Empire, then faith and baptism did not demand severance of prior connections with the Empire. Conversion to Christ did alter the significance of Roman citizenship. Loyalty to the Empire and Emperor fell into a position below faith in Christ and membership in the Church. For Jews, fidelity to Moses and the One above Caesar never had elevated Caesar to the rank of an ultimate authority in this life. Gentiles might have done so. Gentile Christians, depending on the kind of respect or reverence previously paid to Caesar, might be called on to accept the novelty of an ultimate authority of someone besides Caesar when they came to believe in Jesus as Lord. But Paul did not teach renunciation of Roman citizenship as part of life in the Spirit.

Of course, the *civis Romanus* in the post-Republic Roman Empire no longer had a voice in making laws but instead was "someone free to act by law, free to ask and expect the law's protection [with] legal status."[17] Neither Paul nor other Christians could have partici-

---

[17] J. A. G. Pocock, "The Ideal of Citizenship Since Classical Times," in Gershon Shafir, ed., *The Citizenship Debates*, pp. 31–41, p. 37. The legal rather than political status of a Roman citizen inserted non-Romans like Saul of Tarsus into a "community of shared or common law" beyond that of a local municipality. This idea of the citizen, which did not apply to women or slaves, entered into Western political thought.

pated in the exercise of political power in the Empire simply on the basis of their being citizens.[18] Politically, Paul's Roman citizenship was passive whereas citizenship according to the Athenian model of democracy and the eventual American Republic was active (made laws) as well as passive (obeyed laws, protected by laws). And yet the legal status of a propertied Roman citizen whose transactions proceeded according to imperial law, and under its protection, was the ancient forebear of that land-owning proprietor inscribed, for example, in John Locke's political philosophy and the U.S. Constitution. The New Testament, then, does not provide an example of, much less teaching on, active citizenship proceeding under the new orientation of Christian faith in an exercise of participating in self-governance. But living according to even passive citizenship carried Christian recognition and acceptance of the political organization of society. And conversion to Christ did modify that recognition and acceptance on the part of Roman citizens.

Paul's position, for example, was clear. He professed that "Jesus is Lord" (Rom. 10:9; 1 Cor. 8:5–6, 12:3), and thereby weighed in with the powerful demurral that Caesar was not Lord, was not supreme and imperial savior.[19] Nevertheless the apostle declared to the Roman tribune in Jerusalem, "But I was born a citizen!" (Acts 22:28) and more than once claimed legal prerogatives attached to that status.[20] Apparently his own conversion to Christ and renewal of mind in the Spirit was harmonious with some degree of positive regard for his Roman citizenship, as had been the case before his conversion but in a different way.[21] By its nature his conversion affected the whole of

---

[18] See Edward Schillebeeckx, *Christ: The Experience of Jesus as Lord*, trans. John Bowden (New York: Crossroad Publishing Company, 1981), pp. 561 ff. He argues convincingly that the social dimension of the Gospel, its renewal of social relationships as well as personal existence, was actualized during the New Testament period and until Constantine only within the Church, owing to the powerlessness of Christians to reshape the policies and administration of the Roman Empire.

[19] See Richard A. Horsley, "The Gospel of Imperial Salvation: Introduction" and Neil Elliot, "The Anti-Imperial Message of the Cross," in Richard A. Horsley, ed., *Paul and Empire: Religion and Power in Roman Imperial Society* (Harrisburg, Pa.: Trinity Press International, 1997), pp. 10–24, pp. 167–83.

[20] 1 Cor. 6:1–8, however, did not teach reliance on the imperial courts in disputes among Christians.

[21] Positive regard does not mean uncritical endorsement of the Roman Empire. Recent scholarship has focused on Paul's negative evaluations of Roman authorities and the Empire. See, for example, Richard A. Horsley, "Paul's Counter-Imperial Gospel: Introduction," in *Paul and Empire*, pp. 140–147.

Paul's existence so that his discipleship to Christ touched his Roman citizenship too. The result was functionally equivalent, I think, to the "ethic of critical distance" from political authority that Walter Pilgrim ascribes to Jesus.[22] So Paul's position on how to relate to the Roman Empire was complex insofar as it involved not absolute, but conditional, acceptance of a contingent political authority and governance. The condition was that it serve the divine purpose of a just, ordered, peaceful life in society and did not oppose the Lordship of Christ manifest in the existence and evangelizing mission of Christians. Therefore his accolade to standing political authority in Romans 13 was not antithetical, as usually has been thought, to condemnation of imperial tyranny in Revelation 13.[23] Revelation 13 condemned precisely a regime that defaulted on its duty to serve the divine purpose of justice and peace and so did not meet the Christian condition.

Nonetheless, and with that condition firmly in place, the exemplary case of Paul shows that there is a solid New Testament basis for affirming that a Christologically qualified Roman citizenship existed in the early Church as a legitimate manner of Christian life. This was in keeping with what Pilgrim calls Jesus' "ethic of critical distancing" of his mission from political authority.[24] More surprising, between the New Testament period and Constantine, notwithstanding a minority status and sporadic persecutions, many a post-apostolic writer walked along Paul's path of unconditional fidelity to Christ coupled with conditional loyalty to the Empire.[25]

The Commandment and the Paraclete

This section takes up the task of identifying, in addition to Paul's and Pauline writings, two other Biblical sources pertinent to the con-

---

[22]   Walter E. Pilgrim, *Uneasy Neighbors*, pp. 37 ff.

[23]   Both Neil Elliot, "Romans 13:1–7 in the Context of Imperial Propaganda," in Horsley, *Paul and Empire*, pp. 184–204, and Walter Pilgrim stress that Paul's whole perspective on the state cannot be defined by the paean to political authority in Romans 13:1 ff.; Elliot, in fact, argues that even Romans 13 "*does not express a univocally positive attitude toward the 'governing authorities'*," p. 196. Nor does Pilgrim accept the customary interpretation of Romans 13 as an unqualified "ethic of subordination" by Christians to political authority, pp. 8–36.

[24]   Pilgrim, pp. 37 ff.

[25]   See "Introduction," and excerpts from Clement of Rome, Justin Martyr, Theophilus of Antioch, Tertullian, Hippolytus of Rome, and Origen, in Hugo Rahner, S.J., trans. Leo Donald Davis, S.J., *Church and State in Early Christianity* (San Francisco: Ignatius Press, 1992; German original, 1962), pp. ix–38.

junction of discipleship and citizenship. One is the Eighth (or, in other listings, Ninth) Commandment in the Decalogue, "You shall not bear false witness against your neighbor" (Exod. 20:16; Deut. 19:15–21). The other is the Paraclete in John 14–16. Now, the Commandment by itself and without further ado could be brought to bear very profitably on many public matters about which American citizens have to deliberate, starting with the dependence of the judicial system on citizens' heeding the ethical norm of avoiding false and bearing true witness. It could be the perspective from which to raise a question about "false witness against your neighbor" in public discourse. The Commandment on truth-telling about others could direct attention to how types of hidden self-interest generate collective ideologies that amount to "false witness" in public debate. That would be a bracing and far from banal application of biblical morality to American public life. *The New Interpreter's Bible* commentary on Exodus takes this approach when it remarks that, "The major pertinence of the prohibition in our society is the collapse of truth into propaganda in the service of ideology."[26] A kind of "false witness" occurs in public life outside the courtroom if "public versions of truth are not committed to a portrayal of reality, but to a rendering that serves a partisan purpose."[27] This principle deserves more extensive development.

But not here. Discipleship has to be examined first as more than moral orthopraxis. In John, discipleship is constituted by people being drawn into loving belief in the salvific truth of Christ's identity, deeds, and teaching. Consent to and practice of the ethical universals he exemplified or taught did not fully define Johannine discipleship. Yet morality was essential to it and a tendency to set aside the importance of the Commandments seems to have driven a wedge into the Johannine community, with Johannine literature upholding their importance against a secessionist group who separated them from belief in Jesus.[28] Nonetheless, they were re-founded in the reality of Christ.

---

[26]   "Commentary" on Exodus 20:16 in *The New Interpreter's Bible: A Commentary in Twelve Volumes*, Vol. 1 (Nashville, Tenn.: Abingdon Press, 1994), p. 848.

[27]   Ibid.

[28]   Raymond E. Brown, in *The Churches the Apostles Left Behind* (New York: Paulist Press, 1984), pp. 110–117, points precisely to division within the Johannine community over the issue of whether or not obedience to the Commandments in addition to belief in Jesus was essential to discipleship. The secessionists discontinued rather than sublated the soteriological importance of the Commandments, whereas the Gospel and 1 John proceeded from and defended the linkage and thereby preserved the moral reality of norms as elements in a new synthesis.

And in the Farewell Discourse at the Johannine Last Supper, Christ taught on, prayed for, sent, and imparted the Holy Spirit to his disciples. Discipleship stemmed from and revolved around Christ and the Holy Spirit. In John's Gospel generally it was "the presence and activity of the Holy Spirit" that "ensured direct fellowship with Jesus" on the part of generations subsequent to those who followed Jesus up and down the rocky hills of Israel.[29] But Johannine theology of the Spirit as "another Paraclete" in particular (John 14:15–17, 25–26; 15:26–27; 16:7–11, 12–15) contains, it will be proposed, an intrinsic link to the Commandment, "You shall not bear false witness against your neighbor." The link is intrinsic, because the Commandment became internal to the meaning of Paraclete and of Johannine discipleship, not extrinsic as if the Commandment were simply another moral duty incumbent on disciples in the rare event of their being summoned to witness in court. The Commandment and the Paraclete are yoked together with a resulting emphasis on discipleship as bearing true witness to Christ. What is the yoke and what does it mean for discipleship?

The Commandment, or Word, demanded that, "You shall not bear false witness against your neighbor." It formed the whole life of Israel and remains a hallmark of Talmudic Judaism.[30] It was an ethic of truth-telling, a moral obligation to an intellectual act in the social, juridical context of a court of law. Prohibition of "false witness," unlike the other nine Commandments, presupposed rather than grounded a judicial system. It specified the conduct of someone summoned to testify as a witness in a trial. "Each individual is here directly addressed as a potential witness in a juridical forum. . . ."[31] The purpose of hearing witnesses was to determine the truth so that decisions could be made by the judge. Witnesses always gave oral testimony, based only on their own eyewitness, and without an oath. Testimony from two witnesses was required for validity.[32]

---

[29] Karl Rengstorf, *Theological Dictionary of the New Testament*, p. 458.

[30] Nahum Amsel states that "Truth is not just an important Jewish quality. It is called the seal of God . . . the emblem by which God is known, based on the Torah verse [Exod. 34:6] that informs us this is one of God's characteristics," in *The Jewish Encyclopedia of Moral and Ethical Issues* (Northvale, N.J.: Jason Aronson, Inc., 1994), p. 291.

[31] Nahum Sarna on Exodus 20, in *The JPS Torah Commentary: Exodus* (Philadelphia: The Jewish Publication Society, 1991), p. 114.

[32] According to Edwin Hatch and Henry A. Redpath, *A Concordance to the Septuagint, And Other Greek Versions of the Old Testament (Including the apocryphal*

Truth-telling in courts of law has immense significance for any society and this "prohibition . . . is a recognition that community life is not possible unless there is an arena in which there is public confidence that social reality will be reliably described and reported."[33] The Commandment against false witness instilled a principle of social truth-telling, since avoiding false witness actually took place in bearing true witness, testifying without forcing or ignoring one's own eyewitness knowledge, so that the truth of a situation can be known by a judge.

This pre-existing ethical duty comes to the surface in the juridical connotation of "will bear witness" attributed to the Paraclete (15:26) and to the disciples (15:27). Likewise the juridical function of the "Paraclete" (16:8–11) accords with, if it doesn't exactly follow, legal interrogation and a forensic context. A common reference to the pre-existing moral heritage and its juridical context unifies the foregoing verses. And the climactic position of 16:8–11 gathers into focus the juridical connotations in "Spirit of truth" (14:17) who "will bear witness to me" (15:26). In 14:17, 15:26–27, and 16:8–11, true testimony in a conflictual situation of contested truth is central. The obligation to bear true witness is fulfilled, strangely enough, by the Paraclete whose corroboration ("another Paraclete") of Christ's witness takes the form of the Spirit enlightening the disciples on the meaning of Christ. Indeed the Paraclete is described as the true witness to Christ *par excellence*, as Christ had also borne witness to the Father.

The disciples, however, were another story. Just as anyone summoned to the task of serving as a witness in a legal proceeding was selected on the basis of his or her direct knowledge of pertinent facts, the disciples had direct knowledge of Christ. Their problem seems to have been the weak condition of that knowledge. For them to give their eyewitness testimony about Christ was to bear true, not false, witness to Christ (15:27). Bearing witness, however, flowed from a grasp of what Christ had said and done that they did not actually have

---

Books) (Grand Rapids, Mich.: Baker Books, 1998), p. 1061, the English term "witness" translates the Greek (Septuagint) term *marturia* in Exodus 20:16 and *martus* in Proverbs 6:19, 12:17,14:5, 14:25, 19:5, 19:9 and 24:28. John A. Kohlenberger III and James A. Swanson, in *The Hebrew/English Concordance to the Old Testament: With the New International Version* (Grand Rapids, Mich.: Zondervan Publishing House, 1998), 1174 at 6332, point out that the Hebrew word "*ed*" meant "witness" in Exodus 20:16, 23:1, Deut. 5:20, and in the above verses in Proverbs, minus 24:43 and with 24:28 and 25:18. A juridical meaning was paramount.

[33] *New Interpreter's Bible*, commentary on Exodus 20, p. 848.

at the time. Enter the Paraclete. The Paraclete will bring the disciples (14:26) deeply enough into and through their memories of Christ so that they can move from passive accumulation of experience and some understanding of it to deeper penetration of its meaning. This will put them in a position to communicate the truth of Christ.

In John 14-16 the prospect of future witness, however, like the situation of Christ at the Last Supper, involves external opposition.[34] The Paraclete will not come so that at their leisure the disciples can enjoy contemplating the truth of Christ. Rather, the promise that when the "Spirit of truth comes, he will guide you into all the truth"— hearkening back to, "I am the way, the truth, and the life" (14:6)— prepares for a gift received during a time of duress that poses a potential crisis of faith since resistance to the disciples simultaneously puts the truth of Christ's witness to his mission from the Father on trial. The "Spirit of truth . . ." (14:17) "will teach you all things and bring to your remembrance all that I have said to you" (14:26). In 15:26 this act of teaching acquires a forensic, somewhat defensive connotation that makes it an act of providing true testimony (the "Spirit of truth who proceeds from the Father . . . [he] will bear witness [*marturia*] to me") in adverse circumstances. The Paraclete will carry out a true witness to Christ's identity, words and deeds by enlightening the disciples. Their confirmation in belief will occur when the "Spirit of truth" draws them deeper into faith-understanding of Christ's reality. That will equip them for steadfast, not shaky, witness to Christ.

The dawning of deeper truth about Christ within the minds of the disciples, due to the Paraclete, might be construed as an interior Pentecost. The Paraclete, proto-disciple, and co-witness with Jesus, brings about not sensible signs of wind and fire as in the Lucan Pentecost, but an interior re-minding. True witness to Christ before others will be the external effect, while and because, the Paraclete gives witness internally.[35] This interior witness of the Paraclete prompting true

---

[34] In *The Churches the Apostles Left Behind,* Brown stresses the importance of the conflictual experience of the Johannine community for its theology.

[35] This differs from Pauline teaching on passage from an external, written code to an interior norm operating as a new kind of spontaneity moved by the Holy Spirit toward the morally good act. Here, the Paraclete is not New Law but True Witness in the disciples. For a concise statement of the Pauline view, see Michael O'Carroll, "Law," in *Veni Creator Spiritus: A Theological Encyclopedia of the Holy Spirit* (Collegeville, Minn.: Liturgical Press, 1990), pp. 132–133.

witness by the disciples takes the place in them of the written commandment, "You shall not bear false witness against your neighbor."

The foregoing link between the Commandment and the Paraclete is supported by exegesis that looks to both a Jewish background and a legal dimension of meaning in Johannine theology of the Paraclete. Raymond E. Brown remarked that in general, "The Paraclete's special function is to take what belongs to Jesus and proclaim it anew in each generation."[36] But he didn't distance this from legal connotations and held that *paraklētos* has a juridical meaning, along with the meanings of consoler and teacher.[37] The courtroom meaning, however, could not have been "defense attorney" or even "advocate" because in Jewish court proceedings the judge did most of the interrogating in the presence of witnesses but without an attorney for the defense. He concluded that, "If the Paraclete has a forensic function, it must be that of witness."[38] And in Brown's judgment the Paraclete had a forensic function, so the Paraclete was a witness. For example, the Paraclete is the subject of the verb "will bear witness" (15:26–27).

To judge by a recent commentary on the Fourth Gospel, not all exegetes place an accent on the legal dimension of meaning in the word "Paraclete."[39] Francis J. Moloney distinguishes a forensic background behind the term "Paraclete" from the non-forensic meaning in Johannine usage of it. Brown, however, treated Johannine usage and background together. He pointed to a background in late Jewish angelology and to a forensic usage in John. Stated Brown, "Late Jewish angelology offers the best parallel for the forensic character of the Johannine Paraclete."[40] The interpretation offered here follows Brown's focus on the Jewish background and legal dimension in the Johannine usage of "Paraclete," but includes "You shall not bear false witness against your neighbor" in both background and usage.

---

[36]   Raymond E. Brown, *An Introduction to New Testament Christology* (Mahwah, N.J.: Paulist Press, 1994), p. 200.

[37]   Severino Pancaro studied the Mosaic Law in the Fourth Gospel without investigating the theology of the Paraclete in relation to the Eighth Commandment, in *The Law in the Fourth Gospel: The Torah, and the Gospel, Moses and Jesus, Judaism and Christianity according to John* (Leiden: Brill, 1975).

[38]   Raymond E. Brown, *The Gospel According to John (xiii–xxi): Introduction, Translation and Notes* (Garden City, N.Y.: Doubleday & Company, Inc., 1970), Appendix V, "The Paraclete," pp. 1135–1144, p. 1136.

[39]   Francis J. Moloney, O.S.B., *Sacra Pagina: The Gospel of John* (Collegeville, Minn.: Michael Glazier, Liturgical Press, 1998), especially, pp. 391 ff.

[40]   Raymond E. Brown, Appendix V, "The Paraclete," p. 1136.

In this way Johannine theology of the Paraclete transformed an ethical obligation to truth-telling before a judge—something essential to the orderly, just, peaceful functioning of society—into an interpretation of the mission of the Spirit, and no less, into the missionary dynamic of discipleship. I think the best way to understand this transformation is through Bernard Lonergan's concept of "sublation." Sublation is the act and result of incorporating something into a new, more comprehensive synthesis that transforms without destroying a prior element. Referring to religious conversion (any religion) as an act that brings extant intellectual and moral conversions into the new horizon of love for God, there to re-found them, Lonergan explains "sublation."

> I would use this notion in Karl Rahner's sense rather than in Hegel's to mean that what sublates goes beyond what is sublated, introduces something new and distinct, puts everything on a new basis, yet so far from interfering with the sublated or destroying it, on the contrary needs it, includes it, preserves all its proper features and properties, and carries them forward to a fuller realization within a richer context.[41]

Here what is sublated is a Commandment from the Decalogue. The theology of the Paraclete as "even the Spirit of [contested] truth [about Christ]" represents, I suggest, Johannine sublation of "You shall not bear false witness against your neighbor" into faith-understanding of the Holy Spirit. Equally, it represents sublation of the moral force in the Commandment into Christian discipleship where, under the influence of the Paraclete, it became the spiritual impulse to tell the truth about Christ, to bear missionary witness.

Discipleship and Citizenship: Re-minded by the Paraclete

There probably are countless ways for contemporary American Christians to appropriate Johannine theology of the Paraclete. Most likely, more than one application to an exercise of American citizenship is conceivable. Accordingly, this application has arguable probability, not inexorable logical or theological necessity. In fact necessity is all but impossible in appropriating Scripture in a particular context. According to Hans-Georg Gadamer, the dialogical nature of all in-

---

[41] *Method in Theology* (New York: Seabury Press, 1972), p. 241.

quiry becomes evident when understanding and interpretation—always driven by questions arising in specific contexts about matters conceived within particular horizons of understanding—open up the moment of application or appropriation. A scriptural text, for example, cannot guarantee and does not generate its own application. The reason is that appropriation consists in joining the text to an interpreter's (personal and communal) search for truth, meaning and value in reference to concrete issues with linguistic, historical, cultural and social specifications. This brings understanding and interpretation of a scriptural passage into inconspicuous intersection with a reader's total (personal and communal) self-understanding. That intersection comes to the fore in appropriation where a reader's appropriation or application of a traditional text emerges in relationship to the reader/interpreter's cultural context and historical horizon. But that relationship is primarily non-methodical and lived rather than theoretical. And the context, issues and questions of interpreters are likely to differ from those of scriptural authors like Paul and John, for example. This is manifestly the case with a question about Johannine theology of the Paraclete in reference to American citizenship. That relationship did not enter into the origin of the Johannine text and so cannot be read out from it as an implied meaning. So an actual, convenient but not necessary appropriation starts from the question, how does theology of the Paraclete enlighten Christians on their American citizenship?

To begin with, American citizenship has political, civil and social components. The political component can be identified as "the right to participate in the exercise of political power, as a member of a body invested with political authority or as an elector of the members of such a body."[42] This goes back to ancient Greek political experience and theory, though participation in self-governance through the voting rights of American citizenship pertains to almost all adults, unlike citizenship in Athens and according to Aristotle's *Politics*.

The "civil element is composed of the rights necessary for individual freedom—liberty of the person; freedom of speech, thought and faith; the right to own property and to conclude valid contracts;

---

[42] T. H. Marshall, "Citizenship and Social Class," in Gershon Shafir, ed., *The Citizenship Debates: A Reader* (Minneapolis: University of Minnesota Press, 1998), pp. 93-111, p. 94.

and the right to justice."[43] These rights are associated with the courts of justice rather than with halls of a legislature. Much of this can be traced back not just to John Locke but to the *civis Romanus* whose prerogatives after the Republic and during the Empire were outlined by the Roman jurist Gaius in terms of the legal standing of property owners. They acted upon, and through, their property according to laws regulating "acts of authorization, appropriation, conveyance, . . . litigation, prosecution, justification."[44] This was the kind of citizenship exercised by Paul.

American democracy has fused political and civil elements of citizenship. The U.S. Constitution instituted citizens' participation in the exercise of political power by voting for representatives while the Bill of Rights provided a specific legal basis for much of the civil element in the form of enumerated, unabridgeable civil rights. A more controversial "social element" in citizenship has joined that amalgam more recently. It had not come down to the modern West from the classical heritage of Greece or Rome. Nor did it emerge in British law before or during the founding of the Republic but only in the latter part of the nineteenth century. The U.S. Constitution and Bill of Rights did not charter it. The social element of citizenship, said T. H. Marshall in post-World War II England, was "the whole range from the right to a modicum of economic welfare and security to the right to share to the full in the social heritage and to live the life of a civilized being according to the standards prevailing in the society."[45] In the United States this arrived piecemeal in the institution of free public education; in legislation protecting workers' health, safety and bargaining rights; and in guarantees of Social Security and Medicaid, for example, as well as in the system of taxation to support them. Free public education, worker's rights, Social Security and the progressive income tax belong to the social component of citizenship, though not chartered by the Constitution and Bill of Rights.

American citizens live and think all three components of citizenship. Self-governance, by participation in the exercise of political power, seems the most basic component, with the civil element providing the conditions for its operation, and the social component a le-

---

[43]   Ibid.
[44]   J. G. A. Pocock, "The Ideal of Citizenship Since Classical Times," in *The Citizenship Debates*, pp. 31–41, p. 37.
[45]   Marshall, p. 94.

gitimate result of self-governance. Johannine theology of the Paraclete points to a primary way in which participation in the exercise of political power can be a form of public witness to Christ. Precisely the disciple's ordinary ease in acting as a citizen without an established Church providing a pre-defined linkage between discipleship and citizenship offers a primary mode of witness to Christ. Non-established discipleship bears witness, under the influence of the Paraclete, to Christ. How and why? The answer will be undramatic and ordinary.

It follows from the transparency of the Paraclete to Christ. The Paraclete bears witness to Christ, not to the Paraclete. The reality of Christ into which the Paraclete leads disciples includes the startling news in the hymn of John 1:1–14. The conception of Jesus recounted by Matthew and Luke was attributed to the Holy Spirit. Without denying this, the Johannine community's penetration to the mystery of Jesus' identity in relation to the Father led to a hymn celebrating the divine act of Incarnation when the "Word became flesh and dwelt among us." This central content in Johannine faith-understanding, expressed as well in the "I am" statements by Christ throughout the gospel, belongs to the truth of Christ to which the Paraclete bears witness in the disciples. This makes it part of the truth-telling by which the disciples bear their witness to Christ. Under the influence of the Paraclete they integrate that part of Christ's reality into their witness. Being a disciple taught by the Paraclete means witnessing in some way to the Incarnation. This is incumbent on disciples who are American citizens. How can that witness be given as a citizen?

One more thing needs to be included before arriving at the answer. The reality of the incarnate Word, Jesus of Nazareth who works in intimate association with the Paraclete, includes a relationship to creation. The hymn affirms the prior truth about the Word that "All things were made through him and without him nothing was made" (1:3). Consequently, because humanity has come to be as part of "all things," the Word acts in creating cosmically embedded, intrinsically social human nature with an inherent exigence for the political, suprafamilial organization of society. The Word became this kind of "flesh." The effect is a new Creator (Word)/creature (human nature of Jesus) relationship in which the political dimension of human nature has been taken up into union with the Word. On the patristic principle that what has been assumed is (can be) saved, citizenship too, as a particular, contingent expression of the political dimension of human nature belongs to the redeemed human condition of discipleship.

This shows why discipleship has an inherent openness to the political component of American citizenship. In fact, the primary witness to Christ in exercising citizenship, guided by the Paraclete's witness in disciples, consists in the simple, ordinary embrace of the duties of a citizen. The reason is that Johannine theology of the Paraclete can be understood to mean that the union of divine Word and created human nature in the Incarnation of the Logos grounds congruence between discipleship and citizenship. The congruence, then is theological-ontological and not only theological-ethical.

A theological-ethical basis for congruence is a divinely ordered and revealed relationship between two incommensurate goods, discipleship and citizenship. That ordered relationship, found throughout the New Testament, clearly subordinates the political order to the Kingdom of God, citizenship to discipleship. Subordination to discipleship qualifies any exercise of citizenship, and in ethical perspective, requires vigilance so that no reversal of the order occurs in practice. Paul exemplifies and encourages ethical congruence between discipleship and citizenship, despite Romans 13's appeal to an argument from created participation in divine authority. This passage appeals to an ordered relationship of human political authority to divine authority in the order of plan, will, command and activity, not primarily in the order of being.[46]

Theological-ontological congruence between discipleship and citizenship is an actual, already existing human participation in divine being. The theology of the Paraclete contains and promotes a theological-ontological congruence. The Incarnation belongs to the truth of Christ taught by the "Spirit of truth." The Paraclete's witness to Christ transpires as a mystogogical induction into Christ's reality, above all through the Eucharist which educates disciples in practical affirmation of the Incarnation. The Incarnate Logos is Creator initiating a new kind of relationship with creation, including the political aspect of created human nature with its production of various modes of political organization. The personal (hypostatic) union of divine and human natures in the Logos grounds congruence between discipleship that

---

[46] Walter E. Pilgrim stresses the ethical, not ontologoical, content of Romans 13: "His primary purpose is to offer ethical instruction on proper conduct toward rulers, not a political theory on the nature of the state. Paul grounds this ethical instruction in his conviction that governments have been divinely instituted to preserve order and peace and justice in the human community," p. 30. Obedience to government depends in the first place, then, on governments carrying out this ethical purpose.

shares in the wholeness, the unity of Christ, and citizenship that, because Christ's human nature is real and distinct, affirms this distinctness in participating in the created political order that the unity of Christ did not abolish.

Exercising American citizenship witnesses to the Incarnation by showing that entry into union with the Word-made-flesh does not obliterate created, politically oriented human nature any more than the Word dissipated the reality of Jesus' human nature. The personal (hypostatic) union is already realized, actual and salvific. It grounds the congruence of discipleship and citizenship ordinarily expressed by embarking on the tasks of citizenship. Embarking on the tasks of citizenship witnesses to the mystery of the divine encompassing, transforming, and elevating the human without destroying its created validity. Consequently, the kind of wise decision-making implored in the prayer "For Sound Government" gives witness to the truth of the Incarnation. But Johannine theology of the Paraclete implies too that such witness will be due to the influence of the Paraclete who teaches the truth of Christ from within. So a divine answer to the prayer "For Sound Government" comes with the Paraclete Who draws disciples into a sufficient faith-understanding of the Incarnation that they can act in light of the truth of Christ. Their participation in democratic self-governance by competent decision-making in regard to "our society" expresses and witnesses to their faith in the Word incarnate.

And participation in self-governance under the condition of the non-establishment of Christianity gives particularly emphatic witness to the fullness of humanity, including intelligence and freedom, affirmed by the Word incarnate Who acted in its creation. If establishing the Church expresses the primacy of the whole, one Christ whose humanity participates in the Word, non-establishment renders tribute to the distinctness of that human nature and its being filled by the Spirit. That is, an established Church has an institutional juridical format in which the state to some degree serves the purpose of the Church and Christ according to that legal arrangement. But non-establishment allows the visibility of a dynamic ordering of the relation between Church and state that accords with the dynamic ordering introduced into disciples' lives by the Spirit. The personal union of Word and Jesus' human nature is approximated by the institutionalized subordination of state to Church in the religious sphere. But the dynamic ordering of created relationships that is the temporal effect from the mission of the Spirit gains a suitable, contingent method of participation in the political order in a condition of non-establishment.

Application

> You shall not be a false witness.
> Amen. Lord have mercy.[47]

Making wise decisions about our society is a matter first of all of seeking the truth, acquiring adequate information, sorting out true from erroneous reports, in order to arrive at a position for wise decisions. And here too the theology of the Paraclete pertains to exercise of citizenship. For Johannine joining of the Commandment and the Paraclete did not weaken the Commandment's moral obligation to truth-telling in a juridical forum. To the contrary, avoiding false witness became a broad moral mandate to truth-telling about others outside the juridical forum, so that the solemnity of truth-telling before a judge was extended to truth-telling about others when a representative of the legal order was not present. For example, a long-standing moral tradition developed the expansive understanding that "The eighth commandment forbids misrepresenting the truth in our relations with others."[48] In this broadening of the application beyond courts of law, the Commandment prohibits, for instance, rash judgment that assumes truth without verification in accusations against someone, detraction that discloses failings of others to people who did not otherwise know these faults and have no reason for knowing them, and calumny that utters falsehood about others and incites false judgments about them. This ethical framework surely relates to public argument and discourse prior to wise decision-making.

However, false witness can occur outside deliberate private or public acts by individuals and can be a distortion of truth about others encoded into social systems to which individuals belong. And so *The New Interpreter's Bible* wisely commends applying avoidance of false witness to collective mentalities that are ideological. This points a Christian, for instance, in the direction of sounding the social dimensions of existence for collusion in systemic "false witness" in racist

---

[47] From "The Holy Eucharist: Rite One, Decalogue II," The Book of Common Prayer, p. 350.

[48] *Catechism of the Catholic Church* (Liguori, Mo.: United States Catholic Conference, 1994), pp. 591 ff.

structures or violations of human rights. Personal deliberation on public matters, accordingly, will criticize any structural organization of social reality that proceeds from and embodies false witness against others. To go along and get along on the premise that all people are not created by God equal in dignity is participation in false testimony. Sexism and nationalism, for instance, both deny equality in dignity to some people.

But the witness of the Paraclete reaches back into the disciple's own reality in a way that qualifies vigilant attention to false witness carried out by others. The Paraclete's witness generates a habit of mind in disciples that agrees with, and comes to stand in, the gospel truth of Christ's reality as saving, that in particular one's own life stands in constant need of being re-founded in love for God above all and of one's neighbor as oneself. Not for nothing does each Eucharistic liturgy begin with repentant confession of sinfulness and recourse to divine mercy. This counteracts self-justification that undermines faith in and love for God. But self-justification also has the effect of distorting personal deliberation on public matters. A realism gradually attained through repeated repentance and renewed hope for conversion means that a disciple, when entering upon the citizen's task of personal deliberation, does so with the realization that a beam afflicts his or her own eye for law, policy, procedures, cases or individuals.

To accept interrogation of one's situation by the read or preached Scriptures, whether one finds it pleasant or distressing, is a form of docility to the Paraclete. The Spirit guides love for neighbor into personal deliberation that incorporates awareness of one's own defective discipleship into the process of evaluating any public official's performance of duty, for example. And the Paraclete's educating of disciples in the truth of Christ precludes their equating the value and expected benefits from even the soundest political program with those from the Incarnation of the Logos.

The Impossible Commandment

REBECCA ABTS WRIGHT*

*You shall love the Lord your God with all your heart, and with all
your soul, and with all your might (Deuteronomy 6:5).[1]*

*So now, O Israel, what does the Lord your God require of you?
Only to fear the Lord your God, to walk in all his ways, to
love him, to serve the Lord your God with all your heart
and with all your soul (Deuteronomy 10:12).*

*You shall love the Lord your God with all your heart, and
with all your soul, and with all your mind, and with all your
strength (Mark 12:30; cf. Matt. 22:37, Luke 10:27).*

*For the whole law is summed up in a single commandment,
"You shall love your neighbor as yourself" (Galatians 5:14).*

Most of the above quotations are familiar. There is little that could be
considered esoteric on the surface of any of them. They are simple. We
know what they mean. And yet, and yet. Rare is the parish pastor or
priest who has not had parishioners come with a great many personal
troubling issues which stem from these verses and their ordinary
[mis]interpretations. Many difficulties can be paraphrased roughly as
follows: "I know I am supposed to love God with all my heart, but I just
cannot get over/understand/accept [fill in the blank with the problem
or tragedy specific to the individual]."

To love—and especially to love with the whole heart—cannot
possibly be compatible with questions, with doubts, with dislike, with
distrust, with hatred. And so the individuals feel on the brink of despair. Although they may have been able to put up a good front for
others, they worry that if God truly knows what is in their hearts, then
God cannot be fooled. And so they come, some of them, and pour out
their hearts to the priest.

---

* Rebecca Abts Wright is Associate Professor of Old Testament at the School of
Theology, University of the South, Sewanee, Tennessee.
[1] All biblical quotations are from the NRSV unless otherwise noted.

For some in our congregations, the answer is to pray to be filled with the Holy Spirit. They have scriptural warrant that they offer to support this quest, including: "When the Spirit of truth comes, he will guide you into all the truth" (John 16:13a). "By contrast, the fruit of the Spirit is love, joy, peace" (Galatians 5:22).

When one "has" the Holy Spirit, according to these folk, one will both know the truth and be full of love, joy, peace, and the rest of that wondrous catalogue Paul lists for the Galatians. And just as those who are concerned about not loving God with their whole heart when they feel stirrings of unease, whether of doubt or distrust or dislike, those who do not feel joyful and loving and peaceful and all the rest can be convinced that their hearts have *not* become the residence of the Holy Spirit.

Then there are those who are in much less personal pain, if any at all, but may well be more of a trouble to the conscience of their priest. They feel good about God and believe that such warm feelings toward the deity are precisely and only what is required or even requested of them. God has been so good to them it is easy for them to love God back. And if the people in that first glum group would only look on the bright side of things, they too could be happy and love God with all their heart and soul.

Paul in Galatians lists "love" as one of the fruits of the Spirit. This fruit, according to Hans Dieter Betz, "far from being against Torah (cf. 5:23), is in fact the fulfillment of Torah (5.19 ff.)."[2] As Paul describes it, again according to Betz, "love is voluntary and reciprocal, but it involves commitments to be maintained even under difficult and strained circumstances. It is the necessity of commitment and the difficulties of maintaining human relationships that cause Paul to describe the free expression of love as a form of mutual enslavement" (p. 274). That is, Paul is certainly not describing a flighty emotion.

The central problem remains: How can love be commanded? Particular actions can be ordered. Certain conduct can be forbidden. But how can an emotion be decreed? Who can dictate how another person, or even oneself, must feel? And if the greatest commandment is to love God with my whole heart, then I may be doomed before I even get started.

---

[2]   Hans Dieter Betz, *Galatians* [Hermeneia] (Philadelphia: Fortress Press, 1979,) p. 275.

The answer to the apparent conundrum is quite simple, but not at all easy. Accurate as the standard biblical renderings are in terms of being word-for-word translations, these words are not adequate to convey to us what is actually meant. We need to focus our attention on two of the words used: *love* and *heart*. When we look at these terms in the original languages and also trace both the words and the concepts to pre-biblical writings of surrounding cultures, we find the simple answer that "love" in Deuteronomy 6:5 and its later quotations throughout the Bible has little to do with the individual's inner emotional life. Nor does "heart" in Deuteronomy mean the seat of human emotions.

Although William L. Moran states categorically that "love in Deuteronomy is a love that can be commanded,"[3] he is not describing an emotional state. Similarly, A. D. H. Mayes asserts that "love of God is an attitude which can be commanded." He clarifies immediately by adding that for "Deuteronomy it is virtually synonymous with 'obedience.'"[4] He also adds that in the context of treaty making "there also often appears the command that the vassal should love his suzerain" (p. 177).

Love has as many shades of meaning in biblical Hebrew as it does in contemporary English. Someone can say, "I love my daughters," "I love books," and "I love broccoli" without fear of being seriously misunderstood, although those are three quite different uses of one word. As we use the word in English, *love* tends to be something that either does or does not happen. A mother cannot command her daughters' love in the same way she may demand lights out at 9:00 P.M. She may force them to eat broccoli, but she is powerless to compel them to love it. Similarly, a child cannot make a parent love Barney the TV celebrity despite the child's affection for the stuffed dinosaur.

Documents have been found from the eighteenth to the seventh centuries B.C.E. in which the term love is used to describe the loyalty joining kings to kings, sovereign to vassal, king to subject. According to Moran, by the "Amarna period . . . 'love' unquestionably belongs to the terminology of international relations" (p. 79). Defeated rulers pledged fidelity to their conquerors using the vocabulary of love. It is

---

[3]   William L. Moran, "The Ancient Near Eastern Background of the Love of God in Deuteronomy," *Catholic Biblical Quarterly* 25 (1963): 77–87, p. 78.

[4]   A. D. H. Mayes, *Deuteronomy* [New Century Bible] (London: Oliphants, 1979), p. 176.

not very likely that many pleasant emotions were shared, but the vassals knew better than to sign up with another overlord.

There is a long history of comparing Hittite and Assyrian treaties with Old Testament covenant passages. Moran argues in a footnote that there is not as much influence in some places as some believe. However, I think there are many instances where the Old Testament writers borrow a *form* and invest it with different *content*. Regardless of the outcome of this part of the argument, however, the use of "love" to mean "political loyalty" is clear.

> In view of such parallels between Assyrian treaties and Deuteronomy, we may be virtually certain that deuteronomic circles were familiar with the Assyrian practice of demanding an oath of allegiance from their vassals expressed in terms of love . . . we may even assume that they knew of such oaths by Israelite kings (p. 84).

> The vassal must love the Pharaoh; this is only another way of stating his basic relationship to the latter, that of servant (p. 79).

> To love the Pharaoh is to serve him and to remain faithful to the status of vassal. [Subjects] must love their king. . . . A vassal must still love his sovereign (p. 80).

There are biblical examples as well. Joab, in 2 Samuel 19:6–7, bitterly accuses David of "loving those who hate you and hating those who love you." David at this point is grieving the death of his rebellious son and, according to Joab, ignoring his servants who had remained loyal. It is their loyalty that marks them as "those who love you." Thus, it would not be out of line to translate Deuteronomy 6:5 as "You shall be loyal to the LORD your God. . . ." (Cf. also 1 Sam 18:16).

This love/loyalty is to engage all our heart. Now, *heart* is the exactly correct translation for what appears in the Hebrew text. The trouble is that when we hear *heart* once again we think of different things from what was meant long ago by Hebrew-speaking people (and many of their neighbors as well). Human cultures tend to divide the body figuratively, to use particular body parts in figures of speech to stand for particular actions or characteristics. We may say, "she felt the long arm of the law," "he had his nose out of joint," "the students were a pain in the neck." We also speak of "loving with our whole heart," even though we know that the physical organ we call the heart pumps blood and is not the source of the emotions we feel. So far, so good.

The tricky part is that no two cultures/languages use these body parts in exactly the same way. While we say we feel emotions in our heart, the Hebrews used *heart* to stand for the place of thought and will, of decision-making and conscience. Thus, to do something "with all your heart" is equivalent to saying "in all your thoughts and decision making." More evidence of the different connotation of "heart" is pointed out by Moshe Weinfeld: the Septuagint uses *dianoia* "mind," instead of *kardia,* "heart."[5]

The same treaties that specify the vassal is to love his overlord also require that he "fight with all his heart" (Moran, p. 83, n. 35). According to D. J. Wiseman, there are some nine copies of vassal treaties of Esarhaddon extant, albeit some in fragmentary form.[6] Wiseman gives fascinating examples of the use of these two terms.

> If you do not fight for the crown prince Ashurbanipal, son of your lord Esarhaddon, king of Assyria, if you do not die for him, if you do not seek to do what is good for him, if you act wrongly toward him, do not give him sound advice, lead him on an unsafe course, do not treat him with proper loyalty (p. 100, lines 229–236).

> If you do not love the crown prince designate Ashurbanipal, son of your lord Esarhaddon, king of Assyria, as you do your own lives (p. 101, lines 266–267).

> If you, as you stand on the soil where this oath [is sworn], swear the oath with words and lips [only], do not swear with your entire heart, do not transmit it to your sons who will live after this treaty (p. 102, lines 385 ff.).

A collection of ghastly curses follows, called down upon those who do not "love" Ashurbanipal "with the whole heart."

Recognizing that the Hebrew terms used in Deuteronomy 6:4–5 "designate aspects of the human person which do not correspond exactly to English notions," Terrien gives his own translation:

---

[5]   Moshe Weinfeld, *Deuteronomy 1–11* [The Anchor Bible] (Garden City, N.J.: Doubleday, 1991), p. 338.

[6]   D. J. Wiseman, "The Vassal-Treaties of Esarhaddon," *Iraq* 20 (1958). Wiseman's translation with critical apparatus by R. Borger can be found in James B. Pritchard. ed., *The Ancient Near East: Supplementary Texts and Pictures Relating to the Old Testament*, (Princeton, N.J.: Princeton University Press, 1969), pp. 98–105.

> Hear, O Israel, Yahweh, our Elohim, Yahweh is One,
> *And* thou shalt love Yahweh thy Elohim with thy whole mind,
> and with thy whole drive for self-preservation,
> and with the 'muchness' of thy whole being (p. 293).

Weinfeld relates Deuteronomy 6:5 to its use in the synoptic gospels:

> In the NT the element of "mind" and "understanding" is even more explicit in the discussed context [in Deuteronomy]. There we find both the "heart" and the "mind": "you shall love with all the heart (*kardia*) and with all the mind (*synesis*)" (Mark 12:30), and similarly in Matt. 22:37: "with all your heart (*kardia*) . . . with all your mind/understanding (*dianoia*)" . . . "Heart" as "mind" and "understanding" was prevalent in late Hebrew literature (p. 338).

I differ from Weinfeld's conclusions somewhat. It is not so much that "mind" is "more explicit" in New Testament times, but that the writers—quoting Jesus—were making *cultural* translations. The meaning was there in the Old Testament all along in the Hebrew and, as can be seen in the Septuagint, it was understood to be such long before the New Testament. The difference between Septuagint and New Testament may well be that the Septuagint was translated by and for people who were steeped in the Semitic idiom of the Old Testament, as anyone who has ever translated Septuagint and the Masoretic text in tandem can attest!

> The commands of love there [in vassal treaties] are accompanied by demands of exclusive devotion, as in Deut 6:5 . . . . Often we find in addition that the vassal should come to the aid of his suzerain with all his force, that is to say, with his army and chariots. . . . Thus we read in a Hittite vassal treaty, "If you do not come to aid with full heart . . . with your army and your chariots and will not be prepared to die" (p. 351).

To be loyal to the LORD our God in all our thinking and all our decision-making is indeed something that can be commanded because it is outside the realm of our emotional life. Living such a life of loyalty is also tied up with the gifts of the Spirit Paul catalogues to the Galatians. Indeed, it is probably impossible without the gift of the Holy Spirit.

Zacchaean Effects and Ethics of the Spirit

ROBERT B. SLOCUM*

Effects and ethics of the Holy Spirit today can be described in terms of the themes of abundance, hope and community in the story of Zacchaeus. The Gospel of Luke (19:1–11) records that Zacchaeus was a chief tax collector, and rich. He was an outcast, and isolated from those around him by the shameful behavior that built up his fortune while keeping others weak and poor and subjugated to the ruling authority. In the world of his day, Zacchaeus would have been scorned and resented for the abuses of power that made him wealthy. For all his riches, Zacchaeus may have lived with a perspective of scarcity, haunted by the fear that there would never be enough for him. In a world of limitation and not enough, it seemed that he had to look out for himself—even at the expense of the poor and helpless.

Abundance

Things began to change for Zacchaeus when Jesus entered Jericho. Seeing Jesus meant a change of perspective for him. In specific, tangible terms, it was physically necessary for Zacchaeus to change his place of perspective to see Jesus. He was short in stature, so he had to climb a tree to see Jesus as he arrived. More importantly, Jesus' visit to his home made it possible for him to move from a perspective of scarcity to one of abundance. It was an expression of incredible generosity for Jesus to visit the shunned tax collector, and it caused no little scandal in the community.[1]

People grumbled that Jesus had "gone to be the guest of one who is a sinner." But through this visit Zacchaeus realized the nearness and abundance of God's forgiveness, and he responded with enormous generosity of his own. Jesus' visit set Zacchaeus free from his past and

---

* Robert B. Slocum is Rector of the Church of the Holy Communion, Lake Geneva, Wisconsin, and Lecturer in Theology at Marquette University.

[1] For a helpful discussion of Jesus' "scandalous" ministry of reconciliation relative to the parable of the prodigal son (Luke 15:11–32), see Arthur A. Vogel, *Radical Christianity and the Flesh of Jesus* (Grand Rapids, Mich.: William B. Eerdmans, 1995), pp. 66–68 (Chapter 5, "The Scandal of Mercy").

healed him. Zacchaeus's neighbors didn't want his sinful past to be overlooked, but he came away from this moment with a new life. He would give half of his possessions to the poor, and pay back four times anyone he had defrauded.

Perspectives of scarcity and abundance can dominate our lives as well. From the perspective of scarcity, there's never enough. Not enough time, not enough money, not enough energy, not enough life. Scarcity leads to grasping, overprotection, and hoarding. It is a perspective of fear and great insecurity. There may be money in the bank, and investments in the portfolio—but the money may be devalued by inflation, and the stock market may crash. Instead of bringing assurance, having more things can mean even greater anxiety. Maybe someone is taking something, maybe an investment is going bad, maybe a partner is seeking an unfair share. As the Scripture warns, moth and rust do corrupt, and thieves do break in and steal.[2] It could all be gone tomorrow! So the tendency is to seek even more. Perhaps it was that way for Zacchaeus, who seems to have been defrauding people even after he became rich.

Of course, the ultimate perspective of scarcity concerns life itself. We are finite and limited. Many people want more life than they can have, or they want to live a life that is not possible. When they can't hold on to a time of life, or a way of life, or life itself, they try holding on to other things. The grip can tighten as time seems to be passing even faster, with more and more of life slipping away. If only possessions could wall out the changes and the losses! Not too long ago, the maker of a popular luxury automobile promised in an advertisement that "This car will save your soul." Sadly, the luxury car will not save the soul or change the basic terms of mortal existence. But the temptation still beckons—save your own soul, save your own life, get what you need, keep it for yourself. Zacchaeus probably believed that he really needed every coin that he could get his hands on, and he was looking for more. Until Jesus came to him.

Zacchaeus found new life beyond himself in Jesus. In this renewal and conversion, he didn't have to save himself any more. He didn't need to stockpile his resources, or depend on them for hope. He found a different kind of life and a different source of life. Jesus' visit to his home meant a new future for him. As Jesus said, "Today salvation has come to this house." However, for us, unlike Zacchaeus and his contemporaries, it will not be

---

[2]   See Matthew 6:19–20; Luke 12:33.

possible to see Jesus walking into town or sitting down at our dinner table. For us, the abundance of Jesus' presence and forgiveness is made available by the Holy Spirit. As noted by the English theologian R. C. Moberly (1845–1903), "to have the Spirit *is* to have the Son."[3] Or, as stated by the Episcopal theologian William Porcher DuBose (1836–1918), "*All* God's operations in us as spiritual beings are by the word through the spirit."[4]

The answer for us is not found in grasping at additions to shore up our situation, because our situation is not going to be fundamentally changed by more money or fame or personal power. All those things will still leave us in scarcity, and we know it, prompting us to reach out for even more of the same. As Augustine said, our hearts are restless until they rest in God.[5] Nothing less than God will fill the place where God belongs. By the Spirit, we can begin to know the abundance of God's life.

Hope

In all kinds of ways, people seek life and meaning from their "god," and worship the source of their hope. The things less than God that we worship become idols, and our attempts to draw life and meaning from them will prove frustrating.[6] But it may be difficult to let go of the focus of our hope and attention, even when it has repeatedly proven itself to be dry and sterile. A faulty source of hope can

---

[3] R. C. Moberly, *Atonement and Personality* (New York: Longmans, Green & Co., 1905), pp. 168–169.

[4] William Porcher DuBose, *The Soteriology of the New Testament* (New York: Macmillan Company, 1892), p. 56. For a discussion of DuBose's pneumatology, see Robert Boak Slocum, *The Theology of William Porcher DuBose: Life, Movement, and Being* (Columbia, S.C.: University of South Carolina Press, 2000), pp. 74–82.

[5] See Augustine, *Confessions,* trans. R. S. Pine-Coffin (Harmondsworth, Middlesex, England: Penguin Books, 1961), 21 [I, 1].

[6] William Stringfellow and James E. Griffiss both explore the question of idols relative to the temptation of Jesus in the wilderness (Matthew 4:1–11; Mark 1:12–13; Luke 4:1–13). Stringfellow understands all idolatry in terms of succumbing to the claims and temptations of death. See Stringfellow's books *Free in Obedience* (New York: Seabury, 1964), p. 35; *Instead of Death* (New and Expanded Edition) (New York: Seabury, 1976), pp. 109–110; and *Count It All Joy* (Grand Rapids, Mich.: William B. Eerdmans, 1967), pp. 86–88. For a further discussion of Stringfellow, see Robert Boak Slocum, "William Stringfellow and the Christian Witness Against Death," *Anglican Theological Review* 77:2 (Spring, 1995): 173–186 and Robert Boak Slocum, ed., *Prophet of Justice, Prophet of Life: Essays on William Stringfellow* (New York: Church Publishing Incorporated, 1997); see also the section "Meditations on the Idols of our Temptation" in James E. Griffiss, *A Silent Path to God* (Philadelphia: Fortress Press, 1980), pp. 87–108.

seem much better than no hope at all. We resist being empty-handed because it brings us face-to-face with our vulnerability. The assurance of Jesus' presence in our lives makes it possible for us to let go of false hopes. In Jesus' presence, Zacchaeus changed a way of life that was killing him and hurting others. He would no longer put his hope in getting more money and power over other people, and he let go of those idols. He turned from death to life.

Zacchaeus found peace and confidence in Jesus. He suddenly discovered that he could "afford" to be generous. Giving has so much more to do with assurance and inner abundance than wealth. The widow who gave all the money she had to the temple treasury knew about inner assurance and abundance.[7] Those who have seen parish finances from the inside know that the most generous people are not always the most wealthy. A person with disposable assets may want to keep it all for himself or herself, may not want to let go of any of it, and may actually be anxious about what will happen if too much gets away. Zacchaeus was wealthy before Jesus ever appeared to him, but Jesus' presence made the money available to Zacchaeus for sharing. Instead of anxious scarcity, Zacchaeus came to know the abundance of hope.

James DeKoven (1831–1879) once preached a sermon titled "Gathering Up the Fragments," saying, "The Gospel for the day tells of something still that can be done, even for a wasted life, saying, 'Gather up the fragments that remain, that nothing be lost.' The fragments of a life, beloved! The broken pieces of a mighty whole—they may be gathered up again."[8] DeKoven's own life certainly took some unexpected turns, and at times he may well have wondered about its meaning and value.[9]

---

[7]   See Mark 12:41–44; Luke 21:1–4.

[8]   James DeKoven, *Sermons Preached on Various Occasions* (New York, 1880), p. 314 ["Gathering Up the Fragments," preached at Racine College, the last Sunday after Trinity, 1878]. In the Gospel of John (6:1–14), after the miraculous feeding of the 5,000, Jesus directed the disciples to "Gather up the fragments left over, that nothing may be lost." DeKoven was dead within four months of preaching this sermon. For a further discussion of DeKoven, see Robert B. Slocum, "Romantic Religion in Wisconsin: James DeKoven and Charles C. Grafton," *Anglican and Episcopal History* 65:1 (March, 1996): 82–111, 82–96.

[9]   DeKoven was at the center of the churchmanship controversies in the 1870s. He pleaded convincingly for comprehensiveness in doctrine and worship at the General Conventions of 1871 and 1874. DeKoven was elected to be Bishop of Illinois in 1875, but his election was not confirmed by the necessary number of diocesan standing committees in the Episcopal Church. His doctrine of the eucharist was questioned. DeKoven's life is commemorated in the Episcopal Calendar of the Church Year on March 22.

But he knew that in Christ the broken fragments of a life are taken up and drawn into a greater whole, so that nothing is lost. The change of perspective is from despair to hope, from fragments to integration. At times we may seem to be at a dead end, without hope or direction. This can lead to discouragement and apathy. We feel that we can't make a difference—not in the world, not in our relationships, not in our own lives. We can give in to inertia, even just the inertia of routine and business as usual. Zacchaeus could well have rationalized his greed and fraud by saying, "Everybody's doing it, why not me?" Without hope, there's little incentive for change, and limited openness to the future. People who experience this despair can be very dangerous to themselves, and others.

Hope and direction come from beyond ourselves. Zacchaeus saw something new for him when he climbed the sycamore tree and beheld Jesus walking into his world. Jürgen Moltmann offers a moving personal narrative about the movement from despair to hope in *The Source of Life*.[10] He had been a German soldier in the last days of World War II, and he was subsequently a prisoner of war. In confinement he faced the horror of the evil he had not realized he was supporting, and the meaninglessness of the sacrifice of many in his generation. He faced searing memories of combat, including the death of a friend standing next to him in a blast that left Moltmann unharmed. But something very unexpected happened to Moltmann as a prisoner. He came to know forgiveness and hope for the future. Dutch students came from a country that had been torn apart by Moltmann's Germany to offer forgiveness in Christ to the German prisoners. In many ways, Moltmann discovered that Christ's loving presence can touch even the broken and outcast. It meant a new life for him.

Hope, openness to the future, and surprise are closely related. It was a surprise for Moltmann to discover Christ's presence for forgiveness and renewal in a prisoner-of-war camp. Clearly, since he introduces a book on the theology of the Holy Spirit with this story, he understands this to be the work of the Spirit. Indeed, the Spirit is the surprising person of the Trinity. Jesus was conceived by the power of the Holy Spirit, and that was certainly surprising.[11] It is precarious for us to circumscribe what God can do in our world and in our lives.

---

[10] Jürgen Moltmann, *The Source of Life, The Holy Spirit and the Theology of Life*, trans. Margaret Kohl (Minneapolis: Fortress Press, 1997), pp. 1–9. I have used this book as a text for teaching an undergraduate course in theology of the Holy Spirit at Marquette University, and it has served as a theological starting point for this essay.

[11] See, e.g., The Nicene Creed in The Book of Common Prayer, p. 358.

Faith (not diplomacy) is the art of the possible, including the surprisingly possible. As Robert Cooper notes, we may find ourselves to be overtaken by "God as surprise," who "appears among us and acts among us as One who puts life out of human control."[12] We must not wall out the inbreaking of the kingdom of God in our lives, with all its unexpected implications.

For Zacchaeus, the forgiving presence of Jesus in his home was a wonderful surprise, and it led to Zacchaeus's most unexpected generosity to the poor and the victims of his past greed. After this episode, other tax collectors may well have shaken their heads and concluded with regret that Zacchaeus was utterly out of control. And they would have been right. He quit trying to control his own future and guarantee his own security. Zacchaeus quit trying to save himself with his acquisitions and power. He let Jesus in, and opened the door to a new future and a new world that was not under his control. It would be a future with less money in his accounts, but it would be a future with hope. It must have been a joyous moment when Zacchaeus discovered his ability to give.

To sin against the Holy Spirit is the unforgivable sin.[13] But what does that mean? We can understand this sin as rejecting or blocking the means of forgiveness, whereby Christ's saving presence is locked out from our lives and needs. Zacchaeus could have barred the door to his house when Jesus drew near, thus preventing all that was to happen inside. In this regard, our attitude of openness to the Spirit is most important, because the Spirit will not force us to receive life, love or forgiveness against our will. Freedom is essential for real participation in any relationship of love, and the Spirit respects our otherness. Jesus would never have broken down the door to Zacchaeus's house.

To sin against the Holy Spirit is to sin against hope and the future. Michael Ramsey discusses this sin as "'an *aeonian* sin'—a sin relating to the aeon to come."[14] We are on the frontier of the coming kingdom of God as we are led by the Spirit in the way of forgiveness, renewal and hope. We are awakened by God's future in us, and enabled to live new lives. Like Zacchaeus, we may abandon old patterns of behavior

---

[12]   Robert M. Cooper, "The Fantasy of Control," *Saint Luke's Journal of Theology* 33 (September, 1990): 259–269, 269. The word surprise is from the French, *surpris*, overtaken (pp. 264–265).

[13]   See Matthew 12:31–32; Mark 3:28–29; Luke 12:10.

[14]   Michael Ramsey, *Holy Spirit, A Biblical Study* (Boston, Mass.: Cowley Publications, 1992), p. 30 [first published, 1977].

that were harmful. We may allow ourselves to be led in unknown and unexpected directions—as the fishermen by the Sea of Galilee who accepted Jesus' invitation to follow could not have had the slightest idea *where* they were going.[15] To sin against the Holy Spirit is to sin against the new future of God's life in us, and to hold at a distance the unexpected possibilities of God's invitation. To sin against the Holy Spirit is to sin against hope. Zacchaeus embraced hope when he welcomed Jesus and began a new life.

Community

Zacchaeus was lost in the isolation of his fraud and wealth before Jesus came. No one made room for him or offered to help him when the crowds gathered to see Jesus. People grumbled when Jesus came to be his guest. But Zacchaeus's conversion has everything to do with others. With Jesus, in response to his presence, Zacchaeus begins a new life of generosity and reparation. He has been called into a context of relationship and concern for people in his world. As Moltmann states, "The opposite of poverty isn't property. The opposite of both poverty and property is community."[16] Zacchaeus found surprising new wealth in relationship, even as he discovered himself able to share with others in need and those he had harmed. In community, it is not necessary or good for one person to do everything. It was different when Zacchaeus was alone, and had to be the only one watching out for himself. Who would help a dishonest chief tax collector? Jesus' presence restored him to community, and to a way of life that would show concern for others in community.

It is easy to imagine that Zacchaeus's new life was celebrated by a feast, with others present to rejoice that salvation had come to his house that day. When we eat together, we celebrate the community and the food that sustain us. As in the parable of the prodigal son, the reconciliation of the lost is worthy of a feast. By the Spirit, we share that feast of new life and reconciliation in every Eucharist, as we receive the Spirit who completes God's work in the world and brings to fulfillment the sanctification of all.[17] Our fulfillment is made possible

---

[15]   See Matthew 4:18–22; Mark 1:16–20; Luke 5:1–11.
[16]   Moltmann, *The Source of Life*, p. 109.
[17]   See Eucharistic Prayer D, Book of Common Prayer, p. 374.

by the Spirit in the context of community, because we are social beings who cannot realize ourselves in isolation.[18]

The community of the Spirit draws us into a relationship of respect with others and all creation. The closeness of Jesus' relationship with God the Father was expressed when he prayed to his "Abba," which we may translate with the familiar and loving sense of "Daddy."[19] We are to share this loving union of Jesus and his Abba.[20] By the Spirit, we are made sons and daughters of God and heirs of God's kingdom.[21] Indeed, by the Spirit we are drawn into the Trinity's own dynamic community of love and unity, even as we continue in the distinctness of our own personhood. But there are responsibilities that come with this wonderful relationship of love. If we claim God as our Abba, we are brothers and sisters who share the same loving parent. We find ourselves in community with many others who were created and are loved by the same God who created and loves us. The Spirit is manifest in the "*koinonia* of ourselves with God in Christ."[22] The Spirit that binds us together is the principle of unity in the Church, and the basis of the Church's vitality.[23]

As we perceive "the Spirit's tether" that draws us together with others and the Other, we recognize our calling to relate to people as true brothers and sisters—not as objects for our agendas and ambition.[24] After embracing Jesus, it was no longer possible for Zacchaeus

---

[18] See Charles Gore, "The Holy Spirit and Inspiration," in *Lux Mundi, A Series of Studies in the Religion of the Incarnation, Twelfth Edition*, Charles Gore ed., (London: John Murray, 1902), pp. 230–266, p. 243 [first published 1889].

[19] See Mark 14:36.

[20] See John 17, in which Jesus prays for those who come to believe in him through the disciples, "that they may all be one. As you, Father, are in me and I am in you, may they also be in us, so that the world may believe that you have sent me" (John 17:21).

[21] See Galatians 4:6–7, "And because you are children, God has sent the Spirit of his Son into our hearts, crying, 'Abba! Father!' So you are no longer a slave but a child, and if a child then also an heir, through God." See also Romans 8:14–17.

[22] William Porcher DuBose, *The Reason of Life* (New York: Longmans, Green & Co., 1911), p. 149.

[23] Gore draws on Thomas Aquinas to state that his belief "*in the Holy Catholic Church*" means "*I believe in the Holy Spirit vivifying the Church.*" Charles Gore, *The Holy Spirit and the Church* (New York: Charles Scribner's Sons, 1924), p. 357. He makes the same point in "The Holy Spirit and Inspiration," in *Lux Mundi*, p. 243. See Thomas Aquinas, *Summa Theologica*, trans. the Fathers of the English Dominican Province (Westminster, Md.: Christian Classics, 1981), III, 1172 (Pt. II–II, Q. 1, Art. 9).

[24] See the hymn by Percy Dearmer, "Draw us in the Spirit's Tether," Hymn 889, in *Cantate Domino*, compiled and edited by the Bishop's Advisory Commission on Church Music, Episcopal Diocese of Chicago (Chicago: G.I.A. Publications, 1979).

to turn a blind eye to the suffering of the poor or the hardships of the people he had cheated. When Zacchaeus began to realize God's love for him, he could also see God's love for others. His focus turned away from himself, and it was irresistible for him to share generously. He could no longer defraud his brothers and sisters. Of course, if we are sisters and brothers who turn in love to our one Abba, we must also realize that we are in relationship with all creation relative to the one Creator of all. As we turn to other children of God with love and respect, we should also treat the whole creation with care, and never assume that God loves only humanity in all of creation.[25]

By the Spirit, we can know the salvation and open future that came to Zacchaeus's house. We can receive new life and share generously as abundance replaces a perspective of scarcity, as despair gives way to hope, and as we are drawn out of isolation into community with others and all creation.

---

[25] For an interesting and provocative theology of God's love and the relationship of humanity and animals, see Stephen H. Webb, *On God and Dogs: A Christian Theology of Compassion for Animals* (New York and Oxford: Oxford University Press, 1998).

Selected Bibliography
Recommended by the Authors

Badcock, Gary D. *Light of Truth and Fire of Love: A Theology of the Holy Spirit*. Grand Rapids, Mich.: Eerdmans, 1997.

Barrett, C. K. "The Holy Spirit in the Fourth Gospel." *Journal of Theological Studies* 1 (New Series) (1950): 1–15.

Barth, Karl. *The Epistle to the Romans*. Translated by E. C. Hoskyns. London and New York: Oxford University Press, [1935],1968.

Basil the Great. *On the Holy Spirit*. Translated by David Anderson. New York: St. Vladimir's Seminary, 1980.

Bennett, Dennis J. *Nine O'clock in the Morning*. Plainfield, N.J.: Logos International, 1970.

Bennett, Dennis and Rita. *The Holy Spirit and You: A Study-Guide to the Spirit-Filled Life*. Plainfield, N.J.: Logos International, 1971.

Brock, Sebastian. *The Holy Spirit in the Syrian Baptismal Tradition*. New York: Fordham University Press, 1978.

Burgess, Stanley. *The Holy Spirit: Medieval, Roman Catholic and Reformation Traditions*. Peabody: Hendrickson Publishers, 1997.

Burns, J. Patout, S.J., and Gerald M. Fagin, S.J., *The Holy Spirit, Message of the Fathers of the Church*, Volume 3, general ed. Thomas Halton. Wilmington, Del.: Michael Glazier, 1984.

Congar, Yves. *I Believe in the Holy Spirit*, Volume I, *The Experience of the Spirit*; Volume II, *Lord and Giver of Life*; Volume III, *I Believe in the Holy Spirit*. New York: Seabury, 1983.

Craston, Colin, ed. *Open to the Spirit: Anglicans and the Experience of Renewal*. London: Church House Publishing, 1987.

Deissmann, A. *Paul*. New York: Wilson, [1911], 1957.

DelColle, Ralph. *Christ and the Spirit: Spirit-Christology in Trinitarian Perspective*. New York: Oxford University Press, 1994.

Derrida, Jacques. *Aporias*. Translated by Thomas Dutoit. Stanford: Stanford University Press, 1993.

Derrida, Jacques. *Archive Fever: A Freudian Impression*. Translated by Eric Prenowitz. Chicago: University of Chicago Press, 1996.

Derrida, Jacques. *Of Spirit: Heidegger and the Question*. Translated by Geoffrey Bennington and Rachel Bowlby. Chicago: University of Chicago Press, 1989.

Dillistone, F. W. *The Holy Spirit in the Life of Today*. Philadelphia: The Westminster Press, 1947.

Donfried, K. P. *The Romans Debate: Revised and Expanded Edition*. Peabody, Mass.: Hendrickson, 1991.

Dunn, James D. G. "The Christ and the Spirit." *Pneumatology*, Vol. 2. Grand Rapids, Mich.: Eerdmans, 1998.

Dunn, James D. G. "The New Perspective on Paul and the Law." In *Donfired*, 1991: 299–326.

Fuller, R. H. *The Foundations of New Testament Christology*. New York: Scribner's, 1965.

Gavin, Frank. "The Holy Spirit's Province: The Acceptive Attitude and the Inductive Method." *The Living Church* (October 21, 1933): 633–634.

Gelpi, Donald. *The Divine Mother: A Theology of the Holy Spirit?* Lanham: University Press of America, 1984.

Gore, Charles. *The Holy Spirit and the Church*. New York: Charles Scribner's Sons, 1924.

Gore, Charles. "The Holy Spirit and Inspiration." In *Lux Mundi, A Series of Studies in the Religion of the Incarnation,* Twelfth Edition. Edited by Charles Gore. London: John Murray, 1902: 230–266 [first published in 1889].

Green, Michael. *I Believe in the Holy Spirit*. Grand Rapids, Mich.: Eerdmans, 1975.

Gregory of Nazianzen. "The Fifth Theological Oration, On the Holy Spirit." In *A Select Library of the Nicene and Post-Nicene Fathers of the Christian Church*, Second Series, Volume VII. Translated by Philip Schaff and Henry Wace. Grand Rapids, Mich.: Eerdmans, 1972: 318–328.

Gregory of Nyssa. "On the Holy Spirit, Against the Followers of Macedonius." In *A Select Library of the Nicene and Post-Nicene Fathers of the Christian Church*, Second Series, Volume V. Translated by Philip Schaff and Henry Wace. Grand Rapids, Mich.: Eerdmans, 1972: 315–325.

Harkness, Georgia. *The Fellowship of the Holy Spirit*. Nashville: Abingdon, 1966.

Hay, D. M. and E. Johnson, eds. *Pauline Theology*. Vol. III. Atlanta: Scholars Press, 1997.

Henry, A. M. *The Holy Spirit*. New York: Hawthorn Books, 1960.

Holl, Adolf. *The Left Hand of God: A Biography of the Holy Spirit*. Translated by John Cullen. New York: Doubleday, 1998.

Hosmer, Rachel and Alan Jones. *Living in the Spirit* [The Church's Teaching Series]. Minneapolis: Seabury Press, 1979.

Hyde, Lewis. *Trickster Makes This World: Mischief, Myth and Art*. New York: North Point Press (Farrar, Straus & Giroux), 1998.

Käsemann, E. *Perspectives on Paul*. Philadelphia: Fortress, 1971.

Kevan, E. F. *The Saving Work of the Holy Spirit*. London: Pickering and Iglis, 1953.

Küng, Hans, and Jürgen Moltmann. *Conflicts about the Holy Spirit*. New York: Seabury Press, 1974.

Lindberg, Carter. *The Third Reformation: Charismatic Movements and the Lutheran Tradition*. Macon, Ga.: Mercer University Press, 1983.

Mackintosh, H. R. "The Doctrine of the Holy Spirit," in *The Future of Christianity*. Edited by James Marchant. New York: Harper & Brothers, 1927: 125–146.

Martyn, J. L. *Theological Issues in the Letters of Paul*. Nashville: Abingdon, 1997.

Maurice, Frederick Denison. "On the Personality and Teaching of the Holy Spirit." In *Theological Essays*. London: James Clarke & Co., 1957: 246–262 (first published in 1853).

McDonnell, Kilian. *Charismatic Renewal and Ecumenism*. New York: Paulist Press, 1978.

McDonnell, Kilian, O.S.B. "Theological Presuppositions in our Preaching about the Holy Spirit." In *Theological Studies*, 59:2 (June, 1998): 219–235.

McDonnell, Kilian, ed. *Toward a New Pentecost*. Collegeville, Minn.: Liturgical Press, 1993.

McIntyre, John. *The Shape of Pneumatology*. Edinburgh: T & T Clark, 1997.

McKenna, John H. *Eucharist and Holy Spirit: The Eucharistic Epiclesis in 20th Century Theology*. Alcuin Club Collections, No. 57. Great Wakering, Essex, England: Mayhew-McCrimmon Ltd., 1975.

Mills, Watson E. *A Bibliography of the Nature and Role of the Holy Spirit in Twentieth-Century Writings*. Lewiston, N.Y.: Mellen Biblical Press, 1993.

Mills, Watson E. *The Holy Spirit: A Bibliography*. Peabody: Hendrickson Publishers, 1988.

Moberly, R. C. "The Holy Spirit in Relation to the Being of God [Chapter VIII]" and "The Holy Spirit in Relation to Human Personality [Chapter IX]." In *Atonement and Personality*. New York: Longmans, Green & Co., 1905: 154–255.

Moltmann, Jürgen. *The Church in the Power of the Spirit: A Contribution to Messianic Ecclesiology*. Translated by Margaret Kohl. Minneapolis: Fortress Press, 1993 [English translation first published 1977].

Moltmann, Jürgen. *The Source of Life: The Holy Spirit and the Theology of Life*. Translated by Margaret Kohl. Minneapolis: Fortress Press, 1997.

Moltmann, Jürgen. *The Spirit of Life: A Universal Affirmation*. Translated by Margaret Kohl. Minneapolis: Fortress Press, 1992.

Montague, George T. *The Holy Spirit: Growth of a Biblical Tradition*. New York: Paulist Press, 1976.

Moule, C. F. D. *The Holy Spirit*. Grand Rapids, Mich.: Eerdmans, 1978.

Mühlen, Heribert. *A Charismatic Theology: Initiation in the Spirit*. Translated by Edward Quinn and Thomas Linton. London and New York: Burns & Oates and Paulist Press, 1978.

O'Carroll, Michael, ed. *Veni Creator Spiritus: A Theological Encyclopedia of the Holy Spirit*. Collegeville, Minn.: Liturgical Press, 1990.

Opsalh, Paul D., ed. *The Holy Spirit in the Life of the Church*. Minneapolis: Augsburg, 1978.

Rahner, Karl. "Experience of the Holy Spirit." *Theological Investigations*, Vol. 18. New York: Crossroad, 1983.

Rahner, Karl. "The Dynamic Element in the Church." *Quaestiones Disputatae*, No. 12. New York: Herder and Herder, 1964.

Rahner, Karl. *The Spirit in the Church*. New York: Crossroad, 1979.

Räisänen, H. *Paul and the Law*. WUNT 29, Tübingen: Mohr, 1983.

Ramsey, Michael. *Holy Spirit: A Biblical Study*. Boston: Cowley Publications, 1992.

Robertson, Frederick W. "The Dispensation of the Spirit." In *Sermons on Christian Doctrine*. London: J. M. Dent & Co., 1906: 130–141.

Roetzel, C. J. *Paul: The Man and the Myth*. Columbia, S.C.: University of South Carolina Press, 1998.

Schandorff, Esther Dech. *The Doctrine of the Holy Spirit: A Bibliography Showing its Chronological Development*. Lanham, Md.: Scarecrow Press, 1995.

Schlatter, A. *Gottes Gerechtigkeit: ein Kommentar zum Römerbrief*. Stuttgart: Calwer, 1959.

Schweitzer, A. *The Mysticism of the Apostle Paul*. Translated by W. Montgomery. London: Black, 1931.

Schweizer, Eduard. *The Holy Spirit*. Translated by Reginald and Ilse Fuller. Philadelphia: Fortress, 1980; London: SCM Press, 1980.

Schweizer, E. *Theologische Literaturzeitung* (1999): 12, 1242.

Slocum, Robert Boak. *The Theology of William Porcher DuBose: Life, Movement, and Being*. Columbia, S.C.: University of South Carolina Press, 2000: 74–82.

Smith, Huston. *Why Religion Matters*. San Francisco: HarperSanFrancisco, 2001.

Stendahl, K. "The Apostle Paul and the Introspective Conscience of the West." In *Paul among Jews and Gentiles*. Philadelphia: Fortress, 1976: 78–96.

Stuhlmacher, P. *Das paulinische Evangelium*. Göttingen: Vandenhoek & Ruprecht, 1968.

Stuhlmacher, P. "The Theme of Romans." Translated by R. H. and I. Fuller. Donfried, 1991.

Suenens, Léon Joseph. *A New Pentecost?* Translated by Francis Martin. New York: Seabury Press, 1975.

Swete, Henry Barclay. *The Holy Spirit in the New Testament*. Grand Rapids, Mich.: Baker Book House, 1964.

Synan, Vinson. *The Holiness-Pentecostal Tradition: Charismatic Movements in the Twentieth Century*. Grand Rapids, Mich.: Eerdmans, 1997.

Taylor, John V. *The Go-Between God*. London: SCM Press, 1972.

Vischer, Lukas, ed. *Spirit of God, Spirit of Christ: Ecumenical Reflections on the Filioque Controversy*. London: SPCK, 1981; London: SCM Press, 1984.

Wotyla, Karl. *Lord and Giver of Life: Encyclical Letter Dominum et Vivifi-cantem of John Paul II on the Holy Spirit in the Life of the Church and the World*. Washington, D.C.: United States Catholic Conference Office of Publishing, No. 103.

Zahl, Paul F. M. *Rechtfertigungslehre Ernst Käsemanns*. Stuttgart: Calwer, 1996.